327

D0662080

A Guide

to Preaching

A Guide to Preaching

A Practical Primer of Homiletics

R. E. O. WHITE

If you utter what is precious,
and not what is worthless,
you shall be as my mouth.
Jeremiah 15:19

WILLIAM B. EERDMANS PUBLISHING COMPANY
Grand Rapids

Printed in the United States of America

First published 1973, by Pickering & Inglis, Ltd.,
London and Glasgow

First American edition, July 1973,
by special arrangement with Pickering & Inglis

CONTENTS

A primer is for aspirants, not for experts. Experienced preachers will find little for them in these pages, and nothing intended for them. But it is hoped that many who are called to lay leadership in evangelical fellowships, as well as students for the ministry, may find insights and guide-lines to help their progress. In the concluding sections, some who already preach may perhaps find stimulus and direction for continuing improvement in the greatest of all callings—the call to preach the everlasting gospel of redemption through our Lord, Jesus Christ.

'So I will play the part of a whetstone,
which can put an edge on a blade,
though it is not itself capable of cutting' (Horace).

THE AIM

1 CAN PREACHING BE WORSHIP?

TOO GREAT importance can, certainly, be ascribed to preaching. The life of a Christian fellowship may be made to focus too exclusively upon its pulpit ministry. The pulpiteer's pride in his own power, and the adulation of a Christian congregation for a famous preacher, are among the less lovely products of evangelical Christianity.

For all that, preaching holds a crucial place in the life of the church. Christians do not live by bread alone, but by every word that proceeds from the mouth of God: spiritual health soon declines where hungry sheep look up and are not fed. The most diligent pastor will find his counselling ministry limited to an ever-diminishing circle, if he cannot hold a congregation together. The most energetic, enterprising, well-planned evangelistic outreach must fail if those whom we persuade to share our worship find nothing for them when they come.

Unless we are to reduce all Christian worship to ritual spectacle, all evangelism to individual contact, all Christian education to discussion groups in which 'articulate ignorance spreads bewilderment more widely', preaching will always be required, and the good preacher will be sought after by Christians concerned for the work of Christ.

'But good preachers are born, not made.' So are good nurses, good doctors, good writers, good artists. Technique and teaching will never impart the gift. But the 'born nurse' without knowledge of what she is doing will remain helpless; the gifted doctor without adequate training will be dangerous; the uninstructed writer will be incoherent, as the artist without skill to match his talent will remain frustrated and unintelligible.

Without guidance, the most earnest preacher of the gospel hacks away with a blunt knife at the most delicate of operations, his labour vastly increased, his effectiveness sadly decreased, by his lack of method. Of course preaching is a gift. The opportunity is a gift—'Unto me, who am less than the least of all saints is this grace given, that I should preach . . .' And the ability to do it is a gift, as any preacher knows. Sometimes the sermon itself is a gift from heaven, ready-made. But it is poor appreciation of a gift never to unwrap it from whatever hides its value and hinders its use. The least we can do is to invest the entrusted gift with those who may improve it, that the returning Lord may receive His own with usury, and our stewardship be approved.

Paul's answer to his own question, 'How shall they preach?' implies a divine commission—'except they be sent'. Nothing in the following pages will obscure that necessity. But commission without competence is a burden to oneself, to one's people, and to the cause we serve. It is with the acquirement of that competence to do what God sends us to do, that we shall be concerned. Our sufficiency is of God: our efficiency is largely of our own making, the reward of intelligent dedication, and given to workmen who, though they dare not become conceited, take care that they need not be ashamed.

To get the perspective correct, we shall first seek to clarify what preaching is, what a sermon should contain, what it should aim at. Next we shall take note of some special difficulties facing the preacher today, and with them in mind examine some details of technique and method in sermon-preparation. The message on the desk is not yet a sermon, so a chapter will be given to the preaching of the finished product.

Even a primer must acknowledge that to preach better is a lifelong aspiration. Practice achieves much, but steps will be suggested towards the enrichment of continuing ministry, mainly by the persistent discipline of the mind behind the sermon, and the increasing mastery of preaching skills. And something will be added about personal dangers inseparable from the privilege and responsibility of being a preacher of the gospel.

First, however, we must seek to clarify the place in Christian custom and tradition held by this curious practice, the making, preaching, and attending to *sermons*.

For a perceptive observer has drawn attention to an odd distinction between forms of Christian worship. In one tradition, the minister stands for part of the time with his back to the congregation; in another tradition, he stands almost all the time facing them. According to one custom, the focus of worship is the altar, and the place of worship essentially a shrine of the divine presence. According to the other custom, the focus of worship is a pulpit, and the place of worship essentially an auditorium for the hearing of the divine word.

Behind the one attitude lies worship that is God-centred, vertical in direction, preoccupied with a relationship man-to-God, God-to-man, and centring in a sacrifice of praise. Behind the other, we are told, there lies a conception of worship that is man-centred, horizontal, preoccupied with an exposition man-to-man-about-God, and centring in a sermon. And there are those who contend that the horizontal, pulpit-auditorium, sermon-centred experience may be an exercise of real piety, and may have educational value, but it is not worship. Or only worship in a minor key, a very human mood.

The implied criticism is uncomfortably close to common experience. The old gibe, 'if God ever attends a non-conformist service, He usually leaves just before the sermon,' may be cleverly unkind, but we have all at some time felt its point. Modern avoidance of the word 'sermon' in favour of neutral terms like 'address', 'message', 'word', 'talk', is an admission that with the announcement of the text the service of worship seems to move to a lower spiritual plane.

Criticism of the preaching service is of course sometimes expressed far more sharply. A sermon has been defined as a monstrous monologue by a moron to mutes. Nearer the mark is the somewhat petulant question, 'I really do not see why any man who has come to church to worship should have to put up with a few remarks from me'. One can only reply, 'If that is preaching, neither do I!' J. E. Rattenbury's answer was, that no preacher who has felt the fire of God in his bones ever thinks of his sermon as 'a few remarks'.

Moves to eliminate the sermon altogether, and to substitute discussion sessions, teach-ins, question-time, drama, or film, similarly illustrate an impatience with preaching, which stems from confusion about its purpose in church discipline and its significance in worship. That is why we raise the question about what preaching is, and what its rightful place in worship.

Historical Precedents

To answer our question properly would carry us back through Christian history, and beyond into Judaism. We should recall the solemn declaration of the ways of the Lord by the cultic prophets at ancient Israelite shrines, and the many-sided, but always majestic, preaching ministry of the inspired men who brought the Old Testament faith to its culmination in prophetic religion.

The formal recitation of sacred history and its abiding lessons, at the great religious festivals, would take its place in the story of preaching. So would the historic occasion when the collected literature of Israel was read to the returned exiles in the days of Ezra, accompanied by 'the giving of the sense', that the people might know the law and will of God. The continuance of this practice in the regular, widespread synagogue services gave rise to the 'tradition of the Elders' and the teaching ministry of scribes and rabbis, mediating the ancient law and prophetic insights to new generations.

From these synagogue precedents, the whole tradition ultimately derives of expounding written scripture in divine worship. The Targums treasured by later Jewish teachers were summaries of the interpretations offered by the greater synagogue preachers of past days.

The preaching of John the Baptist closely resembled that of the free and directly inspired prophets. But Jesus was often invited to instruct and exhort the people during worship, after the reading of the scriptures, as at His home synagogue at Nazareth. Then He resembles rather the rabbi than the prophet, but men wondered at the graciousness of His speech, and especially at His habit of speaking with direct and personal authority, instead of endlessly quoting authorities, as did the scribes. In this Jesus, too, is closer to the prophetic tradition of preaching, and it was as a prophet that He was popularly assessed—though whether as Elijah, or Jeremias, or some other of the prophets, was debated. That probably means He was unclassifiable! His preaching on the hills and shores and roads of Galilee was a new thing in Israel.

Jesus chose twelve men, expressly that they might first be with Him and then that He might send them forth to preach. Preaching was as much His chosen method as healing: already the sermon was the weapon of the kingdom. No modern preacher needs higher justification for his faith in his work, than the example of his Master.

So the expanding church in the apostolic age 'went everywhere preaching the word'. Paul, like the Master, was invited to give a word of exhortation in the synagogue services of the Mediterranean towns, and those Sabbath sermons from the Old Testament, preached to Jewish and proselyte audiences, formed in many places the springboard of Christian evangelism. Prophets, teachers, and evangelists were the pioneers of the church's growth throughout that first century, and Paul gladly calls them the gifts of the ascended Lord to enrich His church.

It is worth while here to recall the great dictum of Dibelius, exploring Christian origins: 'In the beginning was the sermon'. Research carried out in recent years has recovered from the New Testament the outline of apostolic preaching, emphasizing a remark of Bishop Henson, that Christianity began not with a book but with a preaching. Paul had of course made the point already: It pleased God by the foolishness of preaching to save them that believe.

The primacy of preaching in the expansion and consolidation of the new faith continues to be evident down the long story of the church. Time would fail us to tell of wise and persuasive Athanasius, holding heresy at bay in Alexandria; Chrysostom, 'golden-mouthed', greatest of Christian expositors; the mighty Ambrose, before whom emperors knelt; and powerful Augustine, bulwark of the faith in a dying age; sweet Bernard of Clairvaux, to whom all Europe listened; Peter Abailard, idol of the students; passionate, intrepid Boniface, 'among the best and greatest teachers of the faith' as Lull described him; Jacques Bossuet, 'by common consent among the greatest preachers of all time'; the brilliant Massillon, who searched the hearts of kings—great preachers all!

The decline of preaching brought the decline of the church, as it always does: the clergy becoming indolent and ignorant, the people in their turn became ignorant and faithless. Pope Innocent III approved the fraternities of Francis and Dominic precisely because of their preaching power, the Franciscans as evangelists, and the Dominicans as expositors. In England, Wiclif's lay-preachers, the Lollards, touring the villages with the gospel, foreshadowed the Reformation in Britain long before church politics brought it about.

The Reformation rediscovered the sermon's power perhaps more than Luther or Calvin foresaw. In the new Order of Worship of the Reformed churches, the elevation of the Word was deliberately substituted for the elevation of the Host, exactly as the pulpit, the throne of the Bible, was substituted for the altar in a church's ground-plan. As we shall see, profound theological considerations prompted these changes.

In England, the state-established episcopal church retained the Eucharist as central in worship, yet produced a succession of powerful preachers—Latimer, Ridley, Hooper, Jewel, Hooker, Butler, Andrewes, Donne, Jeremy Taylor head a splendid preaching tradition which continues down to Temple, and our own day. Among the disestablished, dissenting churches, John Owen, Goodwin, Baxter, Robert Hall, Whitefield, Robertson, Dale and Spurgeon lead another fine tradition. In Scotland, Knox, Chalmers, Whyte, Denney, Drummond spring to mind: Ernest Barker says of Scotland that the preaching and the disputation of ministers were themselves an education. The same may certainly be said of Wales, at one time populated by preachers and their hearers! Phillips Brooks, Henry Ward Beecher, Harry Emerson Fosdick are merely a few names that became world-famous, out of an innumerable company of eloquent, persuasive and powerful men whose pulpit ministry made America a church-going nation.

The truth is, that Protestantism flowered in preaching, as has every great Christian movement. The great Awakening, the Evangelical Revival in England with Wesley and his bands of preachers, the Welsh Revival and the Scottish, all soared into fine sermons. The whole modern missionary movement may look back with gratitude to a single sermon preached by William Carey at Nottingham in 1792, of which F. W. Gotch said, 'there has, perhaps, been no sermon preached in modern days, which has had so distinct and traceable an effect on Protestant Christianity throughout the world'. And the same is true of each great evangelistic renewal; names like Wesley, Whitefield, Rowlands, Haldane, Drummond, Sankey, Moody, Graham leave no doubt that preaching has its place in God's plan of redemption.

Even so cursory a review will convince all but the superficial, who mistake the current fashion for eternal law, and the very young, who think wisdom was born and will die with them, that preaching is native and essential to the Christian faith. It will remain in the future, as in the past, a vitalising force in the life and worship of the church. There are, however, deeper considerations which justify the place of preaching in worship.

Protestant Principles

Paul relates preaching and hearing to faith and salvation: the whole Protestant and evangelical understanding of Christianity does so too. Justification by faith alone, salvation by the acceptance of the gospel invitation to trust in Christ, the whole scriptural emphasis upon the knowledge of Christ and man's response in faith to the redemptive acts of God, all presuppose the proclamation of the truth, some continuing witness to the facts.

Of course, the formal sermon is not the only means to that end; probably in most cases of conversion, it is not the first means by which Christ is made known. Yet in the New Testament, and in the church's experience, it is informed and inspired preaching which evokes, sustains, and crowns all other forms of Christian witness, and which instructs and nourishes the faith of converts and maturer saints.

It is the truth which sets men free. It is by the word of truth that we are begotten again. It is the word of the truth of the gospel which brings forth fruit in all the world. That is why Jesus said this gospel must be preached: and why in Matthew 10 we can watch Him giving to the disciple band a large share in His work of preaching, in His authority by which to preach, in His confidence of the divine care for preachers, in His vindication of their work, in His inspiring Spirit, and in His reception by the hearers. And why we may even claim that He died in order to give us a text from which to preach! For He himself said: Ought not the Christ to suffer these things . . . that repentance and remission of sins might be preached.

So Paul, daringly, sets side by side, as two steps in one process, God's reconciliation of the world to Himself by Christ and the preaching of that reconciliation by us. 'God was in Christ, reconciling the world unto himself . . . and hath committed unto us the word of reconciliation . . . as though God did beseech you by us . . .' Paul had no doubt that the preaching of the gospel was part of the plan of salvation.

Writing to the Thessalonians (1 Thess. 2: 13) Paul describes the message he had preached among them as 'the word . . . which works'; and speaking to the elders of the church at Ephesus he refers to the word of God which is powerful. This is the depth of Paul's view of preaching, the insight which lends meaning to P. T. Forsyth's view that preaching is *sacramental*. The background lies in the Old Testament. In Genesis 1 the dynamic utterance of God is shown in majestic, creative action: when God speaks, it is so. In Isaiah, God's word never returns to Him empty, but accomplishes what God wills. 'The worlds were framed by the word of God, and by the word of God the heavens existed long ago.' The law, the psalmists, the prophets and the Master all declare that men live by the words that proceed from the lips of God.

And so in the New Testament, the word spoken with divine authority is a living energy of God. 'But say the word, and my servant shall be healed.' The word grew, and was multiplied; it is living and active, a creative, redeeming, and regenerating seed. Paul actually believed that when he preached the message of Christ, it brought the fragrance of life to some, the odour of death to others. There was decisive spiritual dynamic in the message as it was preached. The gospel *is* the power of God unto salvation—not about the power of God, or an offer of power, but itself a living, pulsating, energy of God, a word that works.

This is the conviction that lies behind the place of preaching in Christian worship. 'What can be more truly described as worship than hearing the word of God as it demands to be heard, with faith and reverence, with penitence, with personal application, dedication, abandonment of the soul to God our Saviour? . . . There ought to be nothing in preaching that is inconsistent with worship, nothing that does not promote it.' So C. H. Spurgeon, prince of Protestant, and Puritan, evangelicals.

And others agree, speaking from other standpoints. The sermon is addressed to man, but it is offered to God, and used by God. Says J. O. Dobson, 'Rightly conceived and rightly delivered, a sermon is a means of grace, whereby worshipping men and women may be led to that self-offering to the divine glory which is worship fulfilled.' And Bernard Manning: 'Preaching is the manifestation of the incarnate Word from the written word by the spoken word.'

William Temple declared that 'to worship is to quicken the conscience by the holiness of God, to feed the mind with the truth of God, to purge the imagination by the beauty of God, to open the heart to the love of God, to devote the will to the purpose of God.' The psalmist suggested that worship has two sides—to behold the beauty of the Lord and to enquire in His temple. How else shall conscience, mind, imagination, will and enquiry be ministered to— or even the heart, and the sense of beauty—except by the unfolding of a divine word addressed to all man's need?

F. S. Leahy stresses that in worship God speaks to men and men to God: so we may define worship in two words—adoration and encounter. 'True preaching, like the word proclaimed, is Christocentric, and issues in crucial encounter between Christ and the soul.' This surely is the heart of the matter, and James S. Stewart expresses it most movingly.

Describing the impact of Jesus upon His contemporaries, how some met God in His mighty works, others in His words, others again in His person, and so were convicted, searched, comforted, transformed, and saved—all 'in the days of His flesh'—Stewart continues: 'But mark this well, *not then only*. For through the apostolic preaching the same thing was happening. Men were still encountering God in Christ. The missionary proclamation of the mighty acts of redemption was in fact a continuation of the divine redeeming activity. When the men and women of Thessalonica, Corinth, Ephesus, heard the preaching of repentance toward God and faith toward the Lord Jesus Christ, it was something more than a religious lecture that was going on: it was God in action to judge and save them by confrontation with the living Christ.'

'So all down the centuries' adds Stewart, pleading that we shall so preach Christ that men and women shall utterly forget us in the encounter with the saving Lord.

Only when something like this is happening, is preaching in any sense 'sacramental', or the sermon 'a means of grace'. Only when preaching is made *an act of worship, in which divine truth is explored and shared, from faith to faith, in the power of the Holy Spirit, with a view to persuasion and decision*, then indeed divine things can happen, and the Word of God be glorified.

That definition of preaching will serve us for a text, though it applies less cogently to evangelistic sermons, which will call for attention later. Meanwhile, we continue to ask, What is preaching ?— but now, from the listener's point of view.

2   THE IDEAL SERMON

THE PREVIOUS chapter closed with so high a definition of preaching that this had better begin with the admission, for truth's sake, that preaching performance often falls far below that lofty ideal. One man preaching religion to others can, in fact, be a very unlovely spectacle.

It can be self-opinionated dogmatism bullying simpler minds. It can be self-righteousness finding disastrous opportunity, or an aggressive ego finding easy, and personally gratifying, self-expression. It can be a hypocritical harangue whose subconscious motive is a defence mechanism against a sore conscience. Or the preacher may be a strutting coxcomb showing off his fine feathers of language, paradox, alliteration, logic-chopping, novelty, daring, debating power, and other gaudy gimmicks displayed in public by the fool intoxicated with his own cleverness.

Preaching can even be the harmless relief of a husband denied the freedom to speak at home. Far too often it is a pleasant intellectual exercise in abstract thought on high themes, substituting reflection for obedience, and pious feelings for active compassion.

Let all this be freely admitted. Nevertheless let us still maintain that earnest and sincere preaching by a man called of God to do it, can be an act of worship, in which divine truth is explored and shared, from faith to fath, in the power of the Holy Spirit, with a view to persuasion and decision. And in re-iterating that high view let us add at once that it exercises an austere, demanding discipline over the man who preaches.

Plainly, the setting of preaching within Christian worship limits severely the themes, the matter and the manner of preaching. *There is no freedom of speech in a Christian pulpit.* On other occasions, the same man may talk about anything he chooses; but his *sermon* can never be free from the constraint arising from the holy occasion, the sacred tradition, the spiritual purpose, the Divine Audience, that attend its delivery.

The setting of preaching within worship likewise excludes all those emotional, but not earnest, people who let the Bible fall open where it will and speak 'off the cuff' to a gathering of worshippers—and think they are preaching. It condemns those who bring ample pages of notes on which are spilled enough ideas to fill the allotted time, who could stop or continue at any point with equal facility, without any gain or loss—and who think they are preaching. It condemns all who use the Christian pulpit to air their personal opinions, to relate their own experiences, to propagate their favourite dogmas, to publicise their personal good causes, to castigate all who disagree with them, to express their own personalities and fulfil their own psychological needs, or just to get things off their chests.

The discipline involved in preaching as an act of worship is a serious matter. Some men dress up to do it, in symbols of intellectual or spiritual authority. We normally stand upon some special structure, or platform, raising us above our fellows, and set within a place dedicated to God—with all the associations, assumptions, and psychological pressures which that implies. We countenance no interruption, no answering back, no questions, on pain of public charge of brawling at divine service. And we commonly appeal to the sacred scriptures and to the name of the Lord Jesus Christ, to lend further weight to what we say. If all this is not done in utter sincerity, with full acceptance of its necessary inhibitions, it is surely the worst form of intellectual humbug, psychological bullying, and religious charlatanism.

To avoid the pitfalls, and to attempt the ideal, it is clearly necessary to get clear once for all what a sermon should be, and should not be.

The Sermon Described

(i) A sermon that is to be a contribution to worship must draw attention to a religious truth which the preacher thinks important and feels very strongly. At divine service I do not want trivialities. Nor do I want academic discussion, examination of some current question in dispassionate, uncommitted neutrality. My opportunity to be at service might be rare, the effort to get there may be costly; in any case, my mood as I come is earnest and serious, and I do not expect my piety to be trifled with. Life outside the church may, for the worshipper, be filled with little, unsatisfying things: in the house of God he longs to be set again among the big truths, the towering ideals, the bedrock convictions, the far distances, that lend new perspective to his daily life.

(ii) A sermon that is a contribution to worship must justify calling my attention to that truth, at that time, by showing its place within the Christian scriptures, that I may feel and acknowledge its authority. If it cannot do that, then however interesting, or forceful, or eloquent, or original, the thought may be, I do not want to hear it *then*. Men and women come to worship seeking a word from the Lord: to offer anything else is to give a stone for bread.

(iii) The preacher must take some pains to clarify that truth for me, and for the young lad and girl in the front seats, for the old man behind me who can hardly read, for the woman across the aisle whose days are filled with meals and laundry and care of children, as well as for the doctor and the business man who took up the collection. It is little to me that the preacher sees quite clearly what he means, unless he makes me see it. And with so varied hearers, clarification needs care. Of course, the truth he is urging may be already so clear, so familiar, so platitudinous, that it needs no clarifying. In that case, almost certainly, he ought not to be preaching upon it.

(iv) The sermon must, most probably, *illustrate* that truth, from scripture, from daily life, from literature, from history, from poetry or Christian experience, or from whatever other source lies to hand. The preacher must make clear its bearings as well as its meaning, if he is to make me understand what he is getting at. The average worshipper already has a head stuffed with religious notions which he well understands but which mean very little in his daily life. Another sermon-full will not help him.

(v) The preacher must take some trouble, if his work is not to be wasted, to make that truth of his memorable. As the service ends, I shall return to home, family, friends, work, and a hundred other preoccupations demanding my attention. The thoughts stimulated, the mood induced, in worship will soon be dissipated if no care is taken, by striking statement and metaphor, by paradox and epigram, by humour and ridicule and story, by dramatic contrast or memorable line, to fire my imagination, and stamp the truth upon mind and emotion. If his message was worth preparing, it is surely worth preserving from oblivion.

(vi) Before he is through, this preacher of the sermon that is part of my worship must apply his truth to me—as well as showing what it has meant, or could mean, to others. At some point, I must see what difference this message is going to make to my life, what significance my presence at this service, this morning, is going to have for my walk with God. At worship I want to hear God speak *to me*: I shall feel passed over, neglected, somehow deprived, if the whole service expires in impersonal generalities.

(vii) Finally, it follows that to become a part of my worship-experience the sermon must evoke from me a definite response. The earnest preacher will leave me no option but to be persuaded, as he was when he started. The politician, the lecturer, the professor, may be content to leave me to do what I will about his offering: no preacher can ever adopt that 'take it or leave it' attitude. Too courteous, as a Christian, to over-press, never descending to brow-beat or bully, he yet wants my full assent, he would win my heart. And yet he must do this, not because he is a forceful and engaging personality, nor even because he is my minister and I owe him loyalty; but because through him I have seen, and have felt, something that comes to me with all the authority of truth, with the inner illumination, the lifting of the heart, the kindling of spirit, that are from God.

All *that* is preaching. Does it seem too much to ask of any sermon, that it shall focus upon some deeply felt truth, state it, clarify it, justify it from scripture, illustrate it, make it memorable, apply it, and evoke my response to it ? If so, what would you leave out ?

This, at any rate, is preaching in the context of worship. And herein lies the work of preparation. Ideally, a man should never prepare a sermon in order to have something to say. He should start his preparation with that already settled. It overflows from his reading, thinking, praying, observing, living the Christian life. What he wants to say is *given* him, kindling and glowing in his mind, crying out to be preached upon. His *preparation* consists in knocking that something he has to say into such shape and order that it will be clear, memorable, persuasive, moving and productive in the hearts of his fellow-worshippers.

The processes of that work of preparation will occupy us in some detail, but we must continue our examination of what a sermon should be by pursuing the question, What may a congregation look for, and fairly expect to find ?

Its Substance Assessed

Analysing what a sermon sets out to do is not the same as assessing its impact upon the listeners. Congregations will rarely listen analytically, nor will they often retain the separate parts and pattern of the discourse when it is done. The overall impression will linger, the impact of the sermon *taken as a whole*. Indeed, the most powerful sermons leave upon the worshipper, not ideas, thoughts, or arguments, or even uneasiness of conscience, but the memory of a spiritual experience. Too often preachers forget that the hearing of the sermon is itself the crucial time. It is *during the service* that the illumination of the spirit, the moving of the emotions, the kindling of new resolution, should take place. And that means that the vital question in assessing any sermon is, What was its impact, as a whole, upon the men and women waiting upon God for His word?

Beneath all the superficial, and pleasant, and partially untrue things that loyal people say about our preaching, certain qualities are looked for with an earnest longing, and their want is keenly felt as a spiritual disappointment.

Many hearers, even in these days, still want to hear something obviously and directly *scriptural*. It may sometimes be merely traditional prejudice against new fashions of thought and speech; more often it expresses a hunger for more than human wisdom, and more than just another man's authority. A passage illumined and made to speak its message plain, will delight the soul upon every remembrance of it.

It matters little whether we take a text to start with, and so proclaim the basis of our thought; or work around a text or passage, letting it appear where it is most effective; or work towards a text, letting all else lead up to it with inevitable logic and force. Just what it means to be scriptural in preaching will cause us some heart-searching: but the total impact of the sermon on many congregations will depend more than we may suppose upon how loyal the message was to the Word they long to understand.

That sermons must be *relevant* we have already hinted, and will urge again and again. The congregation will swiftly judge whether their time is being wasted with purposeless observations on unreal issues, or castigations of things remote from their own experience and thought. The preacher who never gets out of the New Testament into the twentieth century—or even out of the Old Testament; who will harangue the absent; who will discuss world problems with small and helpless people; who will argue about questions his hearers have never thought to ask, and raise problems they have never felt; and the man who will for ever diagnose the world's ills, with never a sign that he knows how to cure them—how he tries his people's patience, and kills their expectancy!

That a sermon should be *interesting* is a demand likely to make the preacher impatient—and perhaps the more impatient, because he suspects he cannot do it. That people have come to service indicates a measure of hope, to start with. Some will be willing to be interested, from habit and spiritual disposition. Others will need to be wooed, captured, and entangled before they know. 'To bore people at worship is not only a failure, it is a sin.' But it is also useless: you might as well be dumb as dull. How to cultivate the art of being interesting, on every occasion—that too must have attention later.

If we add that a congregation has a right to expect that a sermon shall be *profitable*, it is not to repeat again the need for relevance, and the power to evoke response, but rather to remember how sympathetic, even tolerant, many of our hearers are. Preachers are often surprised at the determination of some listeners to find spiritual value, of various kinds, in their sermons—if only we are seen to be doing our best. Mere exhibitions of cleverness will repel; the slick 'outline' that outlines nothing useful will soon disappoint. Skeletons make poor soup. But the eager listener will often find so much in what we said—information, guidance, encouragement, even reproof, correction, instruction in righteousness, kindled memories, wider views, challenge to cherished opinions, new hope and courage— and be grateful. God so often uses us beyond our expectation, or deserving. But that uncovenanted mercy cannot relieve us from the constant obligation to offer what will help and enrich: 'the manifestation of the Spirit is given to every man to profit withal . . . Let every one of us please his neighbour for his good unto edification.'

To urge that a sermon should contain something *new* might appear to contradict the requirement of scripturalness, and the strictures upon striving after mere novelty. There is real difficulty here. The Christian preacher is bound by the faith once for all committed to the saints, and wants to be so. He is still further bound by the attitude of some listeners who strongly resist any restatement of old truths in new terms, or any new emphasis, even upon truths equally scriptural, if it appears to conflict with favourite convictions. Even fresh and disturbing applications of accepted principles will upset some people. Not a few will judge the sermon simply by the faithfulness of the preacher in treading the path which, given that text, 'sound' preachers have always followed.

This attitude kills preaching, as it kills all Bible study, and spells death to all spiritual life, and Christian progress. It is a serious, and just, criticism of much evangelical preaching that it presents no single idea that has not been heard a score of times, perhaps hundreds of times, in different guise, under different texts, within different patterns and headings. Carlyle speaks somewhere of the endless chopping of the straw. If the metaphor seems cruel, it is not inappropriate: so much preaching resembles an utterly foreseeable assembly of evangelical platitudes long worn thin with use, dry and tasteless by familiarity, without weight or nourishment.

What then has become of the *living* truth? What has happened to the spiritual life, fresh, daily renewed, welling up from daily fellowship with the living God, Who loves to surprise His people with new discoveries of grace? Though we inherit the faith from the distant past, we also live by it today, and our preaching of it should carry all the freshness and fragrance of those who walk in newness of life.

'Make it true, make it new, and make it *you*' is said to be the advice once given to journalists, and the secret of truth and of newness is indeed originality—in the true sense of the word. For originality lies, not in thinking differently from other men, but in thinking for yourself. The devout worshipper does want the old, tried, and authoritative truth: but he does not want it in borrowed, out-of-date, imitative, worn and second-hand shabbiness. He wants to hear how you have seen it, felt it, experienced it; he longs to know it again in living power.

Novelty strives merely to be different, originality strives to be true, personal, and fresh. The congregation deserves to be given new insights, applications, emphases, illustrations, testimony, even new information, lest they go away not fed but stuffed with stale residues of outlived thought and faith. Only fresh preaching can refresh the soul. So long as the truth we preach is the old, old truth as we have seen and felt it; so long as the way we put it, clarify it, illustrate it, testify to it and apply it, is our own, it will be new, and renewing. In that sense I preach, as Paul did, 'my gospel'. And my people will never hear that truth, that emphasis, put in that way, from anyone else but me!

Is that not dangerous counsel? Certainly. We walk a tight-rope. Unless something of ourselves be in every sermon, we are actors merely, reciting words not our own. Yet if anything of ourselves intrude, the sermon is destroyed. 'We preach not ourselves, but Christ Jesus the Lord.' Nevertheless, we preach what we do know, and testify what we have seen; 'that which we have seen and heard declare we unto you.' 'Having gifts . . . let us use them: if prophecy, in proportion to our faith.' Or, as Paul had just expressed it, 'according to the measure of faith which God has assigned.'

Congregations always know when we are talking *beyond our experience*, when our books, or our borrowings, are preaching and not ourselves. Clear-eyed and clean-living young people, whose greatest sin has been the stolen apple or a naughty thought, testifying with tears to the depths of sin and degradation from which Christ saved them, may amuse the evangelically inclined, they infuriate all others. So does the man who holds forth upon the sufficiency of God's grace for the worst of pain, or poverty, or domestic bitterness, or bereavement—when all his listeners know he has been the pampered darling of a comfortable home in the best of health all his days. There are many things that we may believe to be true, but *which we have no right to preach to others*. Because our experience has not given us that right; because our special privileges and sheltered circumstances make our words sound hollow; perhaps because something in our own situation, or past actions, disqualifies us to speak on certain subjects.

We do well to listen to ourselves; better still, to listen with the watchful criticism we may expect to meet when others look at our lives, our attitudes, our known actions, in the light of what we say. For all that, a preacher's experience is not entirely limited to his own life-story. If he is also a pastor, he will share many lives and hear many testimonies. And by that wider experience he will often be equipped to share with his people evidence of God's ways which, while not strictly first-hand, is yet within his personal knowledge. But he will want to make that clear when he speaks of it.

What we attempt to do—take a religious truth we feel deeply about, justify it from scripture, clarify, illustrate, make it memorable, apply it and evoke response to it—is scarcely more demanding than what congregations expect of us—something scriptural, relevant, interesting, profitable, new and within our right to say it. Plainly, preaching is no lighthearted undertaking.

But who ever thought it was?

3 'PREACH THE WORD'

NO ADVICE is more often urged upon the preacher, more variously understood, or more rarely explained, than Paul's counsel to Timothy, 'preach the word'. Our insistence upon the place of preaching in Protestant thought, like our description of the ideal sermon, assumed that preaching shall be 'divine truth explored and shared', and its theme justified from scripture as worthy of its place in Christian worship. A. M. Stibbs has declared: 'In the midst of the worshipping congregation of God's people, the original and proper function of the pulpit and the sermon is the preaching and the teaching of the written word of God.'

The same writer has expressed admirably the deepest reason for this: the saving acts of God in Christ, he says, 'because they are acts in history, possess the character of particularity and once-for-all-ness. God is not repeating them in each fresh generation or in every continent. If therefore they are to fulfil their universal and age-long purpose of speaking to all men . . . it is indispensable that they should be worthily recorded, appropriately interpreted, and effectively announced.'

No stronger argument for scriptural preaching can be offered: it recalls the way in which Paul relates 'God was in Christ reconciling the world' with 'God beseeching you by us'. *The preaching of the gospel is the extension through time of the saving event upon which the gospel rests.* There are however other considerations which may be urged.

(i) A period of challenge, confusion, and denial demands a well-educated nucleus of convinced Christians as the best weapon which the church can possess: and nothing produces an informed and spiritually mature church so effectively as preaching which expounds, and applies, the Christian textbook. Great biblical ideas arm the Christian congregation for witness to a critical and bewildered society, while wrong-headed, or deviationist, ideas and theories are not so much corrected as crowded out by positive scriptural exposition of the central truths of the faith.

(ii) Scriptural preaching possesses power. It is astonishing how effective the simple exposition of a biblical message can be. The Bible is indeed a two-edged sword, a living seed, a word of life: the most powerful preaching merely releases the pent-up dynamic of the Word of God into the minds and hearts of men in our own time and language.

Luther's conversion, says Herman Sasse, was a crisis not of mysticism (as that of Boehme), or of obedience (as that of Calvin), or of emotion (as that of Wesley) but a 'discovery in the sphere of exegesis'. The convicting, converting power of the scriptures, clearly understood, transformed his life, and Europe. Alongside this may be placed the testimony of an American business man, reviewing fifty years of constant travelling, two thousand Sundays spent often in two or three different churches each week. Some of these services, he admitted, were so much wasted time. 'However, every now and then, sometimes in inconspicuous pulpits, I have heard messages that meant much to me and to my need. Invariably they were of the expository type. The preacher selected a text or a passage from the Bible, related it in his opening sentences to a fundamental human need, and enlarged upon it in all its helpful suggestions throughout the sermon. Always I left such a church wearing seven-league boots.'

Of course this must not be understood superstitiously, as though the quoting of a text, complete with chapter and verse numbers, exercised some kind of evangelical spell. The power lies not in the words, but in the Word, the biblical *truth*. There is no saving energy in our thoughts, our testimony, our cleverness, our gathered illustrations, our shared experiences, except as these serve to illumine and drive home 'the word that works'. 'Such preaching has power,' says Berkeley Mickelsen, in his massive discussion of hermeneutics. 'Scripture comes alive for those hearing it, for it has already come alive to the minister who preaches it . . . Both hearer and minister are aware of a power within . . . The magnetic power of preaching where the word of God becomes alive is unmistakable.'

(iii) The essence of this preaching power is the note of *authority*. Far too often, pulpit authority is confused with personal aggressiveness and dogmatism, with intense emotion and rhetorical force, with intellectual superiority and scholarship, or with the holding of some office conferring the 'right' to preach. These are substitutes for real authority, which is most clearly felt when truth is spoken plainly and quietly in a manner that permits no argument.

In the pulpit, such authority belongs never to the preacher, but to the truth he speaks. Peter says, 'If any man speak, let him speak as the oracles of God'; on which C. E. B. Cranfield well comments: 'The only words that the preacher can utter are human words, all of them broken and inadequate. Preaching only takes place when the Holy Spirit works a miracle and makes the broken human words become a real witness to the Word of God, themselves a living word of God to the hearers. That is something no preacher can "lay on" . . . he must still follow Augustine's advice, and pray that God may *give* him His good word into his mouth.'

The Bible always authenticates itself. This is the inherent authority of scripture, of which the wise preacher takes full advantage. Some would go further: 'We ought not so much to consider men as speaking to us, as Christ by His own mouth . . . He promised to publish God's name to men . . . He really performs it by His disciples.' This is Calvin's alternative to the authority of priests, church and tradition: by the mouth of the faithful man, called of God, and preaching according to the scriptures, *the living voice of God is still heard* within the church. To be the humble vehicle of that living authority is the highest honour any preacher can desire; fidelity to scripture is a small price to pay for it.

Evangelicals are sometimes nervous of this emphasis, lest too great importance be ascribed to the pulpit, and too much authority accorded to the preaching minister. Yet it was an earnest Puritan who penned the most exalted portrait of the preacher:

> Christian saw the picture of a very grave person . . . and this was the fashion of it: It had eyes lifted up to heaven, the best of books was in his hand, the law of truth was written upon his lips, the world was behind his back, he stood as if he pleaded with men, and a crown of gold did hang over his head. Now, said Interpreter, I have showed thee this picture first, because the man whose picture this is, is the only man whom the Lord of the place whither thou art going hath authorised to be thy guide.

So Bunyan: but to deserve that splendid tribute, preaching must keep very close indeed to the edict from the Celestial City.

In the long run, responsibility for the widespread denigration of preaching must rest upon preachers themselves. Respect for the pulpit is possible, and healthy, only so long as it remains the vehicle for the message of God. Misuse of its privileges, protection, and prestige for purposes alien to preaching the given Word is the surest way to forfeit whatever reverence remains for the calling of the preacher.

> Jeremiah faced a generation weary of prophets, and prone to invent mocking witticisms about the professional 'burden of the Lord' which prophets claimed to bear. What had been for Isaiah the solemn responsibility of carrying the weight of the divine oracle, had now become a byword (Jeremiah 23: 33f.). Jeremiah lays the blame for this attitude towards preaching upon the preachers: 'I sent not these

prophets, yet they ran; I spake not unto them, yet they prophesied . . .
I have heard what the prophets have said, that prophesy lies in My
name, saying, I have dreamed, I have dreamed . . . Let the prophet
who has a dream tell the dream, but let him who has my word speak
my word faithfully'—and not get the two themes mixed up, Jeremiah
means. But if any ask how are we to know what is the word of the
Lord, and not the preacher's dreaming, Jeremiah offers a remarkable
reply: God's word is like wheat that nourishes, compared to the
straw chewed over by the faithless preacher; it is like fire that kindles,
compared with the cold, unilluminating word of the man without a
message; it is like 'a hammer that breaketh even the rock in pieces',
a word of piercing power.

That is why the exhortation still has urgency: Preach the Word.

Must All Sermons be Expository?

Granted the basic reason, and the values, of scriptural preaching,
does it follow that 'only expository preaching is true preaching in
the biblical sense'? So Leahy suggests, and A. M. Stibbs supports it:
'the business of the preacher is to stick to the passage chosen, and to
set forth exclusively what it has to say or to suggest, so that the
ideas expressed and the principles enunciated during the course of
the sermon plainly come out of the written word of God, and have its
authority . . .'

This expresses forthrightly what may be called the *narrower*
meaning of expository preaching: taking a text and preaching
strictly within it; examining it word by word, phrase by phrase,
its grammar, punctuation, overtones and undertones, until its
meaning is exhausted. Stibbs three times uses the phrase 'close-up
microscopic examination' to describe this approach. Much favoured
by the Puritans, the method still delights Bible Conferences and
similar 'teach-ins' for those who already love the scriptures. It has
produced some outstanding preachers, too: men of the calibre of
Alexander Maclaren, and G. Campbell Morgan. Nevertheless, this
narrower view of what it means to be scriptural has some serious
weaknesses.

A. E. Garvie warned that only experts in biblical scholarship
could use this 'absolutely expository' method of preaching with any
effectiveness. The demand for exegetical competence is certainly
most exacting with this approach—but some undoubted scholars
make intolerable preachers. Even more important than scholarship
is the gift of teaching, the ability to impart wide-ranging information
and deep insights in palatable and digestible form. The man who

embarks upon detailed 'microscopic' exposition must needs take great pains to be interesting, comprehensible, and sympathetic.

He must take even greater pains to be *relevant*. Expository preaching is especially prone to remain within biblical scenes and times and language. The expository preacher will often justify his irrelevance by asserting that it is his task to expound the scriptures and leave the listener to apply it for himself, 'with the Holy Spirit's help'. That is evasion of duty. The listener might as well stay at home, with a new translation of the scriptures before him, and wait for a message from heaven. 'The true expositor . . . must "deliver the goods" at the door of men's circumstances and need, to present . . . the biblical statements in such a way that they become the living, relevant, meaningful word of God to the present-day hearer' (A. M. Stibbs).

The besetting irrelevance of much narrower expository preaching stimulated a demand for 'topical', 'life-situation' preaching, in place of scriptural sermons. The antithesis is wholly false. No book is more topical, more direct in its impact upon daily life, than is the Bible. But it is probably true that topical sermons appear more relevant, at the expense of authority; whereas expository sermons preserve authority sometimes at the expense of relevance.

Another way of expressing this issue is to contrast expository and 'prophetic' preaching. Some would liken the modern evangelical preacher, tied to the written scripture and the traditional interpretation, rather to the expert scribe or rabbi, than to a living voice commissioned to bring new truth for a contemporary situation.

L. Nelson Bell makes the point uncompromisingly. 'No one will dispute that the church has a "prophetic" role, or that the Christian ministry has a "prophetic" responsibility, but there is a serious debate at the present time whether either the church or the individual minister has a "prophetic" ministry other than that already made final by the early church and the first century apostles. In the strict sense of the word there is no such thing as 'prophetic' preaching today. No minister can stand in his pulpit and say, I have a new revelation from the Lord. He can only recognise the authority of Old and New Testament writers who spoke, by inspiration of God, *His* message. It is the duty of ministers today to *apply* revealed truth, not to assume the role of prophets themselves.'

We may sympathise with the probable motive behind this, an anxiety over the claims of modern heresies and 'deviations'. But what has become of faith in the continuing presence within the church of the superintending Holy Spirit? This *total* reduction of

the modern preacher to a Christian scribe, expounding ancient
documents in traditional ways, comes near to 'quenching the
Spirit' and denying the promise that He should guide ongoing
disciples into all the truth.

It is doubtful too if the assumptions here made are as true to the
New Testament as they are meant to be. For one clear function of
ministry in the apostolic church was certainly that of the 'prophet'—
the spokesman of God to contemporary needs. If teaching, evangelism, exhortation and prophecy were once separate functions, and
are now combined into one ministry, that is no reason for denying
in the modern church a gift of the Spirit which was, and still is,
of great importance.

Nothing in evangelical loyalty to the scriptures requires quite
this rigidity of outlook, or of preaching method. 'The Spirit breathes
upon the word and brings the truth to sight' is William Cowper's
testimony. And the prayer of Charles Wesley was:

> Come, Holy Ghost, *our* hearts inspire
> Let *us* Thine influence prove:
> Source of the old prophetic fire,
> Fountain of light and love.

> Come, Holy Ghost, for moved by Thee
> Thy prophets wrote and spoke;
> Unlock the truth, Thyself the key,
> Unseal the sacred book.

That Wesley was expressly comparing the scriptural with the
contemporary inspiration is confirmed by the following plea—

> On *our* disordered spirits move
> And let there *now* be light.

In the same spirit, John Robinson, pastor of the Pilgrim Fathers
declared, 'The Lord has more Truth yet to break forth out of His
Word.'

This surely is the true view of the relation of scripture and the
Spirit to the content of preaching. We are led to a *wider* meaning
of expository method than that of microscopic analysis of the words
of a given text. The essence of that wider interpretation of 'exposition' is, *that all we preach shall be expository of Bible truth,* whatever
its method or approach, *and shall bring that Bible truth out of the
past into the present* in the power of the Spirit who first gave it.

Dr Leonard Champion cites Karl Barth for the view that Biblical
preaching is much more than expounding a passage or explaining a

Biblical theme: 'the preacher must seek to understand what the words of scripture meant when they were written. But he must go beyond that study. How energetically Calvin, having first established what stands in the text, sets himself to re-think the whole material and so wrestle with it, until the walls which separate the sixteenth century from the first became transparent. Paul speaks, and the man of the sixteenth century hears.' This is what Professor Ebeling means by 'letting the text *become God's word again*'.

If it is appropriate to speak of a specially homiletic use of scripture, this is its meaning. It strives first to reconstruct the word of God as it came to a past age, and by so reflecting upon that word in that situation to hear the word of God for our time. It would distil out of God's revelation in other times the timeless truth for all times. Mickelsen speaks of this as making 'a good bridge or connection between the biblical meaning and the modern application', preserving both faithfulness to the original, historical context, and relevant application in a modern context. Where this is effectively achieved, the distinction between scribe and prophet, between expository and ·prophetic preaching, has for practical purposes disappeared. The man who faithfully presents 'what the Bible says' in the power of the Spirit who gave it, to the age in which he lives, is become again the voice of the Spirit of prophecy to his own generation.

The discipline of preparation which this demands will occupy another chapter, but the personal discipline it involves may best be expressed in splendid words of Dr Champion:

> We need preachers who, standing within the biblical witness, let the Word of God speak to them, and we need preaching which is then the communication of that Word . . . Here is the problem for the preacher: How can we understand and proclaim eternal truth in a manner meaningful to people conditioned by and involved in the contemporary situation ?

Towards solving that problem, Dr Champion pleads for an understanding of contemporary life-situations in the light of the gospel; for simple, colloquial language; and for an approach which speaks always as a Christian man to men and women—and not, Dr Champion seems to imply, as a mere pedlar of homiletic hand-outs to over-credulous customers!

4 'THE WORD WE PREACH'

TO DEFINE a scriptural sermon as one which 'preaches what the scriptures preach', and the evangelical preacher's aim as 'to be an expositor of the Word of God in the widest sense' may appear simple enough. In practice, it imposes a severe discipline upon all sermon preparation, affecting choice of theme, method of approach, and the way we use scripture to attain our end.

Not many today would imitate the famous sermon against extreme hair-styles for women, based on the phrase *top (k)not come down*, which the preacher professed to find in Matthew 24: 17 'Let him which is on the housetop not come down to take anything out of his house'. Nor would many appeal to Isaiah 22: 23 'I will fasten him as a nail in a sure place' in order to enforce the lesson that sound character demands a clear head, a straight direction and a point at which to drive!

An earnest brother once expounded the power of the Holy Ghost by dexterous use of the scriptural symbols of the Spirit: let the flames of fire at Pentecost be continually fed by the anointing oil of the Spirit, and applied to the living water by which Jesus illustrated the Spirit, and you must get steam, the greatest source of power in the industrial revolution. Such misplaced ingenuity in handling scriptural phrases is not saved from irreverence even by sincerity of purpose.

It is tempting to take the words of Barzillai to David in 2 Samuel 19: 34 'How long have I to live . . . ?' as the basis for a serious sermon on the brevity and responsibility of life, until one notices that in fact Barzillai is complaining of the limitations of old age, and declining to become a burden upon the king. What can one do but 'stand all amazed' when the preacher draws an impassioned and moving exhortation about attendance at the Lord's Supper from the words of Moses to Pharaoh, 'We will go with our young and with our old, with our sons and with our daughters, with our flocks and with our herds will we go; for we must hold a feast unto the Lord.'

What then should we say of a famous message based upon Acts 27: 29? Certainly life is full of storms: in the darkness and confusion that shut out the heavens, the danger besets us all of running upon rocks and making shipwreck of our lives. Certainly, too, the need is for anchorage against drift. Why not then 'throw four anchors out of the stern'—the anchors of the Bible, church membership, faith in God and love for Christ? Why not, indeed, except that these were not what the Mediterranean sailors held on to; and the impression that we do well to throw these Christian ideas overboard was not quite what the preacher intended.

Already, the rigour of 'preaching only what the scriptures preach' begins to give us pause. It is one of the virtues of A. M. Stibbs' plea for expository preaching that he accepts fully the discipline involved. He refuses, for example, to expound the story of Moses and the tree that made the bitter waters sweet as 'prefiguring' Christ and His cross. His phrase 'however ultimately desirable this application of the story may be' reveals how strong was the temptation: but Stibbs proceeds to keep the incident in the setting of Israel's pilgrimage. So with the story of Zaccheus, Stibbs declines the 'natural' tendency to give prominence to the intriguing tax-gatherer and his 'seeking Jesus'. As Stibbs well says, 'the inspired record ascribes the initiative to the Lord Jesus'—and the discipline of exposition recasts the sermon.

How often Jeremiah 18 has been used for a message of unending hope in the patience of the Potter. The divine word in the passage is one of awful judgement, after repeated wasted opportunities. God the Potter is now fashioning a vessel of wrath! (verse 11). Verse 18, too, offers a most attractive text for a sermon of promise—until one attends to what is meant.

A well beloved, and very well-intentioned, brother spent much time and midnight oil on the parable of the Good Samaritan. Memory retains the hard-worked outline in this form:

A man was *going down* the steep and slippery slope from the place of peace (Jeru-salem) to the place of historic battles, Jericho—always an easy descent. He fell among the thieves that ever wait to rob a man of all that is best in life. Notice—

(1) The Extremity of Suffering. He was *stripped*. as we all need to be of the (filthy) rags of our own (self) righteousness. He was *wounded*— for the devil has been a murderer from the beginning. He was left for *dead*—as all sinners are, in trespasses and sins.

Note too:

(2) The Excuses of Sinners. That is, the priest and the Levite. They could plead *the fear of danger*; the robbers might well return. But helping others always involves personal risk. They could plead *the feeling of despair*—'poor chap, he is as good as dead!' What *can* we do for the vicious and rebellious in a wholly permissive society? They could plead *the danger of defilement*, as priest and Levite, naturally preoccupied with ritual obligations; as some Christians are preoccupied with meetings and private devotions when they should be witnessing in the needy world.

Probably the priest knew the Levite was coming—better leave the problem to the young!

Probably the Levite saw the priest ahead—and took his example of indifference from his elders!

Contrast with all this:

(3) The Example of the Saviour. That is, the Samaritan: 'for the parable is told to illustrate Christ's loving compassion toward the lost'. He *spent* not *two pence*, but Himself; He *poured in oil and wine,* the cleansing and comfort of the gospel, the oil of the Spirit and the wine of His own precious blood; He showed the utmost *care,* as Christ ever does in redeeming love; He *took him to an inn*—bringing the sinner into the safety and fellowship of church membership; and He charges all to *take care of him till I come again*—as we shall all answer at the second Coming of Christ for the way we have cared for the lost and dying world.

The earnest evangelical purpose here is plain and moving. Despite a certain disunity of thought, the amount of careful work bestowed is equally clear, from the alliterative headings, the ingenious 'interpretation' on two levels at once, and the wealth of scriptural allusion. The framework is scriptural, and every idea presented is scriptural, except possibly the assumption that the priest was old and the Levite young. Yet the whole is a travesty of exposition, and the effect not so much unscriptural as anti-scriptural.

For the preacher has made the scripture say what he wanted it to say. Indeed, he has made Christ say what he thought Christ should have said. Not a word here about the original setting of the story, the lawyer's challenge, the self-justifying question 'Who is my neighbour?' to which the parable is Jesus' answer, or the final injunction of Jesus. Not a word either about what Jesus actually meant: instead, a new purpose for telling the story is asserted—'to illustrate Christ's loving compassion toward the lost'—which bears no relation at all to the gospel record.

This is not rightly dividing the word of truth: it comes very near to handling the word of God deceitfully. The principle involved is perfectly clear. For the Christian preacher, *the scripture truth is sacred.* To misquote, mishandle, or misrepresent a text, a Bible story, a biblical character, a saying, a psalm or an illustration, or to use a text as a mere pretext, for the sake of your sermon, is as much a sin against the sacredness of scripture as to misuse it to defend a heresy.

Reasons will be offered later for this severe judgement, but first we must explore more fully what it is we are contending for: and this brings us to the depth of our theme.

The Meanings of Scripture

This is not the place to outline the science of biblical interpretation, properly called hermeneutics, which can better be pursued in books like Mickelsen's, already referred to. We are concerned only with those aspects of it which affect the preacher's use of the Bible.

The classical procedure for handling scripture was summarised in the Quadriga, or fourfold rule. 'In the schools of the theologians,' says Luther, 'scripture is to be understood in four ways, literal, allegorical, moral and anagogical' (Skevington Wood). The allegorical meaning consisted of the deeper truth conveyed by a passage; the moral meaning was its effect on the reader; the anagogical meaning concerned the future, the things promised to devout hope.

In general, each passage had a literal and a spiritual meaning. Although only literal meanings were valid in disputes, the 'spiritual' meaning was greatly stressed. 'For a thousand years,' says Skevington Wood, 'the church had buttressed its theological edifice by means of an authoritative exegesis which depended upon allegory as its chief medium of interpretation.' The chapter-headings in the King James Version of the Song of Songs, and of many prophetic passages, where the judgements are apportioned to Israel and the comforts to the Christian church, illustrate the legacy of this method even after the Reformation. So does the 'spiritual' misuse of scripture in countless evangelical sermons.

For only with great difficulty is the habit of seeking occult, hidden, 'spiritual' meanings beneath the sacred text, finally broken. Luther, to whom the right use of scripture was crucial in his conflict with the medieval church, was well aware of the peril involved. 'Mere jugglery, a merry game, monkey tricks,' he called it: 'empty speculations, the froth of the scriptures.' Obviously, any theological or ecclesiastical dogma could be supported from scripture if sufficient latitude of allegorical interpretation be allowed. Yet Luther defends the use of allegory to embellish and illuminate the literal meaning. The habit was too strong! But it is dangerous. By it 'anything can mean anything', and the dexterous quoter of scripture can 'prove' anything from the Bible. It is a wry quip, but a revealing one, which makes the devil the greatest adept at citing texts.

One of Luther's earlier defences against the misuse of scripture was his insistence upon the sufficient clarity of the Bible, its power to make its own meaning clear. The contention that the Bible is too obscure, too debatable, to settle any controversy is still sometimes heard, when scriptural argument is being evaded for the sake of established positions. To make scripture the sole authority in the church, Luther sought to free it from dependence upon theologians, experts, ecclesiastical or other human 'authorities', however ancient. 'That is the true method of interpretation which puts scripture alongside scripture': the Bible is its own light, and one passage finds sufficient explanation in another.

The most tiresome—and lazy—of all preaching methods arises in part from this principle: that of merely listing texts bearing on some theme, or containing some common word, sometimes waiting for the hearers to find them, as though not trusting the preacher to quote them correctly. But the principle itself has serious limitations.

(i) The original readers of each gospel, epistle, or prophecy, possessed only their own portion of the complete scripture; are we to suppose that they could not understand the message they received until the whole canon was complete ?

(ii) Different Bible writers approach similar problems in very different ways, and use similar terms with very different meanings. Full allowance has to be made for wide differences of purpose, of cultural background, of historical setting, even of levels of spiritual insight, before one passage is used to determine the meaning of another.

(iii) Most of the heresies, and the legalistic and prophetic deviations from orthodox Christianity, thrive upon exactly this method of biblical 'proof'—the assembling of phrases and sentences from many parts of the Bible to support what the Bible itself nowhere teaches.

Luther later became aware of the inadequacy of his principle. 'I learn now that it is not enough to throw many passages together helter-skelter, whether they fit or not. If this is to be the way, then I can easily prove from the scriptures that beer is better than wine.' One would like to see that particular 'proof', but we may confidently assume that it would rest upon meanings imposed upon texts and half-texts to support previously reached opinions.

This is the supreme difficulty about scripture exposition. We all find what we look for. None can escape his own presuppositions, his background, his spiritual upbringing, church loyalties, religious temperament. Even our favourite preachers, our sharpest temptations, our personal hopes and fears, are all present to determine the emphasis we give to words and ideas, and to colour our approach to any passage. Says Skevington Wood, 'Much of our contemporary inability to arrive at a satisfying exegesis of scripture has arisen

either from failure to recognise the phenomenon, or from unwillingness to select the right perspective.' Or, we might add, from the
assumption that it is always the other man who is letting his prejudices dictate his interpretation.

The purpose of training in biblical exegesis is precisely to release
the preacher from the personal and subjective limitations with which
he comes to every text and passage, and to enable him to discover as
objectively as possible the viewpoint of the biblical writers themselves.
Unfortunately, it is all too easy for the student merely to exchange
one set of presuppositions for another. When he has learned not to
read everything in the light of his own private spiritual auto-
biography, he may instead come to see in every passage only confirming evidence for some favourite theory of comparative religion,
or socialism, or evolution, or secularism or liberalism, or the latest
theological fad. The manipulation of scripture that results will now
be much more imposing and erudite: it will be for that reason only
the more dangerous and misleading distortion of what the Bible
intends to teach.

So we are driven, by our anxiety to preach what the scriptures
preach, to discover some method of interpretation as objective
and impartial as we can achieve. We need some simple rules or
canons of exegesis which shall become for us unbreakable, habitual,
almost second nature, whenever we handle or quote a scripture
verse. Accepting as the Golden Rule of all expository preaching:

> *Make some scripture statement the basis of your message:*
> *Know what it means:*
> *Preach what it says:*

we now add, as a principle of homiletic discipline, and an expression
of reverence for the sacredness of scripture—

> *The meaning of a passage is never ours to decide, but only ours to*
> *discover.*

But how ?

The Canons of Exegesis

The rules for discovering the true meaning of any scripture
passage are three:

(i) *Examine the precise content of the passage under consideration.*
Try to hear the words as though for the first time. Biblical texts
continually astonish us, if we merely listen to them, instead of

hearing all the overtones and undertones they have gathered during our spiritual pilgrimage. 'The literal sense of scripture alone is the whole essence of faith and Christian theology': so Luther, in his more cautious mood. 'If we wish to handle scripture aright, our sole effort will be to obtain the one, simple, seminal and certain literal sense.'

The obvious way to examine the precise content of a passage is to pause upon each word, and ask why it was used. Almost the whole power of Alexander Maclaren's technique lay in this method. Any text could illustrate how profitable it is: two illustrations must suffice:

Ephesians 2: 8 *'For by grace are ye saved, through faith; and that not of yourselves: it is the gift of God.'*

Paul is explaining how our salvation comes about. Why does he say, first of all, it is *by grace*? Because to him as a Jew, and in all his contention with Judaism, this was the astonishing, crucial point—that men were saved not by works and law-keeping but by the free favour of God. Why does he add *through faith*? Again, because some response by man is obviously necessary if any man's life is to be transformed, yet all that is required to link man to God's saving grace is simply faith—not effort, wisdom, self-reform, righteousness, knowledge or merit. Why is it 'by' grace and 'through' faith? Because the active agency in salvation is God's favour—that is what initiates and accomplishes it: man's faith is merely the channel 'through' which salvation reaches him—faith is not an energy, or a good work, or some form of merit, which in itself can accomplish anything. Why does Paul use the word 'saved' rather than 'forgiven' or 'redeemed'? Probably because in the previous verses he has described the total condition of the sinner from many angles, and 'saved' is the most comprehensive term for all that Christ does for those who put their faith in Him. Why does Paul add 'and that not of yourselves'? The proud heart clings to some vestige of independence, and fondly supposes that it contributes *something* to the process of salvation—the Christian virtue of faith! But Paul will not have it so: faith itself is not 'of us'—God deals to every man whatever measure of faith he possesses. We cannot boast even that we believe. 'It is the gift'—free, unmerited, unconditional—made by love to the needy. And the gift 'of God'— not in any sense a special religious gift or talent belonging to us by nature, but imparted by the Father Himself. The present tense 'are saved', and the direct, personal 'ye are saved'—not men generally, but the readers known to the writer—similarly deserve comment; and so does the final colon, which warns us that the following verse belongs intimately to this one, and must be included in the interpretation. Finally, the first word, 'for', is as important as any other: it reveals the purpose of the whole statement, which is to prove how God in the ages to come will demonstrate the superb wealth of His grace, as revealed in this act of supreme kindness towards us in Christ Jesus.

Romans 8: 32 '*He that spared not his own Son, but delivered him up for us all, how shall he not with him also freely give us all things?*'

Paul is assuring believers of the overwhelming, many-sided confidence in which they may live. The immediate point is that God will provide all needs, one evidence among the many to be listed, that God is 'for us'. The question-form, as throughout the passage, implies that the point ought to be obvious—the onus of proof is on anyone who would be foolish enough to deny it! The confidence rests not upon general considerations about the nature of God, but upon what God has in fact already done—giving the greatest conceivable gift, His own Son: beside whom, all other gifts are trivial. The description of God, as 'He that spared not his own Son' is an argument in itself. The word 'spared', like the negative form—'He spared not'—suggests that God might have been tempted to set a limit to what He was prepared to do for us, but rejected the temptation. Some think that the story of Abraham offering Isaac lies behind the sentence: Isaac was spared, God's Son was not. The same allusion may light up the word 'delivered . . . up'— yielding to utmost necessity. 'His own Son' has special poignancy—it was not a slave or a friend God yielded up, but one dearest of all to His own heart. All this being already done, how can we doubt about lesser things? The giving up of the Son was 'for us all'—God plainly is 'for us' with all His heart! Equally 'freely', undeserved, are all other gifts; but the gifts are not ours without the Christ—they are given 'with him also'. And 'all things' is a Pauline phrase which deserves thorough examination: in this passage alone it occurs in three significant connections (28, 32, 37); it stretches the Christian's confidence to the widest possible application.

To pause in this questioning way upon each separate word and phrase is simply *to listen to what the text is saying*. Some would carry the results into the pulpit and call them sermon-notes: but that is to inflict upon your congregation your undigested homework. So far we are merely seeking the meaning of the text, before attempting to draw from it a message for today. Until we refuse to allow the familiar, hallowed words to slip over dimly comprehending minds, until we attend meticulously to what is said and how it is expressed, we are not yet in sight of the meaning of scripture.

Attention to the precise content of a passage or text is enormously helped if we can read it in the original tongue and not only in some second-hand version. The richness and force of the original, as well as the unfamiliarity of the words, make the Greek New Testament almost a new book, even to those who long have loved the old, familiar versions. Many suppose that the abundance of modern translations has made the original scripture less important, but this is superficial. That so many attempts have been made to render the Testament into modern speech shows how difficult, and even impossible, that task is. The resulting confusion as to what the Bible does say lays upon the public expositor the duty of assessing the rival versions—which he can do only as first-hand knowledge of the original writings enables him to compare their accuracy.

Those who must make do without this equipment will be all the more careful not to choose among modern translations merely by personal taste, or prejudice, or to meet the convenience of a particular sermon. Especially dishonourable is that juggling with many versions which hunts around for some form of words that will 'justify' the meaning you wish to find in some text or story. The preacher dependent upon an English Testament will also pay all the more attention to diction, grammar, and punctuation, and not be too proud to keep a good dictionary next to his modern translation, in order to make sure he understands what he reads.

(ii) The second canon of exegesis is: *Be faithful to the literary and historical context of the passage under consideration*. By the *literary* context is meant, of course, the total passage or writing from which some extract is being taken. As James Black well says, texts are not stray pebbles picked up at random on the shores of the biblical ocean of truth. Their meaning is always in their context. What the writer meant is determined by the subject under discussion, the drift of his argument, his purpose in writing. *The true meaning of any text of scripture is what those words, from that particular writer, would have conveyed to those readers, at that time on that subject.*

Most examples of ridiculous, trivial, extreme, or dangerous preaching will be found to consist of reflections on odd phrases or sentences torn bodily from the scriptures, wrested by brute force from their original context, considered in isolation from all that goes before or follows. Such 'texts' are mere fragments of language, and might just as well have been taken from Shakespeare, the London Times, or the Weather Forecast. What splendid sermons might be composed upon extracts like 'Ye shall be as gods', 'the pinnacle of the temple', 'They have their reward', 'Let us . . . be merry', 'All things are lawful', provided their meaning and place within the scripture be studiously ignored! To make a 'lovely' sermon based upon a wrong exegesis is trifling with the Bible, with your people, and with your own integrity.

By the *historical* context of a passage is meant its place in the unfolding revelation of God, at the time and in the circumstances in which it was given. Scripture means what the writer intended it to mean—all else is invention, not interpretation. But the writer and his readers belong to a given time, stand at a given stage in the divine story, are conditioned by their environment and experience. Ideas, beliefs, meanings of words, which clearly belong to later Christian times must not be read back into the records of earlier centuries. The significance which later events may give to an old prophecy must not be allowed to confuse, or obscure, what the prophet meant as he brought God's word to his own generation. It is inevitable that the Christian preacher will read the Old Testament with Christian eyes and heart: but it is essential that he shall be aware that he does so, and keep clearly distinguished what *he* loves to find there and what the ancient scriptures really *meant*. This is the only honest, and defensible, answer to those who contend that the Bible can be made to mean whatever you choose. It can— in unscrupulous hands. The safeguard is a principle of interpretation which accepts as final and *binding* the meaning which the writer intended at the time in which he wrote.

Said the pithy and perceptive Bengel, whose comments upon scripture are treasured and repeated by innumerable commentators: 'the expositor who nullifies the historical groundwork of scripture for the sake of finding spiritual truths everywhere, brings death upon all correct interpretation.' That is a hard saying, but essential. What that correct, historical, interpretation of the ancient word now has to say to modern people in modern situations is a second, and vital question: but it cannot determine our interpretation of the text. The *meaning* of a passage is not what it says to us today, but what it said to those to whom God first sent it.

(iii) The third canon of exegesis, as it affects preaching, is: *See the text or passage under consideration in the light of the biblical revelation as a whole*. If the literary context and the historical perspective of a passage are properly weighed, this rule should take care of itself, but sometimes a preacher is misled for lack of attention to it. The Bible canvas is exceedingly wide; its story covers a thousand years. Plainly, many details of example, counsel, and warning, many practices and even laws, find a place in so vast a record, without being all of equal importance, nor all of permanent validity. A sense of ongoing revelation, and a balance of truth, are important to expository relevance and effectiveness.

Thus, some Old Testament passages, precious in their time, are superseded by fuller revelation: and the Bible itself is the record of that supersession. Animal sacrifice, circumcision, the seventh 'rest' day, the legal principle of 'an eye for an eye and a tooth for a tooth', are obvious examples of ideals left behind. The Sermon on the Mount explicitly sets forth this historical perspective, requiring that the 'I say unto you' of Jesus shall have precedence over things 'said of old time'.

The same is true of the relative importance of passages. Whatever we make of it, Paul's injunction about women keeping silence in the churches is *not* all that the New Testament has to say about the place of women in the life of the church. The remark of Jesus to the Syro-Phoenician woman is not the total biblical revelation concerning questions of race. Nor is 'Every man shall bear his own burden' a complete Christian insight, but a special example of the danger of half-texts.

This warning to observe the total context of scripture is sometimes expressed as 'observe the analogy of faith'—itself a misuse of a phrase in Romans 12: 6. Luther took 'the analogy of faith' to mean the whole of scripture. Others speak of 'the general norm of the word of God'—a summary of what we think the scriptures as a whole would say. Others again would urge that the preacher should emphasize only those areas of truth which the Bible itself explicitly emphasizes, observing the Bible's own sense of proportion. Safest of all is the rule to read no more into, or out of, a writer's words than he himself intended, and always (in our sermon *preparation*) to bear in mind not only the passage we have chosen but whatever else the Bible has to say upon the same theme.

By this time, the reasons for this severe exegetical discipline will be sufficiently clear, but further emphasis may be necessary. The basic Protestant appeal to the scriptures as the final and sufficient authority in matters of faith and practice makes the attitude of our people towards the Bible a crucial issue. Yet that attitude is determined, for most Christians, not by careful theological considerations, but simply by the way in which preachers use the book in their pulpit ministry.

The widespread assumption that the Bible means whatever you can make it mean is the unhappy legacy of generations of preaching which took isolated phrases, mere fragments of scripture and wove around them whatever reflections or exhortations the preacher's temperament or fancy might suggest. The rise of modern cults, often appealing to the scriptures 'from cover to cover', and quoting them with a dexterity which few could argue against, found many Protestants vulnerable and easily persuaded, largely because this was the way they had heard the scriptures cited Sunday by Sunday—fragment piled upon fragment, without reference to what the original writers intended to say.

Even our Protestant divisiveness arises in part from the assumption that all are equally entitled to their own private interpretations by whatever subjective and ingenious means they choose, uncontrolled by the disciplines of grammar, original purpose, and historical revelation. Whenever the pulpit handles the scriptures irresponsibly, the people are left unarmed and defenceless against any eloquent charlatan peddling ancient heresies in modern guise.

Even so, some will feel that this approach is altogether too academic; that these strictures upon popular use of the scriptures in illustrative and emotional ways, are too severe. What should we make, for example, of a sermon which uses John 2: 1–11 as an illustration of the way Jesus can turn the water of an insipid, cheap, valueless life into the rich and intoxicating wine of discipleship? Or of John MacNeill's use of Luke 5: 1–11 as an exhortation to *Christians* to 'Launch out ... Let down ... Leave all'?

Are we forbidden, under any circumstances, to use the miracles of Jesus as parables of salvation? To see in David's band of bankrupt, hunted outlaws, disciplined at Adullam's cave into a great army by affection for their king, an illustration of the making of the church? May we not play around the imaginative suggestiveness of 'In the place where He was crucified, there was a garden'? Or see Peter walking the waves as 'a Christian with that sinking feeling'? May we not see in Naaman's leprosy a figure of sin, in Joshua's appeal for decision and loyalty, a message for Christian evangelists, in the city's twelve gates facing north, south, east and west and always open, a summons to Christian world-missions? or in the burning bush a symbol of the persecuted but enduring church, from which God speaks—with Moses an enquiring bystander, an 'adherent'?

Some contend earnestly for an inner 'spiritual' meaning everywhere. Others make much of 'typology', where all sure, plain obvious meanings are lost in multiple suggestions, hints, significant parallels, echoes, and two- or three-level interpretations all with elusive symbolic overtones. Others again will allow no meaning anywhere that is not 'Christological', whatever despite is done to original meanings in order to find 'Christ' in some passages. Admirable though the motives may sometimes be, one can only plead that the contenders shall foresee where they are leading, and the resulting chaos of interpretations, when other practitioners of 'double meanings', with other motives, get among their people.

Doubtless, great preachers have found fine meanings beneath the surface of plain texts, and applications of biblical words far beyond their original setting and purpose—and have done great work. Spurgeon laid down certain rules about 'spiritualising': avoid straining the text by 'illegitimate' spiritualising (meaning, apparently, whatever would not appeal to him); avoid perverting a text; never show off, or touch upon indelicate subjects; and always show the original and historical meaning in any case.

If we must tolerate spiritualising, this last rule is the safest. Whatever use you make of a passage, feel it laid upon your conscience to show what it really means, what word of God was in it for those to whom it was first given. If doing that ruins your sermon—so be it! But be aware of what you are doing. To impart a private, personally devised, interpretation to any passage is to evoke the reverence which devout people have for scripture on behalf of your own imported and imposed meanings. If what you want to say is true, and profitable, why pretend it arises from some text that had nothing to do with it? The need, in Christian worship, to justify your theme from scripture does not in the least warrant manipulating scripture to defend your subject. Better, surely, to do without a text, than to invent a meaning for words which God has spoken.

In saying so much about the discipline which reverence for 'the Word we preach' imposes, we do not forget that factors other than grammar, history, context, are involved. Let us conclude with yet another quotation from Luther who led the western world back to the Bible:

> If God does not open and explain Holy Writ none else can understand it: it will remain a closed book, enveloped in darkness . . . Therefore the first duty is to begin with a prayer of such a nature that God in His great mercy may grant you the true understanding of His words.

No one will quarrel with that counsel!

5 'WE PERSUADE MEN'

CONTEMPORARY interest in ancient documents is slight, and a profession devoted to their examination will not excite great enthusiasm in a techno-scientific age. For many, the only utterances that demand reverence are those of tomorrow, not of yesterday. We have already touched upon this dilemma, posed by loyalty to a past revelation versus the urgent need for an up-to-date message. It faced us in the contrast between expository and prophetic ministry; again in the place of relevance in the ideal sermon-pattern; yet again in the definition of preaching as the sharing of truth from faith to faith with a view to persuasion.

Yet our emphasis on exposition of scripture, combined with the insistent temptation to make evangelical preaching a mere exercise in Bible-worship, necessitates further attention to the place of ancient scripture in modern discipleship. Preaching, and the hearing of sermons, so easily becomes an end in itself, a devout mental exercise. It ceases to be purposeful preaching, and descends to evangelical entertainment.

If, as Macaulay said, 'the object of oratory is not truth but persuasion', the object of preaching is *both* truth and persuasion. Motive is of great importance in all public speaking: self-display, self-promotion, self-defence, robs it of all impressiveness. The self-interest obvious in most political speeches, and in all advertisements, discounts at once the fine phrases, glowing eulogies, selected testimonies, manipulated statistics. Just as surely, the absence of any worth-while purpose destroys the value of many sermons.

'The most eloquent speaker is not always the most persuasive,' says a lecturer in elocution; 'for the final test of a speech or a sermon is, what does it make us do—lead a new life? or increase our subscription? A sermon fails if it leaves us merely delighted with its own beauty of eloquence' (Grierson). That is well said: though a sermon may aim not only to make us act in some desirable way, but to encourage or console us, to educate, or to renew. The important point is that it must—to be a sermon at all—aim at persuading us in some direction or another.

Quiller-Couch, that most persuasive of writers, affirms that 'persuasion is the aim of all the arts, and I suppose of all the exposition

40

of the sciences; nay, of all useful exchange of converse in our daily life. It is what Velasquez attempts in a picture, Euclid in a proposition, the Prime Minister at the Treasury Bench, the journalist in a leading article, or the Vicar in his sermon . . . Nor can I imagine an earthly gift more covetable by you, gentlemen, than that of persuading your fellows to listen to your views and attend to what you have at heart.' Unless it be to listen to God's truth, and attend to what He has at heart for men.

Obvious as this task of persuasion seems, we still meet in some preachers the academic aloofness that is content to state an idea and leave it at that; the take-it-or-leave-it attitude, which leaves the congregation as coldly indifferent as the preacher himself; the bullying, 'you had better or else' intimidation, which wins no assent and kindles no high desire; and even sometimes the insufferable conceit which cannot contemplate that anyone can possibly disagree—and so takes no pains to persuade. It was said of two brilliant English politicians, that whereas Fox always spoke to the House of Commons, Burke seemed always to be speaking to himself. That withdrawn, self-absorbed speaking style is met perhaps oftener in the pulpit than in any other public life.

Brethren, 'knowing the fear of the Lord, *we persuade men*', or we are not preachers. And the power of persuasion demands an aim in view, a deep level of communication, and some skill with 'the persuaders'.

Relevance—to Persuade of What?

Plainly persuasiveness presupposes something to be attained, imparted, stimulated, resolved. Jowett (in his Yale Lectures) declared, 'We are not in the pulpit to please the fancy, to inform the mind, to disturb the emotions, to sway the judgement; our ultimate object is to move the will.' Jowett would be first to agree that you will not do the last unless you also affect fancy, emotion, and judgement, but the point is well taken. We can do all and yet fail if the will makes no response.

Professor Edgar Dickie, of St. Andrews, confessed 'We preach always in anxiety, and under tension, since we are preaching every time *for a verdict*. How momentous that Moody so preached a noble and convincing and solemnising sermon that day when one of the audience was the young man who had dropped into the church out of curiosity, Wilfred Grenfell of Labrador.' Even more important, perhaps, was the purposefulness of that unknown Methodist lay-preacher whom the young Spurgeon heard when, delayed by snow, he joined the congregation of seven in a wayside chapel. The verdict which that good man aimed at made Spurgeon the greatest gospel preacher of the nineteenth century.

But the necessity of some aim towards which we persuade men must not be limited to evangelistic preaching. Whenever we preach, it is not for enjoyment of the exercise, for compliments, for admiration, for gratitude, or to deliver our own souls: but for response. That is why we must address only those present—the absent cannot be persuaded to anything. That is why we must not remain in the scripture's world, nor digress to world surveys, theological curiosities, academic hobbies, or any other theme about which any response then and there in the service is impossible to the hearer. It may be very clever, very eloquent, intellectually satisfying: as preaching it is a waste of time; and what is worse, a waste of worship.

Without relevance, our preaching will have little interest, less understanding, no application, no authority, no blessing. It is merely ill-spent breath, and will only confirm the critics' opinion that religion is divorced from real life. Says Fosdick, 'Every sermon should have for its main business the solving of some human problem, a vitally important problem, puzzling minds, burdening consciences, distracting lives.' Ideally, there should always be some clear good reason for preaching that sermon to those people on that occasion.

Later on, we shall suggest that the first step in all sermon preparation is to write down, in one crisp sentence, what it is the sermon aims to do. The great difficulty of doing that, with utter honesty, only underlines its necessity. For the moment, we note only the inescapable fact that without purpose the sermon cannot persuade. Where the aim is lacking, or remains vague and undefined, preaching becomes a mental perambulation through beloved themes, 'the bland leading the bland' in a mist of pious platitudes.

Communication—the Levels of Persuasion

But persuasion implies more than relevance: it demands involvement. The purpose of the preacher has to be communicated to the congregation, to become their purpose also. Something has to be kindled, moved, achieved, while the service proceeds. The truth must be *shared*, not merely passed from one mind to other minds in words, but so that it comes to belong to both, and grips both speaker and hearers. Preaching is 'from faith to faith'—from the conviction of the preacher, to the convincing of the listener before God. That *is* persuasion.

'Nothing more immediately indicates the born orator,' says the ever practical Grierson, 'than the power to get quickly into touch with his audience. He is the person who puts into words with felicity and with the appearance of conviction, what his audience already half-thinks and wishes to believe'—'What oft was thought, but ne'er so well expressed!' Sometimes, of course, the thought, the vision, is wholly new: but the congregation feels obliged to assent because it is so persuasively presented, so convincingly deduced from the faith and principles they already hold.

This is the depth of communication that goes on in preaching. Far too often the sermon is considered in purely intellectual terms, as a pattern of ideas, a line of thought, a communication of truth in words and images. In consequence, we discuss the 'problem of communication' almost entirely as a problem of *language*. Yet Christianity is not communicable in words—else Christ would have written a book. Preaching is ever the attempt to teach the unteach-able. Its communication must therefore proceed upon more than an intellectual level, and involve emotion, aspiration, desire, regret, hope, fear, and faith.

Of course, without intelligibility there will be no communication at all. There are intellectual obstacles, in the hearers' unexamined assumptions, and verbal problems in the differences of language between pulpit and pew. But there are moral, emotional, and spiritual resistance to be overcome too, and this calls for all the arts of persuasive pleading, and for the power of the Holy Spirit.

A great English preacher, Gilbert Laws, with this need in mind, described preaching as 'elevated conversation'. A well-preached sermon is never a monologue. Without mental and emotional talk-back from the pew, there is no preaching—only a lecture, a recital. A written sermon, for this reason, is a contradiction in terms, as lines of printed symbols are not music, and paint and canvas are not art. The 'mass media of communication'—telephone, radio, film and journalism—all in some measure depersonalise human expression and to that extent *diminish* communication. No play-wright would be content to print, as no man in his senses would choose to propose to his beloved by letter. The kindling contact of person to person is of the essence of communication, and most of all in things of faith.

Charles Dickens has a wonderful portrait of a preacher (in Bleak House) which we may enjoy despite its warning. 'It happens that Mr. Chadband has a pulpit habit of fixing some member of the congrega-tion with his eye and flatly arguing his points with that particular person, who is understood to be moved to an occasional grunt, groan, gasp, or other audible expression of inward working, which expression of inward working, being echoed by some elderly lady in the next pew and so communicated like a game of forfeits through a circle of the more fermentable sinners present, serves the purpose of parliamentary cheering and gets Mr. Chadband's steam up.' We take the point. But like all caricature, its power lies in the truth it distorts, and Dickens is saying in one way what Gladstone said in his very different language: 'The orator gives back in a shower what he receives from his audience in a vapour.' Both are confirming the essential point, that persuasion demands involvement, speaker and hearers sharing together in ideas, emotion, imagination, obligation, and response.

The level of this 'elevated conversation' varies in different cultures, but it is always present in some degree in great preaching. Negro preachers have always been able to play upon the mind and feeling of their hearers until the theme of the sermon takes hold and is transmuted into rhythmic speech, movement, and music. So the 'spirituals' were born: 'Go down Moses, let my people go', 'Didn't my Lord deliver Daniel?' 'Swing low, sweet chariot', 'All God's chillun got shoes'—all are said to be the psychological come-back of an entranced congregation caught up in a preacher's message.

In Wales the participation of the congregation was usually less vocal, though often the emotional ejaculation of appropriate responses will at once break and quicken the tension of a service. It is told of one powerful and beloved master of the Welsh pulpit that he so described the inward hesitations of the Prodigal Son as to startle the congregation into wholly involuntary action. The preacher himself sat hunched in a corner of the pulpit, as though bending over a bucket of 'the husks that the swine did eat'. For some ten minutes he was absorbed in self-communing, aloud, turning over all the reasons for making his way home, or staying, every now and then half rising with a tense 'I will arise, and go to my father . . .' but then sinking back as some fresh misgiving assailed him, the wrong he had done, the shame, the attitude of his brother. When at last the resolution was reached, and the preacher suddenly stood, with a determined 'I will arise . . .' two thousand listeners stood up with him, and knew not why.

That is communication at depth. Dr John Pitts records that at a war-time service in central London, Dr G. Campbell Morgan was once interrupted with a burst of hand-clapping, an almost unheard of tribute to great preaching in that sober atmosphere. The spoken 'Hallelujah', the whispered 'Amen', even the quickened heart-beat and the moist eye, are tokens of the working of the truth, and of the presence of the Spirit, which every preacher who knows what he is about prays to see. Preaching, in the setting of worship, is then in truth an experience of God.

Some will dislike this plea for persuasive preaching and deep-level communication, as emotional, even dangerous. Words like 'oratory' 'elocution' may suggest artificial techniques of public speaking unfitting to spiritual work: 'the weapons of our warfare are not carnal'. The means of persuasion will be considered presently, but whatever means are used, there can be no question that our task is to persuade, to move men and women to new experience, new faith, new attempting. *And nothing moves the will but emotion.* More accurately, the word 'emotion' *means* simply 'that which moves'. To cultivate emotionalism for its own sake is indeed superficial, immature, even dangerous in some cases. But to despise emotion, and avoid it, is to condemn all preaching to sterile ineffectiveness.

The 'Persuaders'

The question remains, whether the deep-level, persuasive factors in preaching can be prepared in the study. Probably most beginners rely upon the presence of the congregation, the atmosphere of worship, the sense of occasion, the preparatory time of prayer, to lend emotional and moral force to what they have prepared. But sometimes this does not work. It never works when the sermon itself has been prepared as a mere essay in theology or exegesis. *The intention to persuade must be present from the start*, or the sermon will never get off the study desk into the hearts of the hearers.

Among preparable factors that make for persuasive preaching may be noted:

(i) *The presence of the congregation in the study.* As the hearers, by their responsiveness, contribute much to the effective preaching of a message, so by continually looking over the shoulder of the minister at his desk they contribute more than they ever know to its preparation. They are in his mind from the beginning, so far as circumstances allow, even if only as an imagined group of unknown Christians at worship. The better the preacher knows them, the more powerfully will they influence his choice of subjects, his level of language, his form of argument, his selection of illustrations.

The invisible presence of the intended hearers will often trim away the academic conceits, the obscure allusion, the display of cleverness, and prompt other thoughts more closely related to the business of Christian living. It is a rewarding habit, not only when thoughts dry up and the going is heavy, but at the start of every new paragraph, to hold the pen poised for a moment, and *visualise* the individuals for whom you are preparing. If you are hoping to move them, you had better keep them in mind.

(ii) It follows that to *know your congregation* will greatly assist in preparing to persuade them. The pastor has immense advantage over the guest preacher: some would contend that pastoral preaching is the only true pulpit ministry. Certainly, the same theme, material, style, approach and manner will captivate one congregation and repel another. A sensitive preacher is aware of, and responsive to, the traditions, the prejudices, the level of culture, the commanding interests and problems of every audience.

Obvious differences between city and country-dweller, fishermen and businessmen, soldiers and seamstresses, old and young, will shape the preacher's work without conscious effort. But a little thought before each sermon begins may reveal others, arising from race, prevailing occupation, educational opportunities, religious tradition, recent local events. No honest man will allow awareness of such predispositions to determine the truth he will preach: but it will affect considerably the way he presents it, if his aim is to persuade.

The advice to 'assume nothing' in your hearers may have value: it can also reduce the level of preaching to a puerile string of platitudes which exasperates the most patient hearer. If you assume nothing in the way of biblical and theological knowledge, at the same time never under-estimate the intelligence of your congregation. For them to be in church at all reveals an awareness, and a hunger, above the average. And many will be experts in professional fields; all of them will be watchers and listeners at programmes presented by experts. If they did not completely understand, they will remember sufficiently to recognise that you did not understand either!

Vague, unverifiable assertions, confident sweeping statements, carefully rehearsed and boldly enunciated technical terms and allusions you barely understand, hints at the erudite books and documents you could quote if they were able to understand—all this may inflate your ego but it quite certainly deflates your authority in the eyes of the perceptive listener. To parade superior education before the less educated is, in any case, an unforgivable discourtesy in a Christian.

Overemphasis, too, is always self-defeating. You may bully a few people by this means, but you will fail to persuade the thoughtful. Extreme arguments, exaggerated description, an unbalanced stress upon one aspect of truth, synthetic indignation, always fail to win assent, and increasingly violent language yields diminishing returns in effectiveness. In other public realms, of politics and advertising, speakers may indulge in overemphasis in the hope that when all discounts are made the residual impression will be favourable to their case. With the kind of people whom the preacher meets, and the cause he stands for, the counter-effect is far stronger. He is expected to have a care for truth, and the true will withhold their approval when he is careless of her good name.

The first obligation of the preacher who hopes for respect is to respect his congregation, for their knowledge, their faith, their dedication to God no less ardent than his own, their ability to see through him when he is anything less than genuine. If ever he is to persuade them, he must consider their assent worth winning.

(iii) And *persuasion certainly depends upon sympathy*. You may harangue, lecture, declaim, even after a fashion warn, without it: you cannot preach without it. Said one of the most persuasive of Welsh preachers, Ingli James, 'You must learn to love if you want to win. Jesus preached not as a rabbi or a Pharisee, but as a friend.'

In quite crucial ways, of which we are often tragically unaware, this affects sermon preparation. You will never persuade anyone to face their problem in the way that you advise, if you do not first persuade them that you have felt, and understood, and in some measure shared, what they are up against. You can never effectively warn anyone of the consequences of their ways, if you have not first shown them that you are concerned about what happens to them. Nor will you kindle love for Christ in any young heart that has not first been made to realise that you love him for Christ's sake.

Shame is never evoked by condemnation as it is by your obvious regret and disappointment that such a person could stoop to such things. Faith is never born except in response to a testimony and an invitation voiced with all the earnestness of one who cares. Nor can you encourage anyone whose despair you have not felt, or comfort the bereaved and brokenhearted by long-distance telephone.

The idealist in the pulpit so often seems to resent the ordinariness of the people in the pew: is it surprising that they resent his strictures? A perfectionist preaching is a scarifying spectacle! Said a young army officer to his padre, 'Minister, pray for me when we leave for the front tomorrow.' 'I am coming with you' was the reply. Not his prayers only, but any persuasion he might attempt would carry treble its weight for that remark. Christ's preaching gained much of its unanswerable power because He was content to be numbered with transgressors.

This necessity of sympathy rules out entirely the hectoring, driving, aggressive attitude that the pulpit breeds in some natures. It precludes, too, youth's special gift of scorn and ridicule. It puts out of the preacher's reach some of the sharpest weapons of persuasion—sarcasm, which hurts without healing, innuendo, public reproach, threatening, contempt. Such self-denial may be painful for the impatient man: but the preacher starts beside his listener as a fellow-Christian—or one he would win to be a fellow-Christian—and all his methods and his manner are controlled by that basic love for men that first made him want to bring to them the word of a loving God.

(iv) Persuasiveness is impossible if the preacher cannot be *distinctly heard and clearly understood.* Clarity of style, and a simple, direct form of reasoning, powerfully convey conviction from one mind to others. A man may be as earnest, as learned, even as true, as is humanly possible, but I do not begin to go with him until I see what he means. Of the aids to clearness we must speak again, but its imperative necessity to any attempt to persuade must be realised from the beginning. So many sermons fail to make their point just because the point was never clear from the start.

Of course, clarity of speech is equally important. If it takes much effort to hear what is being said, I have little left to weigh and respond to it. But the secret of being heard, even in the big auditorium, lies rather in clearness of diction and deliberate, measured speed, than in loudness of tone. A man who takes the trouble to make himself clear has already pierced my defences and captured my attention.

Persuasiveness is made difficult, too, if between the preacher and the listeners there intrudes the sheaf of papers which constantly reminds them that the preacher is not really talking to them, thinking with them, but reciting ideas prepared at another time and place. Richard Du Cann (The Art of the Advocate) says many things as pertinent to preaching as to practice in the courts. Among them is this: 'The great advantage of mastery of material, whether of fact or thought or plain rhetoric, is that it leaves the advocate's eye free to gauge the effect of his words . . . It also leaves a part of the mind free to arrange the order of the next sentence. If while speaking he is a prisoner of his writing, the paper on which he relies becomes a barrier between himself and his audience.'

This is authoritative advice, even if it be for many a counsel of perfection. It is well to write sermons, for exactness of thought, clarity of expression, facility with words, preservation of ideas, and (in some delicate church situations) for record of what is said. But to *read* what is written will persuade few—even to listen. To memorise is a great strain, and can inhibit freedom and force. Brief notes can give a speaker liberty of utterance while not tying him to the desk, or to his spectacles. But for the purpose of persuasion, nothing excels the full mind, refreshed within the pulpit from notes, but at the moment of preaching putting all away and talking directly to the eyes of the congregation.

(v) At some risk, it may be added that persuasiveness may sometimes be increased by *re-iteration*. The risk lies in the besetting temptation to repeat oneself, to rehearse one's few cherished ideas to the point where regular listeners could do the work themselves. But re-iteration of a principle, a truth, a warning, or an invitation, is not the same as repetition. An earnest workman will not mind covering the same ground again, from other directions, at different speed, in different intellectual weather, if in the end he can persuade someone to walk with him.

Nothing persuades like persistence combined with patience. Not everyone grasps an argument, sees a point, or realises a need, on first acquantance. Sometimes the new insight or challenge confuses by its newness, and will persuade only with increasing familiarity. By re-iteration of basic ideas through variety of presentation, one can enlist the strange power of habit to hold the mind. The hearer comes to recognise the thought, the challenge—and even to think it is his own! What matters, so long as it has been implanted, and is the truth of God?

Jerusalem was not built in a day: and neither evangelist nor pastor really believes in instant ministry. If you want your people to follow into some new spiritual country, into some novel enterprise, it is well to give them time to catch up!

(vi) Persuasiveness will depend, too, on *particularised, and individualised, appeal*. A direct hit requires expert aim at a chosen target, not a shower of buckshot. The listener must not be left acknowledging in a general way that someone or other should be doing something or other about the preacher's concern: he must feel that he must do something now, and know what. He must realise, before the closing hymn, that what he has heard was just the truth he needed.

At one point of spiritual difficulty, Luther was advised to 'personalise the creed'; not to say 'I believe in God' but 'I believe in *my* God; in Jesus Christ His only Son, *my* Lord; in the redemption of *my* world . . . the forgiveness of *my* sins . . .' A worship-service, with the sense of the divine presence, and a mature and faithful spokesman bringing God's sure word to a waiting and responsive people, should accomplish precisely that for every worshipper. The promises become my treasure, the precepts my guiding counsel, the text is God's word to me, the assurances are my refreshment, and the rebukes my discipline. To achieve that personal application requires, beside sympathy and understanding, considerable courtesy and delicacy, but it makes preaching spiritually fruitful and a means of grace.

An important instance of this persuasive personalising of the message is the appeal directly to conscience. The preacher's sounding-board within the soul is a wide one: mind, feeling, memory, will, admiration for great souls, the lingering fragrance of a pious home, as well as deeper notes of personal bewilderment, anxiety, frustration, regret, guilt, temptation, conflict, fear, hope and aspiration. Yet the one ultimate and effective point of application is the individual conscience.

That is the spot most sensitive, in all the circumstances of worship, to the divine pressure of the truth, and the appeal of Christ. And to that receptor the preacher's persuasion is most persistently addressed. With all our modern psychological expertise, we seem less skilled than some former generations in touching men at this level: but conscience still reacts to truth, and we must rediscover the secrets of soul-surgery if preaching is to regain its former power.

In Paul's finest definition of preaching—'by manifestation of the truth commending ourselves to every man's conscience in the sight of God'—every word is significant; but especially perhaps this leaving of the word spoken upon the hearer's conscience in the presence of God. Of course, conscience is approached through reason, imagination, emotion, argument, appeal: but too often we are content with the means and forget the end. We are satisfied that the argument has been sound, the illustrations vivid, the truth made clear, the service 'enjoyable', but we have not pressed the whole to the point where truth confronts the conscience as unanswerable assurance or demand, with comforting or uncomfortable power.

Yet that alone is where the work is done, the blessing given, and where the conviction of the Spirit may be expected.

(vii) Finally, nothing will persuade until it kindles feeling, and *some touch of passion*, not only in the pulpit but in the preparation and in the material, is essential to a fruitful response.

The calculating Lord Chesterfield advised his son, with a political career in mind: 'Whenever you would persuade or prevail, address yourself to the passions; it is by them that mankind is to be taken. I bid you strike at the passions . . . If you can once engage people's pride, love, pity, ambition (or whichever is their prevailing passion) on your side, you need not fear what their reason can do against you.'

The air of cynicism here repels, but the statements are broadly true. 'An orator,' says W. J. Bryan 'is one who says what he thinks and feels what he says': the evidence that he is an orator is that he makes other people feel it too. 'Feel what you preach' advises Spurgeon, outlining 'rules of success': 'aim directly at the heart'. John Brown of Scotland is said to have preached with such fervour that the brilliant sceptic-philosopher David Hume commented 'He preaches as if Jesus Christ were at his elbow'. It was not intellectual brilliance which evoked that tribute, for intellectual argument was something Hume of all men could arm himself against. It was a soul on fire for Christ—against which there is no defence.

Yet passion must not be confused with noise. It is intensity of feeling which is contagious, rather than its overt demonstration, and only the intensely felt, deeply moving, truth can achieve a *religious* end. 'Loud bawling orators are driven by their weakness to noise, as lame men take to horse' wrote Cicero, one of history's greatest public speakers, who should know. Yet a little Christian warmth of feeling will usually kindle in a congregation an answering warmth that can melt the heart and mould the will in godlier ways.

No one accustomed to Christian thinking and worship will suppose that persuasion to the kind of resolution which the Christian preacher aims at can be manipulated by such aids as we have outlined. Lasting spiritual effects are not to be obtained by elocutionary gimmicks. We have assumed as self-evidently vital the truth of the message preached, and the call of the man to preach it. And with these must be mentioned, as essential to spiritual effectiveness—

the power inherent in all truth to win its way
the contagion of a living faith, effectively expressed
the witness of a convinced mind, persuasively stated
the fervour of a sincere soul, sympathetically imparted
the confirmation of a character at one with the preacher's profession

and beneath, above, and through all else,

the guidance, inspiration, and conviction of the Holy Spirit.

Yet essential as these are, without some care, patience, and skill in persuading men, their power is curbed and their effectiveness needlessly circumscribed.

Even when all these are mentioned, the secret still eludes us. A man of God, speaking in the name of Christ, by the power of the Holy Spirit, may with broken and incoherent sentences, ill-assorted thoughts and clumsy expression, accomplish wonders for the kingdom of God—not because of his inadequacy, nor doing it the better for his want of skill, but in spite of it.

None knew nor how nor why, but he entwined
Himself perforce around the hearer's mind.

Let one soul testify to a lifelong debt, in Christ, to one such faithful teacher.

THE TECHNIQUE

6 CONTEMPORARY ATTITUDES AND COUNTERING TECHNIQUES

SINCE WE are to discuss 'techniques' of preparing and preaching sermons, something should be said in defence of a 'technical' or 'professional' approach to work so spiritual; and about the factors which determine it.

Reference has already been made to the relation of innate gift and vocation to acquired knowledge and skill, in the parallel cases of nurses, doctors, writers and artists. Even 'born musicians' usually have to learn music. But the temptation stubbornly remains, to rely upon personal inspiration rather than methodical toil. Only experience teaches the young preacher that his best results (in the congregations' ears and hearts) will most often come from uninspired hard work.

The high excitement when subject, material, arrangement, and the zest to preach all come as a gift together in a glowing hour of thought and prayer, will always seem to yield the message most satisfying to the preacher. But 'work commands inspiration, and does not wait for it' says one teacher. 'Application is a minor form of genius' replies another. 'Show thyself . . . a workman' said a third. The minister who relies upon being a born preacher, needing no methodical plan of work, deserves to be saddled with a 'born treasurer' who never learned to pay the stipend on time!

Yet labour without direction may be wasted. Hence arises the need for attention to technique—the best attainable method of approach, that will save time, sharpen skill, and avoid pitfalls, through the insight and discipline of an informed homiletic mind. Sound technique never yet made a good preacher, but lack of it makes many poorer than they need to be. Besides, technique is the only element of the preaching art which can be taught: inspiration, integrity, responsibility, grace, cannot be imparted by any human teacher.

Nor will the man who finds his congregation dwindling and his preaching fruitless find help in greater prayer, if prayer is the substitute for honest labour at improving his resources, skill and attainment in the work which God has given him. No man can

consistently rely upon God's blessing making up for his own in-
competence or laziness. Nor is anyone likely to be the least bettered
by listening, week after week, to commonplaces which cost us
nothing. In the story of the church, the men most deeply convinced
of their call from God to preach, and most humbly aware of their
need of divine help to do it, have always at the same time lamented
the paucity of their natural gifts, and have shown their dedication
by the diligence of their toil.

John Wesley in his Journal confessed 'If I had to preach to the
same congregation Sunday after Sunday, even for a year, I should
soon preach them and myself to sleep'. Yet thousands have done
just that, without any soporific effect, but to the upbuilding of
churches and saints. But only when informed methods of labour
have ensured maximum resources and the trained use of them, to
the preacher's increasing ease and the listener's immeasurable
benefit.

The two factors which must guide that preaching technique are
obvious. One is a clear understanding of what the preacher is
about, of the ideal at which he aims, which we have tried to describe.
The danger here is that the *beginner* may honestly strive to get the
purpose and ideal of preaching clear in his mind, and then forget it,
as familiarity and habit dull his sense of wonder at what he is doing.

The other factor shaping technique is an acute awareness of
the special conditions within which, in these days, that ideal has
to be served. Of these we must now speak, however briefly: for the
contemporary preacher will not make much impression if he fails
to reckon with attitudes adverse to preaching, which he may well
face within his congregation, and not only among the younger members.

The preacher today must not be surprised to meet:

(i) persistent *suspicion* of his motives and his sincerity. In most
churches, the preacher is usually a salaried protagonist of a cause on
which his personal interests obviously depend. He is no impartial
or disinterested witness to what he claims. In truth, he is a preacher
because he so believes, and not *vice versa*: but that will not satisfy
the critically inclined.

A certain inbuilt distrust of propaganda is one of the legacies
of war, with its definition of *truth* as 'the assertion that best serves
the cause', and of news as 'not something objective that you report,
but something you handle and mould, invent or suppress, in the
interests of policy'. Linked with this is a widespread 'back-lash'
against advertising, which automatically discounts any confident

assertion, any proffered evidence, or enthusiastic commendation, as selfishly motivated special pleading.

One manifestation of this attitude is resentment at being 'talked at' without opportunity to challenge; in sympathetic listeners, it prompts requests for discussion of the sermon. This raises serious questions about the true function of the Christian preacher, whether he is one arguing a case, or one proclaiming a divine gospel.

Whatever the preacher decides about that, the modern atmosphere of suspicion towards all 'publicists' must considerably modify traditional pulpit attitudes. A conciliatory spirit, and a wholly undogmatic approach, are plainly essential. Reasonableness of argument and attitude, and something nearer to a conversational style than the declaiming harangue of earlier decades, are also demanded. Humility and diffidence will in these days prove far more powerful than arrogance and assertiveness—even if Christian standards of conduct did not exclude these in any case.

Aware of the anti-professional attitude of many, the shrewd preacher will also draw his examples and illustrations constantly from the lives of lay-people in ordinary world-environed situations, rather than from the inner history of the church or from biblical figures. In this way, he answers the objector without seeming to, silently making the point that what he is saying is as relevant to lay-folk as to parsons.

(ii) The modern preacher will of course expect to meet much *indifference*, both towards himself and to what he wishes to say. This is a relatively novel situation for the Christian pulpit, which has often been opposed, occasionally reviled, oftenest tolerated with pretended respect, but only rarely treated with indifference or contempt.

One obvious result, as serious for the quality of preaching as for its influence and opportunity, is the smaller congregations. 'The first necessity for good speaking is a large audience' says Anthony Trollope. The consequence of small audiences is often a discouraged, pedestrian preacher who finds no inspiration, no sense of occasion, to give his hard-won words any wings.

The truest cure for this wholly mechanical depression by numbers is an honest recognition by the preacher of exactly what is happening to his own spirit. Often he feels hurt, neglected, slighted, by his constituency: the root may be pride. A better valuation of the faithful folk who are still loyal, and a remembrance of the Master's reverence for the few, and His many attentive conversations even with one soul, will help.

The realisation that, at any rate, there is no cure for the small congregation but to preach better the fewer there are present, will also brace his courage. It would be mere self-pity to imagine that all the blame for poor attendances lies with one's own inadequacy. Many factors beyond the preacher's control, or the church's, contribute to the drift from true religion. It may be added that some speeches upon which human lives and liberties depend are often delivered to gain the verdict of only twelve 'good men and true'.

Yet indifference will demand of the preacher more than courage. He must set about circumventing it, and acknowledge it to be part of his duty to overcome it. To presume upon interested attention is to invite rejection. He must learn to kindle interest, to sustain interest, to cultivate the expectation that he will be interesting, and to use interest as a weapon of persuasion; and he must be quick to detect, in preparation and in preaching, the point at which interest flags. For lost interest means lost hearers.

Some earnest men recoil from this obligation to arrest and hold attention, despising the light, anecdotal, entertaining sermon as trivial, irresponsible, 'mere religious music-hall'. This attitude may be justified, it is certainly understandable, within the Christian circle: it is no help at all in gaining the ear of the indifferent and unconcerned. Granted that the purpose on hand is the most serious in the world, the indifferent are not to be coerced into attending by dourness and threatening. Whom we would persuade, we must first entice to listen, and there is no compulsion we can use but that of a man's own alerted interest. Only so can we lead him, unawares, to entertain ideas he had not intended to hear.

(iii) A third factor in the modern situation is the widespread *aversion to anything unpractical*, irrelevant to life, merely academic. This, too, is a new situation, as the great sermons of a former generation will show. Delight in theologising for its own sake, in philosophic and logical analyses, even in speculation on matters beyond human knowledge, often prompted long and exceedingly abstract disquisitions. Among the most valuable, Butler's 'sermons' were delivered to public congregations, though today they are prescribed philosophic texts. And Liddon, Dale on Christian doctrine, even Spurgeon in his more Puritan moods, achieved a level of pure intellectual interest which few dare attempt today.

Intense social concern, finding few solutions to desperate human problems; the moral pressures of a turbulent, permissive, and increasingly violent society; the challenge to accepted standards of behaviour, and the emergence of sharp new practical problems with every increase in man's knowledge and power—all contribute to the demand for practical leadership and relevant counsel. Many are impatient of thinking for thinking's sake. Even more clearly, applied science has taught our generation to believe that the only profitable end of knowledge is use, and to test all research by technological applications. To know is no longer important: to know-how is everything.

In this climate, pragmatism, which erects the *results* of a doctrine or an idea into the proof or disproof of its *truth*, has become an almost universal assumption by which to evaluate education, law, politics, philosophy, and religion. The preacher as theologian and scholar may wish to oppose this attitude with high arguments about intrinsic truth and the value of knowledge for its own sake. The preacher as citizen may wish sometimes to comment upon public problems, though he will not attempt to discuss world affairs as though his hearers were the United Nations Assembly. But the man-in-the-pulpit setting out to persuade the man-in-the-pew will always reckon with the climate in which he preaches and the unconscious assumptions of his hearers.

So he will strive constantly to bring the high doctrines into the market-place, and the soaring theology of the New Testament into the home, the church, the workshop, the social environment, and the individual conscience. He will do so all the more readily if he observes how the Master preached, and how Paul counselled his churches. But *do it he must*, whether readily or reluctantly, if he would catch the ear of our time and carry with him the assent of the modern listener. Most congregations like their preachers to be scholars, but not to sound like them.

(iv) Yet amid all this, perhaps the most obvious characteristic of the time in which we preach is the decline in the listener's power of concentration upon the spoken word. For two generations at least, education has been highly visual and concrete in method, with models, illustrations, films, slides, graphics, cartoons, diagrams, and varied techniques for physical involvement, participation, and discovery.

Even the weather forecast is depicted, not spoken, and road signs abandon words for symbols. The great classics of literature are visualised for us on screen or strip magazine, and great newspapers tend to become picture albums with ever shorter captions. The expert journalist is he who can 'say' most in briefest headlines. Advertising has long given up both reason and speech, relying upon pictorially presented association and suggestion, which permits no logical analysis or contradiction. Characters in modern plays become steadily more incoherent, even inarticulate, reflecting a trend observable also in daily life.

Three results stem from this essentially non-literary nature of our present culture. Except for the poets (and even in part for them) we have largely lost the sense, the feel, the precision, delight, and mastery of *words*. We grow poor and slovenly in vocabulary and speech. That all examples which might be given are fleeting is part of the malaise: but at one time everything good, attractive, exciting, highly coloured, romantic, expensive, satisfying, melodious, up-to-date, popular, or different, is just 'fab'—which used to be 'fabulous', which used to be 'fabulously good, attractive, exciting, and the rest'. Simultaneously, all speech and writing become steadily more violent, coarse, exaggerated, because each word is devalued by imprecision. Words inevitably lose their spell in a visual culture.

There is loss, too, of the power of *imagination*. The great books, plays, speeches, have ever been those which could evoke pictures, scenes, characters, and create the total situation described, by the power of words over the mind of the reader. Once that is done for us, in cartoon, film or television, we *see* how the hero was dressed, the splendours of ancient Rome, the tender expressions of first love, the horror of Macbeth. That all was achieved by grease-paint, practice, twenty retakes before the scene was right, and tons of papier mache and cardboard, matters little. The price we pay for mass-produced, ready-made images is the loss of imaginative power and the decay of imaginative response.

> Anthony Trollope could convey all the poignancy and passion of a love scene, involved in a disparity of social levels and a tangled story of false accusation overshadowing the girl with family shame, against which the noble loyalty of the young squire is proved faithful. He does it by means of a downcast eye, a fluttering whisper, and a repressed half-sentence. Yet he makes us *feel* the poignancy, he calls up in us the passion and the joy. Today we laugh at the sentiment. But the modern writer just cannot do it—with all his sensuous imagery, his double entendre, his detailed descriptions of figure and dress, and his all-too-explicit account of the mental and physical relationship involved. He tells you everything—and does not get half the emotional or imaginative result in intensity of sympathy. All he can stir is lust, or so it seems. Hence modern language grows ever more unrestrained and uncensored, striving to regain the lost effectiveness in creating images in the mind of the responsive reader.

Poverty of words and poverty of imagination make it difficult for many to sustain listening, or reading, for any length of time, or to retain what they hear or read. There is widespread loss of *capacity for concentration*. In almost any popular newspaper, the news articles, leaders and features get progressively shorter. Each paragraph dwindles to one or two sentences, never more than three; and each sentence is simple, brief, rarely more than ten words, sometimes mere ejaculations of three or four words. And always—one thought at a time! Editors know their readers.

In her study of Winston Churchill, Lady Violet Bonham Carter has a vivid comment upon the decline in capacity for *listening*. She says, 'In those days of the small electorate, speeches were not only eagerly listened to, but were reported verbatim and avidly read. When I think of the patience and apparent pleasure with which vast audiences would follow close-knit argument buttressed by hard dry facts— import and export statistics and Board of Trade returns—I realize how impossible it would be to get the same attention for the same matter nowadays. I remember hearing that the Newcastle Hippo- drome, holding some three thousand people, was sold out for several nights in succession while the Free Trade v. Protection case was debated by a distinguished but rather dry and academic Liberal . . . and a Conservative protagonist of Tariffs. No Hippodrome in England could be half-filled, even for one night, by such a performance today.' In fact, the 1970 equivalent, at the British General Election, con- sisted of five or ten minute interviews with leaders, visually presented with films and diagrams, on television.

These consequences of cultural changes around us affect deeply the milieu in which we preach. The technique of preaching has to reckon with the difficulties of the hearer—but what can we do? Some would substitute for sermons, religious film-strips, visual aids of many kinds; some would act plays, or process round the church in gorgeous vestments, adorning the premises with pictures, images, and sacred symbols. Some clamour for an imaginative, colourful, and non-literary ritual. Most of us could make far more than we do of the priceless acted-gospels we already possess in baptism and the Lord's Supper, both perfect teaching-spectacles. But what of preaching itself?

This question will occupy us at length. But it is immediately obvious that the preacher who would grasp and hold his hearers must learn to exploit the mind's capacity to see what is clearly described. He must learn to project his thoughts on to the screen of the mind in colourful images, clearly focussed. Other devices to meet the lack of listening concentration and retentive power include a well-ordered, memorable outline; and the deliberate kindling of emotion—without which nothing said will be vividly recalled. The purely intellectual sermon is acceptable only to 'eggheads'—whose major problem in religion is not an impaired power of concentration.

Variety, too, is essential, in face of this inability to listen and retain. Much will be said of this also, not pleading for variety for its own sake, but as *necessary* to catch and hold a modern listener's attention for any useful length of time. And the preacher must learn to get his effects with great economy of words. Shorter sermons usually demand greater preparation and self-discipline in preaching, and those who highly value their calling find it hard to concede the demand for brevity. Yet if the extra five or ten minutes *diminish* the impact, because the hearers just cannot contain all that is offered, we have gained nothing and lost what we had!

In the end the preacher's only answer to decreasing time, capacity, and opportunity, is ever increasing efficiency.

(v) A fifth characteristic of the church in which we preach is harder to describe and to reckon with. It is an emotional, and half-conscious, *materialism* to which the spiritual world is almost wholly unreal. This often underlies the demand for preaching that is relevant to *this* world. Talk of immortality, for example, is almost meaningless to most modern people, except in the context of bereavement, where the immediate relevance of the Christian hope is felt and acknowledged.

Even those who 'firmly' believe in God, in the living and ascended Christ, in heaven and hell, in the moral law, the power of truth, of beauty, and of goodness, the victory of faith—even these find it hard to realise—that is, to make real to themselves—what their beliefs mean. And for many modern people, all religious talk is purest make-believe.

The preacher cannot, of course, come to terms with this complete antithesis to his own thinking and attitude. But he must remember how deeply it affects his listeners. Reckoning with it, he will endeavour at all times to use specific, precise language, avoiding woolly and mystical approximations to what he thinks he is trying to express. A foggy imprecision plays at once into the scepticism of those who profess to be unable to make sense of his message.

The preacher will, in the same shrewd way, constantly emphasize the utter mystery, the inexplicable paradoxes, the sheer miracle, of the known material world. He will press earth's wonder, the multitude of things we cannot explain in the natural world about us, to the boundaries of thought, where religious questions of origin, nature, purpose, and destiny, inevitably arise. He will continually remind his listeners of the constant interaction of physical and historical facts with moral and spiritual ones, in the unfolding of human life and destiny.

In social and political affairs, in morality and welfare, in humanistic concern and scientific understanding, and in all relationships of people, the influence of character, faith, courage, vision, self-discipline and the clear foresight of desirable ends, is undeniable. So, often and again, the alert preacher will imply, and sometimes demonstrate, how man's attitude to timeless spiritual facts and influences affect for good and ill his daily life in the 'real' world. His choice of themes, his approach to them, and his care in the use of language, will often reveal how aware he is of the infirmity of his people's spiritual imagination.

We might extend this description of the world to which we preach, indicating other features such as—the growing impatience with organised religion, the intensifying awareness of personal relationship, the increasing concern with the quality of life, the steadily developing unsureness about moral permissiveness and liberty as sufficient bases for socially rewarding behaviour. The truth is, that the age changes all the time. The preacher needs to cultivate watchfulness, an alert mind and a sensitive spirit, and so to draw from the ceaseless flow of books, articles, talks, plays, films, protests, slogans, cliches, reports, fashions, magazines, popular songs and all the rest, hints and clues to the changing mood of his time. He will often detect the underlying longing, the deep misgiving, the half-hidden sadness and confusion, beneath much that is raucous and brash. Often he will give voice to deeper things than his contemporaries knew they meant.

Of course, many of these features of our time involve much deeper questions than merely the technique of preaching. But they also determine this. For if 'the Christian man must live with his contemporaries', equally certainly the Christian preacher must speak to them, where they are and in their terms, if he would be heard. This is the justification for speaking of 'preaching technique' at all: it concerns the method by which we realise the ideal of gospel-preaching in the sort of world to which we are sent.

Technique, in fact, can

help a man organise a sufficient storehouse of ideas and of material;
can assist him in the arrangement and pruning of that material to the best advantage;
can suggest varied ways in which he can bring the sermon to a successful and effective conclusion;

can illumine and sharpen the introduction, in which so often all possible interest and attention are killed from the outset;

can lend understanding and skill to the business of illustrating, impressively and memorably, the ideas to be communicated;

can teach a man how to use the sources of interest open to a public speaker at all times;

can improve beyond all expectation his dexterity with the tools of his trade, with words, their meanings, their overtones and power;

can even enlighten him about the elements of the ancient art of rhetoric, of which—whether he likes it or not—he is a public practitioner;

can assist him as the years pass in constantly sharpening his mind and replenishing his resources, so that his last wine is more mature than his first;

can remind him, profitably and self-critically, of the self behind each sermon, the personality behind the preaching—the personal faith and character that are the first requisite of progress in preaching.

We shall begin at the beginning of the homiletic process, with the gathering of ideas, themes and materials. We shall trace the work of sermon preparation, step by step in elementary fashion, to the crowning moments when the message so toilsomely prepared, so earnestly prayed for and prayed over, is presented to the waiting worshippers. And then we shall glance at some of the ways in which the elementary stages may be left behind, and the beginner advance to power in the greatest calling in the world.

7 GATHERING MATERIALS

THE REGULAR preacher soon discovers that he *must* organise his resources of themes, ideas, quotations, illustrations, facts and reflections, if he is to avoid becoming repetitious, and is not to feel barren and hard-pressed as the next preaching engagement draws relentlessly nearer. 'Sermons, like rivers, require a vast watershed;' said Dr F. W. Norwood, 'the best of them are fed by streams we had not noticed on the map. A man cannot live for two sermons a week: they should be the mere spill over from a full thought-life.'

Having learned that, a man becomes either an inveterate jotter-down on old envelopes, book jackets, letter margins, committee agendas, and shirt cuffs; or a disciplined and meticulous recorder and indexer of all likely material, in ever-growing rows of notebooks, each duly cross-referenced and dated. Or he settles for something in between, now one and now the other, always wishing—when the choice idea or quotation eludes him—that he had learned to do it properly.

There is no ideal and universal method. A man must know himself, his own strength of memory, or weakness of mental association. *But collect he must.* The endpapers of most books are useful to record page numbers where preachable facts or thoughts occur, provided that at the same time the idea and the book title are entered in the sermon-book. Thus T. R. Glover's *Paul of Tarsus* may have on its end-papers an entry like 'Paul's *sun*-compounds 178f.' (the *sun*-compounds being Paul's coinages like *fellow-worker, fellow-soldier, fellow-prisoner* and others). The sermon-book will then have a note: 'Paul on togetherness, team spirit: Glover's *Paul*'. There are many more complicated methods of recording one's finds.

It is however with the point at which the watershed begins to flow into a sermon that we are here concerned. Two things must be emphasized.

(a) The best sermons *grow*. This is true, even though the message given completely in a single inspiration is so enjoyable to preach. More often than not it has been growing half-consciously; even so it is sometimes less rich and profound than those over which we have laboured and prayed with little reward for weeks. The cost usually determines the value.

To enable sermons to grow we must cultivate a seed-book, where *every* idea for a sermon gets *written down*, fixed, captured, and recorded, without fail, as a matter of conscience. It is useless to expect God to give you a message twice, if you cannot take care of it first time. Equally useless to suppose that bright ideas will return at your bidding, if you gave them short hospitality when first they knocked your door.

The sermon seed-book will never be put away, but lie on your desk within reach. It may have a small brother in your pocket, and even a second cousin beside your bed: but these can be a snare unless you regularly transfer the contents to the main desk-copy. What goes down is the main idea, with any related text, or illustration, or source, or sudden reflection, or reason for storing it, or possible application, or tentative way of developing it, or anything else that might be useful. Each idea gets a new page: a ring-book will allow extra pages to be added as required.

Thereafter, all kinds of information, comments, quotations, and other material will gradually assemble around that seed-idea. Your reading, your conversation, your off-duty thoughts as you wait for trains or drive alone, and not least your subconscious mind, will throw up thoughts that clarify, elaborate, or correct, what you have noticed and noted for future use. Everything will get transferred in due course into the seed-book, and a busy pastor will be steadily accumulating material on perhaps fifty different themes at once.

Thus will be discovered yet a new application of the saying 'Unto him that hath will be given'. The idea will grow if you plant it, and die on you if you do not. Some of these themes will never be preached, some will die of further study: but a man is never left groping in the barren, feverish darkness of an empty, tired mind, struggling to get started. As the engagement to preach approaches, he will run through his seed-bed, after prayerfully thinking about the place and the people, and *something will be given him*.

(b) The other point demanding emphasis is that it is a poor sermon that has no footnotes, that is literally 'all your own work'. One of the most coveted of all compliments on great preaching expressed this: 'He was no giant thinker, but every sermon opened windows to my awakening mind.' To study James S. Stewart, H. E. Fosdick, R. W. Dale, and many like them, is to gather an astonishing range of facts, biography, testimonies, Christian history, apt quotations, fine insights beautifully expressed, biblical background, poetic gems, all scattered lavishly by the way.

So, the congregation is introduced to great characters, and stories, to historical events and explanations, to the source and background of hymns, and the heroism of the saints, all by way of illustration of other themes. Of course it can be overdone, as the preacher crams in everything he has ever read or heard or borrowed, to show how erudite he is! But so can it be underdone, and the congregation left with one poor mind, one narrow experience, one limited man's shallow thoughts and insights, for their weekly fare.

To widen a congregation's outlook to include two thousand years of Christian experience and thought, and a world-wide church's variety and enterprise, is no mean aim for their preacher, even though he attempts no formal educational scheme, and keeps close to what is relevant to their own lives. He will endow his homespun lessons with so rich a background of faith and story that simple people will see their lives in a new perspective, and grow in Christian stature.

But all this is not done without care, and organisation, and method. Nor should literal footnotes be despised. The actual sources and authorities for statements made should always be available, both for those who challenge your accuracy and for those who wish to pursue your thought. By the time the sermon is preached, the seed-book will have lost its page, but the sources should be noted on the back of the sermon-notes. In later years, when perhaps you will revise that theme, you will be grateful to have recorded your authorities.

Beside the standard dictionaries of the Bible, and of the Church, and an encyclopaedia, for checking his assertions, the young preacher needs some such survey as F. C. Gill's *The Glorious Company* (Epworth Press), or the Penguin *Dictionary of Saints*; and a good Dictionary of Quotations (Oxford, or Stevenson) for checking even the most familiar saying.

Sources of Ideas

(i) By far the most fruitful source of sermon themes is, of course, *the alert reading of the scriptures*. No sermons are so fresh and unforced as those spurred by texts which leapt from the page demanding to be preached upon. Suddenly, in a familiar passage, you notice something you never noticed before—

the four ages mentioned in Matthew 19
what Jesus did *after* cleansing the Temple, Matthew 21: 14,23
the variant use in the gospels of the same proverb or saying of Jesus,
    e.g. Matthew 13: 12; 25: 29; Mark 4: 25, Luke 8: 18; 19: 26

a surprising or vivid metaphor, as 'Let the peace of Christ be umpire in your hearts'; the apostolic nursemaid in 1 Thessalonians 2: 7; the returning Christ as burglar, thief, reveller, boss.

a succinct summary of great ideas, as Colossians 3: 15–17, or the Trinity in Ephesians 2: 18

stabbing phrases like 'By these things men live'—kept in its context of a man narrowly escaped from death: 'not I . . . but sin; not I but the grace of God; not I but Christ . . .'

a little noticed character—Silas, Nathan, Jonathan, Dorcas, Andrew, Barzillai

the negative statement of a truth—'If I had not come . . .', 'If Christ be not raised . . .', 'If it were not so I would have told you'

the other person in a familiar story, the one rarely noticed—the elder brother, Barabbas, Martha, Reuben, John Mark

even an unexpected order of words 'Amen', and only then, 'Hallelujah' Revelation 19: 4

Only practice develops this alertness, but a few hints may hasten the process. *Read expectantly*: there seems no good reason for the familiar advice not to read always for sermons. Why not? God may give a word at any time. Read very brief portions, to savour each sentence. The shorter, the more striking. Soon, novel things will strike you in every passage.

Read varied translations. Nothing so often picks up the too-familiar-but-never-really-noticed thought or phrase and raises the inner eyebrow, as do some of the modern versions. Always it is necessary to confirm the offered new expression, lest it be in fact a mistranslation, or some individual scholar's personal fancy: but by that time the mind has already been alerted.

Better still, of course, to *read the Greek Testament* itself. No book in the world is more full of sermon ideas! Simply to wrestle and hunt and compare until the exact shades of meaning become clear, and the emphasis in a sentence sets its thought in a new light, or the history of a word suggests more clearly what the writer had in mind, or the repetition of a word in different grammatical form throughout a passage illumines the thought-process—how infinitely rewarding it all is! No mere translation can quicken the mind to all the overtones and undertones, the beauty and the sharpness, the nuances and the echoes, that kindle sympathy between the mind of the writer and the mind of the reader. There is literal and exciting truth in the confession of a Bible student, that he knew what it was to bury his head in a lexicon and lift it in the presence of God.

It is well to get competent tools. John Wood meditates in rewarding fashion on a single word in Hebrews 2: 1, led by no less an authority than Westcott. But his examples of the uses of the word are drawn from Plato, Plutarch, Aristotle, and Hesychius, who span nearly 800 years, only Plutarch speaking in first-century terms. Though this might not be as misleading for Hebrews as for other New Testament books, it is essential to use a Lexicon of first-century common speech, not of classical Greek. Abbott-Smith's *Manual Greek Lexicon* is among the best. For most words this is also a Concordance to the Greek New Testament, which enables the student to notice and pursue various references to the same *Greek* word by a given writer—linking texts together by their use of the same *English* word can sometimes distort meanings disastrously. Note for a positive example how the same Greek word links Matthew 17: 2; Romans 12: 2 and 2 Corinthians 3: 18—and a sermon is born!

(ii) Particular attention is necessary to one aspect of the alert reading of the scriptures for sermon-themes: the Christian preacher's *use of the Old Testament*. For the Old Testament is too often neglected, or abused, or merely distorted into a kind of word-puzzle where pious ingenuity may find Christian truths in astonishing places. Simple reverence for a great literature, not to mention reverence for God's unfolding revelation to His chosen people, demands that we accept the Old Testament for what it is—God's word to Israel, before we begin to rewrite it as a Christian anthology of types, glimpses and foregleams.

That the timeless truth which flowered in Christianity was pressed upon Israel, at sundry times and in diverse manners, as they were able to bear it; and that much of the gospel is therefore implicit, and even explicit, in the old covenant revelation, is unquestionable. But this does not at all justify our distorting its original meaning in order to yield far-fetched cryptic foreshadowings of Christian ideas. The sword set in Eden was not the earliest appearance of the blade-and-hilt shape of the cross of Jesus, Joshua 5 does not really throw light on the true relation of Christian baptism and confirmation. The twenty-third psalm is not a believer's testimony to Jesus.

Apart from loyalty to truth itself, the issue at stake in this frequent distortion of the Old Testament is the immense loss we suffer when we do not listen to what the book actually says. The values of Old Testament preaching are numerous. Its breadth and variety lend immeasurable richness to any man's ministry—and variety, we said, is essential in these days. Its gradual development of truth, from stage to stage leading up to Christ, is likewise invaluable, for there is a sense in which each generation has to come the way Israel came, growing in its comprehension of God, of Messiah, of sacrifice, of morality, of suffering, and of God's providence in history.

But there are also passages of utter perfection in the Old Testament, truths nowhere better expressed. The saints in Israel knew the living God, as surely, if not as completely, as Christians do. Psalm 51 is the perfect analysis of penitence, Psalms 23, and 73, and 103 are unsurpassed expressions of confidence and faith. Isaiah 40 cannot be written again, nor can Isaiah 53. Jonah is one of the great books of the world. The spiritual personality of God, the essential morality of religion, the dangers of institutional, state-established piety, find no clearer voice than in the Old Testament prophets. And who shall say we Christians can leave all this behind?

Moreover, a religion of private soul-emotions, as evangelical Christianity tends to become, needs the social conscience and corporate loyalties, the historic sense of God's world-purposes, that lie within Old Testament faith. If, as the whole biblical story implies, much in the Old Testament is sub-Christian, and all is pre-Christian, yet all may provide material for comparison, contrast, preparation, or illustration of Christian truth, and much is so plainly presupposed in Christ that we neglect it only to our great impoverishment. Our alert reading of the scriptures must, then, explore the whole book, and not just favourite passages.

And there is so much for the preacher to explore! The Old Testament is full of glorious texts—

One thing have I desired . . . to behold . . . to enquire (worship)
The sheer beauty of holiness (carefully translated)
The Lord will go before thee . . . and be thy rearward
Thy statutes have been my songs . . .
Show me Thy way . . . I will show thee my glory
If the Lord command thee, thou shalt be able to endure
They went out to go into the land of Canaan, and into the land of Canaan they came

—but the list is quite endless. There are, too, innumerable character-studies offering material for psychological and moral analysis. Mere analysis, without some relevant religious *point*, will of course be pointless: each study must illustrate a theme or truth. Yet the study should come first, and the theme only emerge from it—even though in preaching the order be reversed. Be human, be fair (especially to the Bible's bad characters) and be sympathetic. Try to look at each individual as if for the first time. The more clearly he is seen, the more plainly will the meaning of his life, and the reason for his place in scripture, be understood. If the study begins with the lesson to be illustrated, the familiar pious 'explanation' of the man, firmly in mind, then the result will be not a living person wrestling with God and with life, but a cardboard cut-out, a diagram to illustrate a lesson.

To give examples is dangerous, if that inhibits a preacher's own analysis of each story, its motives and its consequences. But to tempt others by showing the wealth available: Esau is the 'profane' man, in contrast to the docile church-attender! David recalls middle-aged moral dangers. Samuel is loyalty personified, Gideon is impatient youth arguing—even with angels—until told to go and do something himself. Abraham shows faith restless and unaware, but responding; Isaac, faith waiting, marking time; Jacob shows faith redeeming the almost lost; Joseph shows faith enduring, and God over-ruling at the last. Ahab, Nathan, Aaron, Micaiah the son of Imlah (the non-conformist!), Nehemiah the pedestrian plodder, Jeremiah the most Christ-like character in history—all beckon to discovery.

The man who knows his Old Testament will sometimes turn to it for the answer to great questions and for the best approach to urgent themes. On the place of religion in the State, Micaiah will provide a framework; on racialism, Jonah will say nearly all that can be said. On facing a hopeless task, see Jeremiah; on oppression of the little man—ask Elijah or Naboth. To understand revenge, read Nahum or Obadiah. To describe the tasks of reconstruction, set Haggai, Zechariah and Joel side by side—as history did. Can God abide sin?—Hosea has an answer different from the one that springs unconsidered to our minds.

Does religion pay?—see Psalm 73, and for a man beset not with problems but with God, read Psalm 139. To feel God abroad in His world, study Psalm 111, and to realise what the word of God can do, read Psalm 29. A wonderful story underlies Psalm 40—and Bunyan illustrates it. And no spiritual psychiatrist understands depression better than Psalms 42–43.

Even special church occasions may send a man back to the earlier Bible pages for a starting-point. Peter found his Whitsunday text in Joel, and so may we. Psalm 48 is an Anniversary poem about visiting God's house. A pastor's settlement or anniversary may recall the special qualities of a preacher's *feet*—and why. Both Good Friday and Easter Day are in Isaiah 53, as Christmastide is in Isaiah 9 and 11. Palm Sunday was shaped by words of Zechariah. Citizenship Sunday recalls Jeremiah 29: 7—and in contrast, Judges 21: 25, after 18: 1 and 19: 1. Harvest Festival is everywhere, but Psalm 24, and Habakkuk 3: 17, demand attention.

The closer one keeps to Old Testament meanings, the richer the message becomes. 'Every scribe who has been trained for the kingdom of heaven is like a householder who brings out of his treasure what is new and what is old.' Our justification is, that what is old, too, came from God. But what is old must come alive: 'Unless these Old Testament stories grasp us round the ankles, they are irrelevant' (T. Kerr Spiers).

(iii) Alert reading is not the only source of scriptural themes and material. Sometimes one must search out truth, and not wait for it to strike. One obvious method of doing this is to *choose a book, or a series of topics*, to be covered in a deliberate plan of preaching, and then to set oneself resolutely to fulfill the self-imposed task. The educational value of this type of preaching is obvious, and so is the impression of earnest, thorough and planned ministry, which your people will quickly respect. But the value is even greater to the preacher himself.

Much time spent in searching for topics is saved if at least one, and probably two of the weekly addresses form part of a series. The next paragraph of a book, the next subject in a series, is there awaiting attention, and usually escape is impossible—one must get down to it. Strange as it may seem, the resulting work is often far better than that which springs from impulse or 'inspiration'. Moreover, one is led to topics that otherwise one might avoid—to discuss money and Christian offerings, in going through 1 Corinthians; or to consider adultery in studying the Commandments. The only excuse needed is—that the subject is there, in the way. And at least you are forced for a time to abandon the well-worn hobby-horse!

There is no need always to announce what you are doing: people will feel pleased with themselves if they notice about halfway through that you are following a plan. There is no need, either, to make the series weekly, or even regular: the order may be important, but not the intervals. Nor will the studies in a set biblical book always be of equal passages: the subject-matter must determine each sermon. Sometimes you will linger on a text, sometimes discuss a paragraph, sometimes quickly review a whole chapter; occasionally you will miss a passage with a brief reference only to its obvious meaning. Occasionally you will be well into a gospel or epistle before it is necessary to touch questions of its background and purpose.

Some biblical books are best expounded by problems (as 1 Corinthians); some, by persons, or places, or events (as Acts, or Samuel, Judges); some will yield to a series on great sayings of Jesus (so James' epistle), or on themes of salvation (Romans), or the tests of life (1 John), or the religious man's many moods

(Psalms), or by representative stories (Genesis). Variety is every-thing, and only a few books (Philippians, or John) will fall easily to verse-by-verse, paragraph-by-paragraph exposition.

The ten foundation stones of social security—the ten Command-ments—provide a series at once biblical, practical and exceedingly relevant. To take ancient prophets to modern problems, expounding the main message of each prophet in a modern setting, will lead to unfamiliar biblical pastures. A study of the Apostle's Creed, but taking the great biblical passages for basis, would broaden and deepen faith for many. The sayings of Jesus about His death may bring new meaning to the Lord's Supper through a whole year, while collecting 'What Jesus said' on various urgent subjects, or 'Questions Jesus Asked', will bring out the sharp urgency of His teaching for our contemporary world'

Self-discipline of this kind will doubtless involve harder study and careful arrangement. On the other hand, a row of such 'seeds' growing in the seed-book help to fertilise each other. And the diligent searching of the scriptures for the message God has appointed, never fails to bring its reward.

(iv) A second method of searching for subjects, instead of waiting for truths to strike one, begins at the other end. Usually we seize upon a theme and ask how this applies to our people. The preacher serious about his responsibilities will often *begin with the people* and their known needs.

The pastor visits, converses, listens, watches and reflects: it is his charge, this 'cure of souls'. So he is acutely sensitive to the spiritual state of his friends, to their odd reluctance to give to public charities; to their strange unawareness of the problems of the district; to lingering echoes of old quarrels that still spoil fellowship; to the difficulty new people have of feeling themselves at home—or the time it takes for young converts to be accepted. He may be aware that the long suffering of a loved saint has started in some minds bewildering questions about God's ways. Questions may be asked of him, concerning something happening in the church at large, or about sceptical broadcasts. He may feel his circle is somewhat intolerant, or that their knowledge of the wider world is scanty, or that they seem rarely to consider the missionary obli-gation and vocation, or that they are short on Christian joy.

With love and hope—not criticism—in his heart, he will sit and think of these, his colleagues in the kingdom, with his Bible open on his knee. What does the Bible say about illness, or almsgiving, or intolerance, or bereavement, or immaturity, or whatever else is causing concern—or should be. And so, as he searches memory and scripture for the answer, a sermon is born, directly out of pastoral awareness of a people's present needs. The visiting preacher, though he knows one church far less intimately, will often know general situations of the same kind, and proceed in the same way.

Two pitfalls need to be avoided. One, certainly, is the temptation *to invent problems*, uncertainties, needs, that only the academic, the preaching scholar, would see. The need, if it is to spur a real sermon, should be a felt need of the people, not a theoretic need which the theologian, or the expositor, thinks they *ought* to feel. Occasionally even that approach will be demanded: but then he must create the sense of need—and the whole method will be different. To deal with questions no one but the preacher would think of asking, to labour to solve problems your people have not yet felt, is to exasperate your best hearers and move your critics to amusement.

The other pitfall to be avoided is the temptation *to reveal how the sermon was born*. It would be fatal to pastoral confidence to begin with 'Visiting this week someone who has been ill a long time, I was faced with the question . . .' That poor soul, so quickly identified by those who saw your car outside the house, will never ask another question that troubles her heart! It would be fatal to all sympathetic listening to begin: 'I have been thinking how prone some of you are to go about from church to church . . .' The natural reaction would be to say—'And next Sunday we will be off again!'

Preach what the Bible has to say about the need that you have noticed, and the truth will make its own way all the more powerfully because you do not try to force it. Why antagonize by a personal, and offensive, diagnosis, when all that really concerns you is to cure? We preach *to* people, where they are: we refrain—if we are even a little wise—from ever preaching *at* people.

(v) An important further source of themes for preaching is an honest *review of your own ministry*. Twice a year a man should look back over his carefully kept record of texts and topics, and note what is *absent*. There is a balance of truth to be observed, and a perspective of faith and ethics. There is a whole Bible to expound, and a total view of salvation, of discipleship, of social responsibility, of church-loyalties, to be taught. There are young listeners as well as old, and some middle-aged as well. You are the steward of the whole truth of God, and not simply of your pet themes and passages, your favourite and easiest subjects. And you are minister to all kinds of people.

Often the review of your work will shock you. Months pass, without mention of some great Christian doctrine, some important element in Christian experience, some plain but easily neglected duty. We find we have been in the epistles far more often than in the gospels; or we discover we have been concerned with churchly matters to the exclusion of outside responsibilities. The review will be more thorough, and perhaps more impartial, if a check-list of matters which should be included in any balanced year's ministry is faithfully used. And among the questions to be asked should be included—How would the young people feel about this quarter's subjects? And how do the old react? What have I been returning to too often? What am I unconsciously avoiding!

Such a process may sometimes be depressing, but it must always be beneficial: often it will lead to a new care in planning ahead for the next six months. Rarely indeed will a self-critical examination of recent work fail to stimulate one or more lines of reflection which conscience demands you share with your congregation.

(vi) It should not be necessary to mention *the Christian Year* as an almost compulsory source of themes. The pattern of festivals, from Advent through Christmas to Lent, the Passion, Easter, Ascension, Whitsun and Trinity, is surely the finest aid to Christian education, and to Christian witness, that the church has ever devised. It is comprehensive, fundamental, objective, and recurring. Used as an annual rehearsing of the basic articles of belief, it cannot fail to produce a congregation well instructed in their faith, its bearings, and its joy.

Certainly it is possible to make too much of the 'holy days', and some churches are suspicious of pre-Reformation emphases. Few would want to recover, in evangelical circles, the saints' days and epiphany, though Paul's conversion, Bible Sunday, and the church's birthday, have reasonable place in a church's celebrations. But there is no need to over-stress the pattern, or even to publicise it at all— simply to follow it in your own silent planning as an aid to balance and comprehensiveness. Nothing but good can come of an intelligent syllabus of truth.

(vii) Themes and subjects are not the only materials that must be safely harvested against the lean times: much more is needed to make a full meal for the Christian soul. Richness comes from fullness, and fullness from continual replenishment. A man must read and listen, think, observe and pray, if he is not to expose in every sermon his own impoverishment. Yet what a man reads and retains is so much a matter of his general education that little useful help can be offered in a manual: only a reminder that the field is the world and all life is a library.

Ingli James once advised men to have by them, all the time, a book that informs—the textbooks, commentaries, and such like; a book that kindles, presenting new thoughts with authority and freshness; and a book that stretches the mental muscles with unaccustomed exercise, demanding more concentration than is easy to give. It would be well to add, also, a book that one expects strongly to disagree with—provided only that it be read with fairness of mind. So much needs no emphasis.

But the preacher who wishes to be relevant and understanding will need to notice what other commentators on his time are saying, and will strive to grasp how personal and social problems appear to other minds very different from his own. This type of reading and listening will often be far less congenial: therefore it must be the more diligently cultivated.

Newspapers, magazines, broadcast discussions by all kinds of speakers, political propaganda, advertising trends, and current 'documentaries' all reflect the scene, and give voice to the thoughts and feelings, amidst which the preacher must work. He may not find their deliverances attractive, consistent, or even credible—but he will listen, and record.

Many public bodies, professional groups, research teams of experts, business corporations, and societies with social or reforming aims, pour out white papers, blue books, statistics, surveys, analyses, reports, prophecies, warnings and pamphlets, on everything from education to the population trends, from world-pollution to world literacy. To attempt to absorb them all would be silly. To ignore them all must lead to ignorance unforgivable in those who claim to have a message that matters.

Usually the preacher must be satisfied to have others review and summarize, and indicate for him the things he ought to read. He must select, and record—if only the sources to which he can turn if he needs the facts, and the authoritative opinions. All the time, fresh ideas, unusual angles, restatements, new presentations of problems, and unfamiliar information, will accumulate in his notebooks—some finding their way at once, by the 'homiletic habit of mind', into the seed-bed of sermons where potential themes are growing.

Those who dislike, or abhor, the stage and the screen, will be content with reading plays, and skimming reviews of current productions: none will wisely neglect what the most powerful pulpit in western society is saying. Even those who are content to cater for the lowest public taste are making their own kind of comment upon what that taste is. Those serious dramatists and artists who seek to form public taste often say things which society needs to be told, and highlight problems society prefers to ignore.

The preacher will wish to broaden his own experience and understanding, and he will also be aware that his hearers have often shared in discussions, at home and at work, which were provoked by film or play. Only the properly qualified will make explicit comment, but awareness of what is being said and shown will often provide clues to prevailing opinion and problems. Younger listeners, at least, will be glad to know that the preacher knows the world to which he is trying to speak.

The preacher will often lack time, inclination, or patience to attend much to contemporary fiction. The study of great literature is the study of life, and the serious novelist will do more to enrich experience, awaken imagination, sharpen observation, and explore character, than any other teacher. Here too a man will probably have to rely upon reviewers to keep him aware of what is being written, and to guide his own selection. The main point is that he will want to know—because his people do.

Bradley's studies of Shakespeare's handling of the human tragedy; Shakespeare's own exploration of ambition, power, justice, jealousy, obsession, romance, love, statecraft, joy, and everything else that makes up the tragedy and comedy of man; Thomas Hardy's wistful pessimism, retaining the Christian temper without the Christian hope; George Eliot's examination of avarice—redeemed by a child, and of character triumphing over circumstance; Trollope's superb analyses of motive and relationships;—such are random examples out of hundreds, of the way a preacher will gain enlargement of view from those who interpret life by creative fiction. Douglas Stewart's *The Ark of God* contains studies of James Joyce's Apocalypticism, Aldous Huxley's Mysticism, Graham Greene's Catholicism, Rose Macaulay's Anglicanism, and Joyce Cary's Protestantism. With such a guide the beginner will soon learn how to read with patience and with profit.

The fifth source of wider understanding and awareness will demand still more insight and skill, and in many cases still more of patience: but the result may be correspondingly rewarding. The deepest reflections, clearest observation, and most moving reactions in any decade are those expressed in its poetry, and few who think and speak can afford to deprive themselves of the refreshment, rekindling, faith and beauty offered in the great heritage of verse.

But poets of our own time, too, have relevant things to say—and no one can say them better, with more acute sensitiveness to changes in social climate, or with greater sympathy. Much illuminating comment—and often quotable comment—will be found in the odd corners of some magazines and the slim paperback pamphlets of 'collected verse'. Some of it may not last, because it is so contemporary. But that may be its value to the man who earnestly wants to understand the mood to which he ministers.

From such varied tributaries is that river of the mind fed which overflows in public speech. But all needs to be garnered. Perceptive, or memorable, sentences, slogans, observations of human reactions and behaviour, character studies, typical situations, excuses, compromises, consequences, social comments and almost anything else that strikes the reader as true and fittingly expressed, may be pinned down—with source and page—to be transferred at the right time into some accumulating sermon-outlines.

By such methodical mental husbandry a man's pulpit ministry is delivered from that impulsive, arbitrary, and sometimes desperate last minute search for something to preach which some people call 'waiting for the Spirit'. Too often this means that mood and habit dictate the message. There is no ground whatsoever to suppose that there is more of the Spirit's guidance and power in a ministry that is haphazard and unplanned than in one carefully and prayerfully prepared, balanced, and purposeful.

No man will allow the syllabus he has drawn up, or the seed-bed of sermon-thoughts, or the Christian year, or even any announced series of subjects, to become a chain, a strait-jacket, a mental prison. Congregational events, sudden needs, a clear leading of the Spirit, may at any time interrupt prepared plans and themes: flexibility is essential in the work of God. Yet the exceptional must be kept exceptional. If you prepare a plan prayerfully, you will feel bound to fulfil it loyally. And far more often than might be expected, the conscientious workman will find that God has provided beforehand just the word for the need that could not have been foreseen.

8 SHAPING THE MATERIAL

NO MAN should prepare a sermon in order to have something to say, but because he has something already, and must say it. Where that 'something' comes from, we have discussed at length: the next question is, how to say it. The subject settled, there will be six or ten ways in which to present it: 'preparation' consists in choosing and carrying into effect the right way for that theme and for that congregation, with that purpose in view.

The basic rule here is, that the way the sermon came to you is almost *never* the way in which you preach it.

Although 'How to say it' is a secondary question, it is still important. We named seven things a sermon must attempt: it must take a religious truth that is deeply felt, justify it from scripture, clarify, illustrate, make it memorable, apply it to my situation, and persuade me to respond. Each of these seven aims must be considered separately for seventeen-year-olds, for twenty-seven-year olds, for fifty-seven-year-olds, and for the over-seventies. The preacher will make his point briskly and crudely for the teen-agers; precisely, authoritatively for professionally trained people and for students home for the vacation; picturesquely, with charm and imagination, for the housewife and the man of words; reminiscently for the old saint who saw it long ago more clearly than the young preacher sees it yet—but is glad to be reminded of it, all the same. By the time the preacher has attempted all seven things differently for four types of listeners, he will not despise preparation!

That is exaggeration, of course. But truth lies in it. The preacher in earnest about his business will teach himself that the way that comes easiest to him is not necessarily the way that appeals to the people he wants to win. And while there are as many methods of preparation as there are preachers—and no one can copy another, or be told how to go about it—the principles involved in sermon-preparation deserve attention. A great deal of good, wholesome spiritual food is ruined in the baking.

The main questions that arise are obvious—knowing what I want to say, in what order shall I put it? How explain, illustrate, apply it? How shall I begin? How shall I end? But certain preliminary questions are vital. The first page of a beginner's sermon is never preached. It contains the answers to three 'ritual' questions, which even after years of experience a man will go on asking as he approaches each new message:

(i) *Who is this sermon for*?—for old or younger listeners; for believers, unbelievers, or half-believers; for the committed, the half-committed, the enquiring; for the ungenerous, the unforgiving, the idle, the bewildered, the disconsolate; for vacant people looking for a vocation? This is where the congregation crowds into the study. If the answer must be 'mixed'—*define the mixture*. And glance occasionally at your definition as preparation proceeds.

(ii) *What am I trying to say*? There is much to be said for the oft-quoted counsel: Get the heart of the message into a single sentence. If the point of the message is not clear to me *from the start*, it never will be clear to the congregation. The preacher has failed who wins only the charitable comment, 'I think I see what you are getting at!' The preliminary page should state it, stark and crisp. And it should then control all the preparation.

(iii) *What am I aiming to do*? Every sermon should have a practical purpose, a reason for being preached—lest a worship-session be wholly wasted. The target should be set within sight, and within practical reach, on the sermon's first page—and it too must be allowed to determine, and to discipline, the process of preparation.

The preliminary page completed, the next step is to assemble all available material, and let it ferment—phrases, ideas, verses of poems, illustrations, references to events, stories, quotations reserved for this theme, biblical connections, parallels, instances, suggested applications, alternative ways of developing the main thought. Time, prayer, imagination, a receptive, and retentive, mind are needed here: and patience—the refusal to finalise anything. Just collect all possible material.

This is the stage for research, for checking translation, searching out unfamiliar words, consulting authorities, glancing at commentaries, re-reading the chapter before and after the text, and recalling the circumstances of the writer and readers. How very often that last remembrance, of how the message was first received, will lend light and vividness to what we say!

Assembly is the stage, too, for 'boxing the ears of the text with questions'. Why does the prophet, the apostle, say it in just that way? Why that odd expression, that unusual word? Why is he so emphatic? or so sharp? How would I have said this to my young daughter? How would I say it to my wife, or to old Mr ——? How does it apply to a church like mine, in an age like this?

Much of the material will lie ready to hand in the seed-book sermon-plot, but all must now be passed through the quickening mind, with a congregation and an occasion in view. James Black has well defined the tools at this stage as the spade, the rake and the riddle. We dig into the subject (and the seed-bed) for the heart of its meaning. We rake together all available ideas, suggestions, quotations and illustrative material. And then we sift it through, saving the fine thoughts and stories that are not strictly relevant, and preserving them for future use. The result will be pages of well-considered notes, rich with reading and reflection, from which a worth-while message has yet to be distilled.

This assembly of the material is usually the most enjoyable part of the process: the mind is awake, ideas flow, the scripture is full of suggestion and significance, the message is moving your own heart. You wish you could preach it, there and then. This stage can be dangerous, too, for sometimes we fall in love with the process, and miss our original theme. Some people never attempt this step, but start right away to write out their sermon and let ideas come—and the result reveals the omission. Others mistake this assembly of material for preparation itself—but that has still to come.

The people envisaged, the theme defined, the material assembled, we can begin to prepare for the pulpit, arranging all we wish to say in the most effective order, the most persuasive pattern. Which raises the controversial topic of outlines and their management.

The Value of Outlines

A heap of ammunition is not a victory, any more than a pile of ingredients is a cake. The more rich the meal, the more necessary is some care in the arrangement of the courses, and while the out-pouring of a well-stored mind in eloquent freedom and spontaneity may be very enjoyable to the trained listener, most hearers will find the total fare somewhat undigestible.

Let us without reluctance admit that outlines and arrangements can be tortuously overdone. 'As a woman over-curiously trimmed is to be suspected, so is a speech.' John Watson tells of sermons *manufactured* as a carpenter makes a table—each section separately selected, turned, shaped and finished, and the whole neatly constructed with all the signs of the workshop and the smell of glue about it. Watson prefers the sermons that grow, organically, naturally, inevitably, by the processes of a clear mind's thinking.

Sermon divisions in more leisurely, more patient days often ran

to twelfthly, and fourteenthly, with two or three symmetrical sub-divisions under each. In our time, sermons may be all outline: the mere headings mistaken for a message, and slogans substituted for thought. Most of us have suffered, too, from the over-clever headliners, who indulge in alliteration for its own sake, in puns and facetiousness and rhyming words, and all the rest—but say nothing in the end. Skeletons are dry, angular, dusty objects, never very nourishing.

All this is true. But to react against it by eschewing all orderly arrangement of material, simply letting the ideas come as they choose, is equally extreme—and self-defeating. There is more to be said for preaching to a clear and explicit outline than may be said against it.

(i) We have stressed the decline in most people's *capacity to hear and retain* what is conveyed in words; the visual character of prevailing culture and the consequent demand for shorter sermons, or none at all. One of the ways in which we can meet the psychological conditions in which we preach, and help our hearers, is to provide the memorable outline, by which the thoughts can be grasped and carried away. Say, if we will, that the visible outline is a mere clothes-line, a crutch for lame listeners. But our hearers *are* lame in this respect in these days: why not be Christian, and help them? The outline will not be all the help they need—but without it, other help may be in vain.

(ii) It is true that *a clear remembering* of what is said is not the main purpose of preaching, but rather an immediate response to the truth presented. Yet that response is likelier to come, and to last, if the ideas that evoked it can be recalled. The sermon-outline is a set of shelves upon which the main thoughts can be arranged in the listener's mind. It becomes a basket in which he can carry most of the material home. It may even become a pocket-book from which, at work in the middle of the week, he can extract the remnants of what he heard, and be blessed again.

Some people will recall the striking sentence. Other minds are so fashioned that they will recall most easily the progress of the argument. Others again cannot recall anything but the vivid illustration, the story. But all will remember more if they are given a framework on which to arrange it. A reader can turn back a page to recall a point, a step in the discourse: repetition of a heading may give the hearer the same help towards continuity.

Why should the average listener, as he struggles to understand you, and perhaps struggles at the outset even to hear you, have also to memorise your message as you go along? Why not, for the truth's sake, help him? If you cannot, because you skimped the preparation, your sermon will be as ephemeral as it deserves to be. If you will not, because you think intelligent people ought not to need it, you have ceased to *serve* your congregation.

(iii) For a third consideration, the careful arrangement of material enormously adds to the *clarity* of the whole. Although you began by setting down in one clear sentence what you intended to say, you will use many sentences to say it persuasively, imaginatively, emphatically. The danger always presses, that the pith and point of the message will be lost in the multitude of words, obscured and buried in the material with which we intended only to adorn it. The hearer is not really responsible for catching the gist of what you dimly feel and blunderingly hint at! The plain fact is, that until you have arranged your thoughts in orderly fashion, you have not thought them through. Even if we use notes, we should never preach to others a sermon we cannot *think through*, as a whole, on the way to the service, or during the choral anthem. It is not a matter of memory, but of clarity and mental grasp.

(iv) The orderly, progressive arrangement of ideas adds greatly, too, to the *interest* of a sermon. We have all endured preachers who dribble along—a kick with one foot, then the other, then the first foot again, doubling back, side-stepping, and retrieving—and never a decent shot at goal in the end. The common complaint that sermons are too long generally means that they are boring, and the chief reason for that is want of any visible progress.

'No preacher irritates or grows wearisome', says Dr Gilbert Laws, 'so long as he is climbing . . . Weariness is not in length but in circularity . . . in motion without progress.' A clear and cunning arrangement, with mounting tension, renewed surprise, unexpected application, steadily built-up argument, will often carry the listener along with such attention that he looks at his watch at the end with something of astonishment.

(v) Linked closely with this is the *mental relief* afforded by an explicit plan of discourse. The reader can pause, and put his book down. He can poke the fire, mark the page; he can talk to himself, or go for a walk. He starts again where he left off just as soon as he wishes. The listener can do none of these things, he is hurried on at the pace the speaker chooses. When a section of the sermon is plainly completed, and the speaker pauses to brace himself for the next point, the listener also is grateful. His mind relaxes, he registers a corner reached on the road he has to travel, he feels a certain satisfaction at having followed successfully so far, and he takes breath for the next stimulating idea. Such ease in attending is a considerable part of the 'pleasure' which good preaching imparts to an appreciative congregation.

Taken together, such considerations surely outweigh the dangers of over-emphasizing the need of explicit and memorable arrangement of ideas. The question remains, how the sermon outline is to be handled, for the best effect.

The Management of Outlines

Whether to announce your headings, and if so how, depends upon several considerations. As aids to memory, to clarity, and to a sense of progress, the more clear the headings are, the more effective they will be. The listener can see where he is going, and can tell how far he has come. But there are factors that tell on the other side.

By announcing the sermon's divisions beforehand, the preacher forfeits at once all element of surprise, and usually of expectancy. He also commits himself publicly to a plan, and if he fails to fulfil it, his failure is plain to all. Sometimes, too, the outline is so obvious that the congregation are ahead of the preacher from the start. They long for him to finish his self-appointed exercise, and let them go home. If on the other hand the outline is intriguing, or unexpected, the announcement will kindle interest instead of destroying it. If the outline challenges contradiction, the congregation may find new attentiveness by silently arguing with you as you proceed. And if your hearers have grown to expect from you a reasoned and relevant exposition, close to the text, the announcement of a plan that seems to be far removed from your subject will set them trying to foresee how you reach that outline out of such a passage!

There is therefore no general rule governing how or when you let your skeleton appear—or even whether you do so at all. Everything depends upon what is right for that particular message. An attempted illustration may show how a decision on strategy is arrived at.

Suppose you have noticed the place of hope in the epistles of Paul, in Peter, and in the letter to the Hebrews especially. From this has grown a new appreciation of the lack of hopefulness in modern life. But your congregation is one of mixed ages, and you have said rather a lot lately about the message of Christ for the old and infirm. This sets you searching the texts upon hope, and you find an anchor, a helmet, a hope that saves, a hope that abides, a hope we are begotten to, a hope in which we die, a hope without which we are of all men the most miserable—with Watts' blind cherub with one star and a one-

stringed lute haunting your mind. Clearly there is in the message of
hope something for all ages and all sorts of people.

So, you will speak of the importance of Hope, for the young, for
the middle-aged, and for the old. But will you announce it so? Few
outlines could be so flat, discouraging, and hopeless! Nor are you much
profited if you do not announce it: for when you have finished with
the young, and move to the middle-aged, the congregation will leap
ahead to the most obvious of the three, and feel somewhat older
themselves by the time you catch up with them.

Something will be gained if you invert the obvious order, and announce that you will speak on the importance of hope to the old, to
the middle-aged, and to the young. The young will then mentally
go for a walk until you reach their section; and the diligent, faithful
listeners will mentally comment—'Hope for the old is obviously
important; hope for the middle-aged is stretching it a bit—but the
importance of hope for the young? He will never persuade them of
that!' They may listen to see how right they are—and be glad to be
proved wrong.

Even so, the outline is still unexciting, pedestrian. So you try again—
without changing for a moment the content of the message given you
to preach. The trouble is the obviousness of saying that hope is
important at the end of life: yet you want to say just that to some
fearful older saints within the fellowship. So make a virtue of the obviousness: set it in contrast with the other less obvious points—and
something emerges. Make your announcement not a list of headings,
but a statement of this contrast. You will need a carefully arranged
sentence to make this point and announce your pattern—you may
draft it several times before the right words come. But in the end you
have it:

'I want to suggest to you the importance of hope . . .'—not I am
going to speak: they know that already. 'I am going to suggest . . .'
at once invites them to consider it with you, as something you are
not quite asserting, but putting forward for discussion. 'I want to
suggest to you the importance of hope, not only for the old (that
pays them the compliment of conceding they could have thought of
that for themselves) . . . not only for the old, but for the middle-aged,
in life's testing and searching years . . . (the mental comment may well
be, 'That is an unusual point, yet obviously he is right!') . . . Not
only for the old, but for the middle-aged in life's testing and searching
years, and especially, though we rarely realise it, for the young, at
life's beginning, with all their plans to make.'

And off you go: . . . 'Hope is important for the old, because then
the past seems everything, and is gone; the future is short, and
frightening . . . and a dreaded end begins to remove our friends . . .'
The old among your listeners will feel at once you have thought how
they feel, and have a word of God for their hearts; yet the younger
listeners will feel that you have conceded the triteness of this point,
and are really hurrying on to what you will say to them! 'Equally
important, we said, is hope for the middle-aged, against the encroach-
ing cynicism, the multiplying disappointments, the frustrations and

fading dreams . . . then to keep your hopefulness is an anchor of the soul, sure and stedfast . . .' The old will still listen, remembering what you are describing; the young will see that this sermon is pretty close to life, after all. 'Yet most of all is hope important for the young, because the hopes you cherish, and strive for, determine your life from the beginning, shape your character, sustain your courage, . . . the young live by their dreams . . . and the Hope of the World is Jesus.'

Much more than this, of course will have to be done to clothe the framework with profitable truth. But we have in one sentence announced our theme, mapped out the journey, put up some shelves on which the ideas may be arranged, and at the same time, though the three headings are tame and platitudinous, we have so arranged them and so announced them as to point a contrast and challenge to agreement.

Every sermon will demand this kind of tactical exercise in deployment of ideas—though practice marvellously increases the facility to see, or to feel, how it should go. The method, the timing, and the type of outline, will depend upon the content and the aim. Hence will arise again that coveted quality of variety. Your people will never quite know how you will tackle any theme—until you tell them.

Whether to recapitulate the outline at the end will depend in part upon the outline, and in part upon the preacher. An obvious outline, like the one just studied, would only be weakened by repetition. To recapitulate the unforgettable is irritating! But sometimes, to gather the headings together in a single view has cumulative power. Where each division was a step in an argument, or offered evidence of the theme, or took an insight or an application to some new stage, recapitulation is almost necessary to reap the harvest sown. Again, it depends upon the sermon.

But also upon the preacher, for some men cannot recapitulate their headings without re-preaching their sermon. And that is disastrous.

But whether the preacher announces the divisions or not, whether he forecasts the steps, or announces them as he goes, or lets them appear at the end, or announces them at the outset and gathers them up at the end, or whether he relates them in a sentence, or leaves them in a bare list—

the divisions must be there, for the preacher's sake;
the divisions must be seen to be there, for the listener's sake.

At what precise point in the process of sermon-preparation the outline will emerge and begin to control the structure, must again

vary from sermon to sermon. Here the vital rule must be, that the
divisions must grow out of the message, and never the message
out of the divisions. The student who said 'I have two wonderful
points for a new sermon, and I cannot get a third—do give me one!'
is still remembered after thirty years for that odd request. That
'wonderful sermon' should plainly have had just two 'wonderful'
points—a third would be mere appendix, verbiage, trifling, obscuring
what was in his heart to say. Always the message comes first, and
must determine the arrangement—never *vice versa*.

So, the clear definition of the hearers, the summarising of the
essential truth, and then the assembly of the material, must all
certainly precede the fixing of an outline. But at some point in
the assembling of ideas, a programme will begin to arrange itself.
Ideas, quotations, applications, will fall into groups, find their
logical place, build themselves into divisions. The whole will be
pondered, and mentally reshuffled, several times, but the simple
and natural order, when all is properly digested, will always show
itself. Then, only the polishing of headings into memorable phrases
needs attention.

> The outline which comes first, and leaves the preacher to hunt for
> what to say under each sparkling heading, will profit no one. Someone
> describes the potted 'sermon-outlines' which sometimes appear in
> religious papers—a series of figures and letters, with three- or four-
> word headings, and no more, as 'a bundle of dry twigs, and no fire'.
> They are dehydrated fodder. Unsatisfactory, too, is the outline which
> comes first and determines the whole. John Wood offers with approval
> an outline which, in the setting of the total sermon, was doubtless
> rewarding and true, but which—considered simply as an example of
> homiletic technique—shows a clever and accomplished pattern
> leading somewhat far from the true meaning of a great saying of the
> Lord:
>   on John 12: 24—
>   1. The *immeasurable possibilities* of a single life—one corn of wheat
>   . . . much fruit
>   2. The *irreducible price* of a fruitful life—it must fall into the
>   ground and die
>   3. The *infinite pathos* of a wasted life—the seed not sown abides
>   alone.

Very neat. One only wonders if these were quite the thoughts
in the mind of Jesus as He spoke.

Whether a man thinks the process here described is too laborious
and time-wasting, will depend upon the real value he assigns to
the work he tries to do. It may depend also on the measure of his
self-conceit. Certainly, with practice and experience what is here set

out in detailed steps becomes a mental discipline, which economises effort considerably, and telescopes the process into a 'homiletic art'. Yet the most gifted preparer of sermons will sometimes find a theme unyielding, and will return to the method he was taught before he will give up. And the most accomplished at the work is always aware that what comes now with comparative ease is but the reward of years when he toiled laboriously at each message, and often despaired.

9 CAPITATION

THE MATERIAL assembled for a sermon will 'fall' into its most effective order more readily if example and practice have made familiar a number of possible patterns. Since the content of the message should determine its shape, there is no end to the variety of outline. Yet personal habit, and sometimes the tradition of a church or of a period, tend to concentrate on one or two types of sermon as the 'right' or the 'best'; those pattern-outlines then become hackneyed and well-nigh invariable. What is worse, they come to control what is to be said. Some men would preach on the four horsemen of the Apocalypse with the habitual 'three heads and a tale'.

Classical authorities on public speaking, like Aristotle, divided every speech aiming at persuasion into four parts:

The exordium, which states the subject and aims at awakening attention, curiosity, interest, surprise, good humour, or even anger (at some outrage, or at government policy!)

The narration, which explains the present position, the history of the matter, the causes, and other necessary background to the subject

The proof, which indicates the steps now proposed, and the reasons for them, how they will overcome the evil and promote the good which the speaker has in view

The peroration, which reviews the whole case, kindles emotion, and evokes response, decision—or a riot.

Aristotle is willing to interweave narration and 'proof', but the most important section is the peroration.

Something like this classical form had great place in the history of Christian preaching, especially in the development of numerous 'propositions', each with its exposition and its proof. For the modern audience, and for the modern sermon's material, it is much too heavy—and certainly too intellectual. The famed 'Negro' sermon-pattern follows Aristotle fairly closely—

> First I tells 'em
> Then I 'splains to 'em
> Then I rouses 'em
> —then they'd better!

While the supposedly Welsh sermonic habit is almost its opposite—

>Begin low,
>Proceed slow,
>Aim higher,
>Then fire—
>>and sit down in a storm!

This however pays no attention to content—nor to typical Welsh preaching, either.

Almost obligatory, in some circles, is the three-point sermon with introduction and formal conclusion—the 'three-pronged fork' as Alexander Maclaren called it. 'It is only natural', someone has said, 'that the Lord's fishermen should flourish a trident.' But the familiarity of the 'three-decker' sermon is due as much to habit and to laziness as to any belief that it is right.

Yet gibes about this form are not all justified. It is a fact that most people can remember three things with little effort. Ask them to remember four—four figures, four names, four dates—and they will probably get two right, though the same people would get three out of three. Moreover, the basic form of argument is threefold—two premises, and a conclusion drawn from them. Most people can retain this easily:

>All gems are valuable,
>This is a gem.
>Therefore this is valuable.

The three-point sermon-form is therefore certainly not to be avoided.

What else could one do with a message on 'The kingdom of God is not meat and drink, but righteousness, peace, joy in the Holy Ghost'? Some passages are especially rich in truth, and it is well to limit the lines of thought in any sermon on them to three, even though much remains unsaid. The context of the superb declaration 'God is love' (1 John 4) would provide spiritual fare for a month's ministry, but at one meal three dishes are plenty—

>If God is love, then
>>Life is good
>>Love is right
>>Tomorrow is a promise.

On the other hand, to deal with the Woman of Samaria and the wonderful offer Jesus made to her, under the headings—

>The Woman
>The Well
>The Water

reduces the story to bathos as deep as Jacob's well! Similarly to summarise the Prodigal Son's experience as—

> He went away
> He stayed away
> He came back

is to offer husks that the swine might refuse. A clever variation

> Sick of home
> Homeless
> Homesick
> Home

is an improvement just because it breaks from the lazy three-form, and shows some thought. But not much.

Some excellent sermons have just two main points, and when these are related in some way, by contrast, or paradox, or logical inversion, the effect can be powerful. A third heading would ruin all. One of the greatest sermons preached in the past two centuries, we have said, was that preached by William Carey at Northamptonshire in 1792. It had but two main thoughts.

The text was Isaiah 54: 2,3—
Enlarge the place of thy tent, and let them stretch forth the curtains of thine habitations: spare not, lengthen thy cords, and strengthen thy stakes; for thou shalt break forth on the right hand and on the left: and thy seed shall inherit the Gentiles, and make the desolate cities to be inhabited.

Here obviously is material for more than two sections, but very wisely Carey omitted all that would obscure the main intention. Isaiah does in fact say two things—what *shall* happen, and what therefore Israel *ought* to do. Carey keeps strictly to that: since God intends immense enlargement, Israel must prepare a larger camp—longer tent-cords and stronger tent-poles. So Carey insisted—

> Expect great things from God
> Attempt great things for God.

And the order of the headings is all-important: reversed, they cease to be truly evangelical—we must fasten faith upon God before we make any of our attemptings.

It was the best pair of shoes that the Northamptonshire cobbler ever fashioned. How they fit, and how they match—it is no wonder that in them Carey trod the world, leading thousands.

A third thought would have tripped the preacher up, and the danger should be noted. Psalm 27 : 4—

> One thing have I desired of the Lord, and that will I seek after; that I may dwell in the house of the Lord all the days of my life, to behold the beauty of the Lord, and to enquire in his temple

appears to contain several things. In fact it is one thing desired, and named, and then analysed into two parts. He desires to worship constantly, to live among holy things in the presence of God: but he sees worship as essentially—

> to behold the beauty of the Lord
> to enquire in His temple.

To behold is to lift up one's eyes to the divine loveliness; to enquire is to open one's mind to the divine word. That is worship—just that. Two legs will carry all that should be said. The couplet is again complete.

1 John has a phrase twice:

> *God is greater than our hearts*—to forgive, when sometimes neither others, nor we ourselves, can forgive ourselves;
> *Greater is He that is in you* than he that is in the world—to overcome for us when we can scarcely any longer put up a fight!

The two sides of defeat, guilt and helplessness, are thus eclipsed by God's greatness, and we can be assured. Nothing can usefully be added to those two ideas.

But what can we do with Paul's way of salvation, in Romans 10 : 9—

> If thou shalt confess with thy mouth
> That Jesus is Lord
> And shalt believe in thine heart
> That God hath raised Him from the dead
> Thou shalt be saved.

That almost demands a four-step sermon, lest we distort the basic theology. Salvation, Paul says, comes to those who *confess* Christ's *Lordship* and *believe* that He is *alive*. This is a striking instance of the imperative need to expound what is there—neither adding anything nor omitting anything. And of the need to keep the four headings unified: together they make *one* way of being saved—four headings of one message, not four distinct themes.

This is important. A fourfold message extends the modern listener unless the unity of the whole is kept quite clear. Acts 2: 42 gives us a description of the original, 'essential' church, at its earliest beginning:

> They continued steadfastly in the apostles'
>   doctrine,   (= the church and Christian education)
>   and fellowship,   (= the church as incorporation of believers)
>   in breaking of bread   (= the church and worship)
>   and in prayers   (= the church as vehicle of divine energies).

Again the four ideas in the text demand four divisions in the sermon, if the description is to be balanced and complete. But there is obvious danger of chasing four hares at once, of preaching four dovetailed sermonettes, on education, fellowship, worship and prayer, and losing *the church* altogether. The uniting idea—the infant church at its purest and best—will, if kept clear, carry the other four thoughts upon its back.

The more the headings, the more imperative this unity. Once a year, perhaps, a man may permit himself five points, and even—once in a ministry—six: but then they must be strictly subordinate to a main theme so dominating that the total impression cannot be lost. A character-study, for example, or a dramatic historical incident, may be so sub-divided. To attempt it with an abstract theme, such as 'sanctification', or 'faith', would almost certainly mean that listeners pick up one stray thought and let the rest wash over them. Any address with more than six points is not a sermon, but a series.

It is *an excellent rule* never to preach two sermons in four which follow the same pattern. If morning sermon last Sunday had three points, neither the evening sermon, nor either sermon on next Lord's Day, should have three. That seems a counsel of perfection, and the over-riding consideration must be to let the *content* determine the *form*. But to have that counsel of perfection laid upon one's conscience is healthy, if only to remind us that a congregation obliged to put up with one face, one voice, one manner, and type of mind, week after week, does deserve all the variety we can provide. To ring the changes continually upon

> two-legged runners
> three-pronged forks
> four-legged tables
> five-finger exercises

and just *occasionally* a simple, unstructured meditation on a single theme, will keep them guessing, and stimulate interest, not only by what you say but by the care you give to how you say it.

There is however another source of variety, and one offering great increase in total impact, in the way the several headings relate one to another. A few examples will, with practice, suggest others, for the possibilities are endless.

Patterns of Structure

A sermon may have well-defined divisions, yet lack any coherence of structure; it may have 'points', but no pattern—like a packet of pins. But when the separate points are seen to belong closely, inevitably, together in a total pattern of thought, the effect is enormously enhanced. The 'pattern of thought' is the message given of God for a people, with its intended effect upon their lives: the separate points are not meant merely to break it down into manageable units, but to enforce it, step by step, with gathering momentum, until the whole message is laid upon the conscience of the listener. If the separate points are really separate, unrelated, the effect of the whole is more likely to be dissipated, than increased.

(i) *Cumulative divisions* illustrate the value of relatedness most simply. Here care is taken that the content of the divisions is not—so to speak—on the same level of interest, or thoughtfulness, or familiarity: and that order of points is chosen which will 'pile on the pressure', moving from the obvious and familiar to the unexpected and debatable, or the more important.

In Romans 1: 16 Paul declares, with some heat, that he is not ashamed of the gospel of Christ. Remembering Rome's magnificence and might, and Paul's Jewish background, it is interesting to ask how he would defend the gospel, to such a city. Assuming that his reasons would emerge in what he goes on to write, we may expound Romans 1: 16 thus:

Paul is not ashamed of the gospel because—
  (a) *It is utterly reasonable*—the letter is one long *argument*, from history, from experience, from ethical results;
  (b) *It is entirely relevant*—the letter discusses social, personal, and moral problems, not academic theories;
  (c) *It is inherently revolutionary*—it works, it is *power*, the power of God, as chapters six to eight will show.

So Paul has no need to be ashamed, though Rome boast her intellectual pride, her practical skill, her political might. Nor have we.

Here the first point sounds somewhat hackneyed and a little remote; the second is (to a modern congregation) much more important, if it can be proved; the third is a little startling, and the greatest claim of the three. In this order, any effect would be cumulative: alter the order, and the whole is weakened.

Another outline offered on the same text runs:

Paul is unashamed of the gospel because it is—
(a) *The Gospel of a living Personality*—Christ, and His story;
(b) *The Gospel of a Redeeming Energy*—'power', negative, positive;
(c) *The Gospel of an Ethical Revelation*—'righteousness revealed'.

This follows the order of ideas in the text itself, and includes verse 17, as Paul intended. But how it 'tails off' into less gripping areas of thought—important though they are in theory. Simply reversing the order would greatly improve the whole by a steadily *increasing* interest and impact.

In 1 Corinthians 14: 1 Paul summarises the message of chapter 13 in a word which means, literally, 'pursue—chase after—love'. Love then is no mere feeling, impulsive and fitful: nor something which happens to you; Christian love has to be pursued with deliberation and persistence. What is it?

(a) *Love is an attitude*: so through chapter 13, and the gospels;
(b) *Love is an art*: a sensitive, imaginative spirit—so in 13, and in Jesus;
(c) *Love is an adventure*: hence 'pursue'—an adventure of the spirit which leads to unforeseeable gain.

Here again, the first idea is somewhat prosaic, though important. The second idea is more attractive, requires some care and insight. The third is more provocative, and the real message lies here—we must adventure in love for Christ's sake. The impact accumulates.

An outline attributed to James Denney seems, very unexpectedly, to ignore the cumulative principle:

On Matthew 11: 28—Our Lord's invitation was addressed to people who—

(a) Found their religion to be a burden;
(b) Having no religion, carried the burden of futility;
(c) Carried the heavy burden of a bad conscience;
(d) Felt life itself to be a burden grievous to be borne.

Doubtless Denney would develop each point, and relate each to the text, in his usual convincing way. Something must be allowed, too, for the change in priorities since his time: to his hearers, a burdensome religion, and a sense of guilt, were more immediate problems than to most people today. However, that outline for our own time seems to gain greatly if we take the four groups in the order (a), (c), (b), (d) as *widening circles* of modern people.

(ii) *Argumentative divisions* have obvious force, though this pattern comes very easily to certain types of mind, and congregations can grow very weary of being argued with every Sunday. Two examples may suffice:

Romans 8: 17 presents the great Christian argument of hope:
(a) *If children*—the basic premise—and we are, by birth, by adoption, by the witness of the Spirit to our spirit;
(b) *If children, then heirs*—to family life, and love; but we have not all as yet—texts on the inheritance reserved for us;
(c) *If heirs, then joint-heirs with Christ*: texts on *His* inheritance—which includes resurrection, ascension, immortality, glory: 'Because I live, ye shall live also.' He has joined us with himself in the heirship!

1 Corinthians 15 on the same subject, urges that we see the logic involved in our doubts. They are too dangerous to play with. Let us be quite clear, and consistent (verses 14–19):
(a) *If Christ be not risen, the whole gospel falls* (14): we have nothing to say to men;
(b) *If the gospel falls, all our experience is a delusion* (14): we are wholly misled;
(c) *If Christian experience deludes, then nothing is solved* (17): our sins, problems, evils, are unaltered;
(d) *If nothing is solved, we are desperate* (19): the world knows no alternative.

We must, then, count carefully the cost of not believing the Easter faith.

This type of message can be very powerful. It has one serious pitfall, to judge by experience both of preaching and of listening: the mind full of the total argument tends to run ahead and anticipate the way the whole case leads. The result is confusion. What should be a cogent, relentless theorem descends to a mere muddle. It is essential, in this pattern, to keep the steps entirely distinct, and to be satisfied with establishing one point at a time, letting its importance to the whole appear when the sermon is complete.

(iii) *Telescopic divisions* have a curious interest, difficult to define, which can hold attention to an unusual degree. Perhaps the sense of progress is part of the fascination. In this pattern, the text is shown to establish one main truth, and the divisions of the sermon develop subsequent ideas *each drawn from the preceding one*, like a telescope. A. E. Garvie offers an example:

On John 3: 16—

(a) *God's immeasurable love*: God *so* loved, and loved *the world*;
(b) *The Supreme Disclosure of that immeasurable love*: God gave His son,—His only-begotten Son;
(c) *The Transcendent Purpose of that supreme disclosure*: that whoever believes might not perish, but have everlasting life.

This develops Garvie's thought a little, but the telescopic pattern is his, and its effectiveness is evident. The successive steps constitute not so much an argument as a continuing discovery.

Alexander Maclaren, for once deserting his gift for exposition in the narrower, 'microscopic', sense, offers us the following meditation on Romans 8: 17—

(a) No inheritance without sonship
(b) No sonship without spiritual birth
(c) No spiritual birth without Christ
(d) No Christ without faith.

—an almost perfect example of the telescope being steadily extended to its full length, most effectively.

Revelation 3: 20 is most significant when its context is allowed to control its use—for it shows Jesus standing at the door of the Laodicean *church* begging admission to a fellowship of which He ought to be the very centre! Yet 'begging admission' is a wrong phrase: for John uses a very strong word 'Look, I stand at the door and *rap*!' We may therefore arrange the truth thus:

(a) *Christ's position* 'I stand at the door'—He confronts us.
(b) *Where Christ stands, there is pressure*—'I knock—rap!'—He is not to be ignored.
(c) *Where Christ presses there is promise*—'I will sup with him and he with me.'

This is the order of the text, and closes with invitation. The true burden of the Laodicean message, however, is rather warning to a 'sickening' church that it will be utterly rejected if it does not change. The invitation is to individuals within the decaying church to let Christ into it, before it is too late. They, at least, may then sup with Christ. If the sermon is to keep close to this intention, points (b), (c) would be reversed, and the phrasing adjusted. In each case the telescopic pattern is effective.

One can look through a telescope either way! Sometimes it discloses larger and larger views; sometimes it can reduce a total situation to a point. Such is the following:

Ephesians 5: 25 declares that Christ loved the church, and the whole epistle provides illustration of how much He did and suffered for His love. This basic, broad position yields this narrowing pattern:

(a) *If Christ loved the church, we cannot love Christ without loving the church*—loving what He loved;

(b) *We cannot love the church without loving the real existing churches*—one cannot love intellectual abstractions!

(c) *We cannot love the churches at large without loving one local, particular church*—the church on our doorstep, in reach;

(d) *We cannot love the local church without loving its people, its work, its services, its good name*—there is nothing else to love.

Though the impression here is of a sustained argument, the actual form is rather of a series of thoughts each focussing on part of the one going before, until attention is concentrated on the individual member in his own church-fellowship.

(iv) *Contrasting divisions* have already been suggested, as in William Carey's couplet about expecting and attempting great things. Such contrast can illuminate and balance truth. Sometimes those who readily assent to one thought will be much helped by having to consider an opposite emphasis, or an application less welcome to their minds, set forth as its necessary counterpart.

John 18: 26 records the challenge to Peter in the High Priest's courtyard: 'One of the servants of the high priest, being his kinsman whose ear Peter cut off, saith, Did not I see thee in the garden with him?' A clear contrast is implied, for on the one hand Peter's presence in the garden with Christ, and his zeal in Christ's defence, argue one thing about Peter; his presence here, warming himself beside a hostile fire, already denying that he knew Jesus (verse 17) argues quite another. The sermon-form may then comprise contrasting questions:

(a) *Have you ever been into the Garden with Jesus?*—following into sacred and intimate places, professing loyalty, sharing peril, one of the inner three—or has it always been a distant loyalty, holding off, uncommitted?

(b) If you once were there—*What are you doing where you now are,* beside the world's fires, denying Him, betrayed by your company, your conversation, your cowardice?

A message for backsliders, one would think—though sympathy, not judgement, must always inspire preaching.

Four verses contain the phrase 'But God' with slight variation. Each describes God breaking into life, in a dramatic and transforming way. But the situations into which, in each case, God powerfully enters, are vividly contrasted:

(a) *God breaks into a world confused and doomed* (Galatians 4: 4)
(b) *God breaks into a personal situation, baffling and disheartening* (2 Corinthians 7: 5–7)
(c) *God breaks into a career selfish, materialist and self-satisfied* (Luke 12: 20)
(d) *God breaks into a life sinful and lost* (Ephesians 2: 4).

Here is probably too much material, with the usual danger of offering four unrelated themes. To combine the two personal situations, (c), (d), as an inbreaking in judgement or redemption, would probably improve the pattern, but all will depend upon keeping the instances firmly subordinate to the main unifying idea: that at any moment in any man's life, God may do the unexpected.

It is tempting to use the device of contrasted headings to present a paradox, or a direct contradiction. The famous pair in Galatians 6: 2,5

Bear ye one another's burdens
Every man shall bear his own burden

tempts to a contradictory structure. The twin sayings of Jesus—

He that is not with me is against me (Matthew 12: 30)
He that is not against us is for us (Luke 9: 50)

almost compel a paradoxical outline. Such patterns can be intriguing, but they demand great care: what seems clear in the study can sound very confusing in the pew. As in the second instance, a unifying viewpoint is essential—the impossibility of neutrality, which has two sides, one of warning and one of encouragement.

Given that care, and clarity, a contrast may illumine truth rewardingly. Galatians 6: 7,8 very solemnly warns that a man reaps precisely what he sows; Deuteronomy 6: 10–11 assures Israel that God will give great and goodly cities which they did not plant, houses full of good things which they did not fill, wells they did not dig, vineyards and olive trees they did not plant . . . Two very different areas of human experience are here brought into sharp comparison: it seems man may elect to live upon one level with God —or the other.

One use of contrast rarely fails to hold attention, that of setting side by side two carefully chosen characters: Jacob and Esau, Paul and Barnabas, Peter and John, David and Jonathan (a fascinating pair!), Amos and Hosea, Elijah and Jeremiah (both were likened to Jesus). Here the difficulty is an embarrassing wealth of material, and rigid self-discipline is necessary. It is best to choose only one or two particular points in the parallel, and those closely related.

Peter and Andrew as sons of one home, subject to similar experience of Christ; Peter in denial, with Barabbas in betrayal; Samuel's loyalty and Saul's inconstancy—such make manageable contrasts that offer interest as well as usefulness.

(v) *Unpacking divisions*, practised by a master expositor, can yield the most satisfying preaching of all. In any man's hands, the method will especially delight lovers of scripture, given only conscientious investigation and some care for presentation. The intellectual and spiritual reward, for both preacher and hearers, closely resembles that of opening a Christmas parcel. One of the great sayings of scripture is presented, in all its richness of association, mystery, beauty of language, depth of promise, and then one by one the wrappers are slowly removed, each revealing new and unexpected treasure, until the whole divine gift lies before the mind, to be accepted by faith.

Robert Menzies does this with words as familiar as John 10: 9—
'I am the door: by me if any man enter in, he shall be saved, and shall go in and out, and find pasture.' First the text is related to the context: the blind man, now healed, is excluded from the Jewish synagogue, by self-appointed shepherds of God's fold, presuming to be guardians of the eternal doors. The meaning of the Shepherd in scripture, and the implied authority in Christ's claim to be the true Shepherd of God's fold, are quickly explained. Then the practical consequence is drawn: whoever, hearing Christ's voice, will enter by Him, the Door for the sheep, will find

(a) *Safety*—'he shall be saved';
(b) *Liberty*—'he shall go in and out';
(c) *Satisfaction*—'he shall find pasture'.

Obvious—when you see it done: but how the meaning of the words has grown under the preacher's hand.

A. E. Garvie does the same with still more familiar words, John 3: 16—

(a) *The nature of God's love*—He gives
(b) *The measure of God's love*—His only son
(c) *The objects of God's love*—'whosoever'
(d) *The need for God's love*—'perishing'
(e) *The claim of God's love*—believe!

To reduce the result in this way to a mere skeleton-outline is especially unfair to this type of sermon, precisely because it is the skill in developing each successive disclosure of depth which makes the message so rich. If we try to imagine James Stalker, with all his wealth of knowledge about the thoughts and ideals of the first century, patiently unfolding the implications of 1 Corinthians 1: 30, unpeeling, as it were, the layers of Paul's meaning, we may catch the thrill of a spiritual feast.

'Christ Jesus, who of God is made unto us wisdom, and righteousness, and sanctification, and redemption . . .' comes at the close of a chapter in which the attitude of Greek and Jew to the message of the cross has been the main concern. Paul has also reminded the Corinthians of their own unprepossessing background, when Christ called them. How different peoples find different things in Jesus, is therefore close to Paul's intent: and Stalker follows this clue, in something of the following manner:

(a) *Christ is made widom*—for the Greeks, and all like them, who are concerned for intellectual understanding, seeking life's *meaning*;

(b) *Christ is made righteousness*—for Romans, and all who like them are concerned for social justice, seeking *solutions* to man's problems;

(c) *Christ is made sanctification*—for Jews, and for all like them who are concerned for man's religious hunger, and seek blessedness, and God;

(d) *Christ is made redemption*—for all men, sinful, afraid, sad, seeking peace, pardon, immortality.

Christ, in fact, is Everyman's answer!

Here again one must clothe the bare framework with a great scholar's exposition of the four main concerns of ancient peoples, and of humanity at large; and also remember the quality of his Scottish audience. But even in this dehydrated skeleton of a message, is not the text transformed?

So important is this sermon structure, of disclosure by analysis, that one detailed example of the thought-processes behind it may be offered:

1 John 3: 1-3 is one of the great gospel assertions familiar to every lover of the New Testament. For ordinary public services, it probably contains too much for any expository sermon, but in specially favourable conditions—at a Bible Convention, for example—patient attention might be given to a detailed examination. At first glance, the important ideas are plain: love shown us, sonship given us, and likeness to Christ expected. A certain tone is felt, for the writer has broken into a fairly close-knit argument with an exclamation; and this is repeated in the term of address in the middle of the utterance, 'Beloved . . .!' The word is appropriate, for the readers are those who have received the love God has shown—yet the address just here seems to call attention to something unexpected, almost incredible: 'Beloved, . . . would you believe it! . . .' This yields our title, and introduction; the main ideas must then determine our divisions. (As only an outline can be given here, no gathered thoughts from a seed-plot are assembled to elaborate the treatment: in this type of message, for this audience, elaboration is less necessary than in public sermons. Pressure on time would exclude it, in any case). The treatment might run like this:

The Apostolic Wonder

Introduction: Even apostles, living in the midst of daily triumphs, surrounded by a vital and ever growing church, sustained by the recent memories of Jesus, close to the fountain and source of pentecostal power—even they could never quite conquer their surprise, their sense of perpetual wonder, at what had happened. 'Behold! . . . Beloved, can you believe it ? . . .' 'O the depth of the riches, both of the wisdom and knowledge of God . . .' exclaims Paul; 'What shall we say to these things ?' That is how John felt. What moved him to this apostolic wonder ?

(a) *The Cause of apostolic wonder—the munificence of divine love.*

(i) *'What . . . love'*—love is always wonder-full, in sweetheart, or wife, in parent, or the answering love of a child: but especially is there wonder, a sense of surprise, of unexpected, undeserved privilege, in the knowledge that we *are loved*—it is the great wonder in life.

(ii) 'What *manner* of love . . .' (literally, 'from what country', that is, of something unfamiliar, strange, needing explanation). Used of the astonishing stones of the Temple (Mark 13: 1); of the astonished reaction to Jesus' stilling of the storm (Matthew 8: 27); of the astonishment of Mary at the salutation of the angel (Luke 1: 29). In each case it might almost be translated, 'What on earth . . .!'—What on earth sort of love is this !

(iii) *'The Father . . .'* There is a love of obligation like that of a merely grateful son; a love of compassion, like charity; but there is a warmer, more personal, affectionate love, that of relationship— and such is God's love, the love of a Father whose 'good pleasure' is in His children.

(iv) *'Bestowed on us'*: love can be felt, even by the inarticulate; it can be told, even when actions and attitudes are clumsy and mistaken; it can—further—be shown, in a score of kindly, generous, gentle ways; John seems to mean yet more —a love so active, positive, strong, as to be actually communicated and to become the basis of a reciprocal relationship—rather as Paul speaks of His love shed abroad in our hearts.

So amazing is the divine love which kindles wonder in apostolic hearts !

(b) *The Object of that munificent love, the Conferring of Sonship.*

(i) God's love wills *that we should be called* children of God: God 'owns us' to be His—not as the elder brother who disowned the prodigal ('This, thy son!'). 'He is not ashamed to call us brethren.' That the world disowns us, knows us not, is unimportant, since 'it knew Him not'—the Son. God places us alongside His only Son, whom He acknowledged at baptism and at transfiguration, and at resurrection (Romans 1: 4). This is *the status* to which munificent love has raised us !

(ii) Yet more wonderful *'such we are'*: sons of God by birth and by adoption, partakers of the divine nature. We 'belong': such is *the relationship* to which munificent love has begotten us.

(iii) And still more wonderful, we shall be recognised, one day— though now the world deny us. Much we do not know about the future—'it doth not yet appear'. But this we know: 'He shall appear', whom the world did not know; this too we know, that *we shall see Him*; and this yet again we know, that we shall bear His image, be like Him, be recognised as belonging to the same Father by the family likeness we shall bear. This is the *magnificent hope* which munificent love has kindled within us.

Such was God's object, and so He has achieved: that we should be acknowledged, and actually be, and one day shall be seen to be—His sons.

(c) *The effect of that conferment of sonship, a Christ-moulded character.*

(i) Our hope is here focussed, and fastened, *upon Christ*: He is the drive, the motive, the ambition, and the explanation, of all our life. ('Hope' probably does not mean only the hope of His appearing: 'this hope' sums up the whole confidence of the passage. The original makes clear that the hope is fastened upon Christ, not 'every man having . . . in himself'). The perfect Son is the idol of all the sons.

(ii) Our standard, and definition, and ideal of purity and holiness is Christ: we have seen, and know, and declare, that *'He is pure'*—this is what purity means! His purity condemns, but also inspires. He *is* the Perfect Son.

(iii) So the Perfect Son is the pattern for the family: *we purify ourselves,* because the life and likeness of the family has become our controlling impulse. We are to be conformed to the image of God's Son, because we are sons—that He might be no longer entirely unique in moral character, but the firstborn among many brethren. In conferring sonship, the love of God has bestowed an ideal, a standard and a likeness—in Christ the perfect Son.

It amounts, then, to this: the divine love is wonderful, breathtaking. But the aim of that love is not that we should be moved to wonder, but lifted to sonship; not that we should be surprised, but that we might be sanctified; not that we should stand transfixed by astonishment that God could so love us, but that we should live transfigured by the spirit of His Son reproducing His likeness within ourselves.

Behold, what manner of love . . . !

This full example illustrates the danger of the unpacking-pattern: it can become so full that main ideas are obscured. Normally, the preacher would need to select among the thoughts the text offers him, those that his congregation can absorb at one sitting. Though it must be remembered that the listener has the text before him—and he is very likely to comment afterwards that the preacher did not say anything new!

Further, all the examples offered have scrupulously followed the order of ideas in the suggested text: this is not necessary, and often not wise. A text may be unpacked in any order, so long as the

plain meaning is not thereby distorted. Sometimes the main thought
of the text is in its tail, and the remaining clauses explicate it, or
qualify it, before it is stated. In that case the sermon will need first
to clarify the main point, and take up the earlier clauses in any order
that sustains interest.

> Acts 2: 33—'Therefore being by the right hand of God exalted, and
> having received of the Father the promise of the Holy Ghost, he
> hath shed forth this, which ye now see and hear.'—would require
> such re-arranged 'unpacking'. The main thought is clearly Peter's
> explanation of Pentecost to a startled and enquiring city. Its miracles,
> its meaning, its (preached) message, and above all its changed men,
> all require explanation —and Peter's explanation is simple: *Christ
> hath shed forth this*. We may then choose for title, 'Pentecost Ex-
> plained', and our introduction will stress the events in the city, and
> the things that need explaining—then and now. Peter declares that
> what has happened before their eyes is Jesus at work—He shed forth
> this! And he unfolds that assertion as follows:
>
> (a) *Pentecost was the fulfilment of a promise*—'the promise of the Holy
> Ghost': new, but not unforeseen; strange indeed, but full of promise,
> not fear;
>
> (b) *Pentecost was the gift of the Father*—'received of the Father':
> culminating gift of five—Bethlehem, Galilee, Calvary and Easter, now
> 'this'.
>
> (c) *Pentecost was the act of the exalted Christ*—'being by the right hand
> of God exalted'—the city had last seen Him high upon a cross: He
> sits now high at God's throne, and on the side of power. They still
> have to reckon with Him they crucified! They witness the mani-
> festation of His victory, and the fruit of His intercession ('I will pray
> the Father, and He will send another Comforter . . .')
>
> (d) *Pentecost was the unchallengeable fact to which now they cannot but
> respond*—'which ye now see and hear'. The unanswerable witness of a
> Spirit-filled church!

Here the textual order would have been much weaker. With this
matter of order we may close our discussion on the assembling of
materials. Many a good message is spoiled by disorder: but many
also by a *wrong* order. So often a man will dispense in the first five
minutes all the thought that really gripped him, stirred his imagination, attracted him to the subject. The rest of the sermon is repetition, or padding, filling in time. As a whole this is poor, and betrays
skimped preparation. But if it be all he has, at least let him improve
it by keeping the best wine until last. Let the weightiest thought,
the richest insight, the new angle or application, be led up to, not
launched at once and then obscured by trivialities. As a general
rule, for beginners, it is well to preach a sermon in the reverse
order to that in which it occurred to you. The interest will then

mount, instead of flagging as soon as your freshest ideas are exhausted. Better still, of course, to have enough ideas to excite attention, then to hold it, and then to leave it wanting more!

One mere trick of method will both underline, and facilitate, this care for the most effective order of division. It is *always to take a fresh page* as you begin to assemble ideas for a new division. Let the sermon-headings always head the pages. Then, when the assembly is done, before you rake over, sift, and discard the superfluous, *always shuffle the pages*. Try the points in another order—in every possible permutation of pages!—until the most effective, and sustained, pattern appears. Only then proceed to write out the finished product.

10 IN CONCLUSION

THEME CHOSEN, purpose and hearers defined, materials gathered, sifted and arranged, the first part of the sermon to be actually written out in full will be the conclusion. One of many prescriptions for great preaching runs this way: 'Make sure of your first sentence; make sure of your last sentence; and put your first sentence and your last sentence as close together as you possibly can.'

Aristotle, we may recall, held that the peroration was the best remembered section of any speech, because it is the last to be heard. But he added that no fine peroration can redeem a lost beginning, and no final flourish accomplishes much if it is not built up for, all the way.

Without doubt, conclusions are usually the weakest part of all sermons. The probable reasons for this are illuminating. Sometimes it is because both speaker and hearers are spent, minds tired and attention wandering. The cause may well be that the preacher was growing weary when he reached that part of his preparation, and this is reflected in his mood as he preaches, in the quality of the closing passage, and in the diminished responsiveness of the congregation. To avoid this, strength and thought must be reserved for the final assault. That is why, as a matter of habitual technique, the conclusion should be written out while the mind is fresh and eager.

Sometimes the conclusion is weak because the message never really gripped us deeply. In our heart of hearts we did not truly believe in it—as a message given from God. Such want of conviction always glimmers through: our hearers realise that we have conscientiously done our best, but our heart was not in it. And so the pattern of thought is presented, and left with them—to accept or reject. All unconsciously, our manner of ending suggests it will not make much difference! The cure for that, of course, is greater care in deciding upon our theme.

Curiously enough, the opposite attitude, also, can leave us with a weak conclusion. We may feel very deeply indeed about a given message; in the study we are eager, sure that this is a word our people need to hear; we face the pulpit with anticipation—but we neglect to prepare to the end. We rely upon the inspiration of the occasion, sure the best way of ending will 'come to us' as we preach. We depend upon the flood tide of the sermon to carry us onward in triumph! And we go over the weir—splashing and floundering to the bank in numerous 'last' sentences that dissipate all effect. The unprepared conclusion nearly always shows.

But possibly the commonest reason for weak endings is the most serious. We have no strong conclusion because we had no clearly defined aim: it is impossible therefore for us to arrive with any flourish or finality. We can only flicker out like a dying lamp, because there is no direction to concentrate the beam. Like a car without brakes, a sermon with no end in view can come to a stop only by loss of momentum.

This is why it was emphasized that the third preliminary question to every sermon should be answered at the outset with a definition of purpose. Abstract explorations of a text or a theme or a character, elaborate diagnoses of problems, and all the other aimless meanderings among irrelevance that sometimes pass for sermons—all these are mercilessly exposed by the speaker's inability to find a place where his talk must naturally stop. The cure in this case is brutally to ask oneself *why* one is preaching at all.

Occasionally, of course, there may be good reason for not having a formal conclusion. When an argument has sufficiently made its point, to recapitulate is to weaken. When the pattern of thought is so closely woven as to need no ends tied up, to dribble on is to subtract effectiveness by multiplying words. But much more often, a quick summary leaves the whole message on the mind as the worshipper departs; a positive appeal makes the relevance of the whole sermon urgent and pressing. A few very detailed and practical applications may suddenly illumine the significance of the truth for an individual life.

An excellent sermon expounded the need, and value, of zeal, understood as enthusiasm—the enthusiasm of Paul, and his personal right to urge it upon others; the buoyant enthusiasm of the apostolic church, so joyously infectious; the enthusiasm of so many who have accomplished much, and endured much, in the Christian story; the way enthusiasm lends zest to daily Christian life; the debt we owe to Christ, to be enthusiastic in His service: then came the conclusion 'Let us then *be* enthusiastic!' This remembered summary does no justice to the excellence of the exposition, the illustration, the sustained interest, the examples and the earnestness of that message. Yet it ended with a sense of disappointment. Reflection suggested that what went wrong was the lack of a focussing conclusion. How can anyone set out to 'be enthusiastic'? An improved conclusion might run: 'So then, are you being asked to do some new piece of work, and are you hesitating?—Go and do it, right away, with enthusiasm. Are you on the point, this very morning, of giving something up, of resigning, pulling out?—Don't do it! Be enthusiastic. Have you let the years go by just waiting to be asked?—go out and find your work for God, and get on with it, with zeal. Is there something on your conscience, even as I speak, that you have been doing half-heartedly, or shirking altogether?—commit yourself now to God to go and do it properly. Are you everlastingly pleading, every time you are offered a task that you just 'can't'?—change your tune, and TRY. For be sure of this: All our excuses are confessions of a lack of zeal. Enthusiasm is not a feeling—it's a *decision*, persisted in, against all odds, because zeal for God has eaten up your heart.'

Let it be admitted that the contrived conclusion can ruin a sermon, too. Worst of all is the kind that drags in the cross of Jesus, somehow, inevitably, every time, however incongruously. Similarly with the evangelistic appeal, tacked on to the end of a message that in no way prepared for it, simply because it was required by the promoters of the meeting, or expected of an evangelical preacher. The artificiality of such a proceeding exposes its essential dishonesty.

Hardly better are conclusions that struggle to retrieve the lost opportunity; or that appeal for the belief which the sermon lamentably failed to kindle; or strive to explain again what the sermon never made clear; or urge people to 'remember' what was never made memorable.

A truly disastrous sermon-ending is that in which the real motive behind the sermon is suddenly revealed, and proves to be unworthy, entirely personal, even spiteful. A high-toned discourse on the value of the Lord's Day and the sacredness of God's House that descends at last to a scolding for last Sunday's poor congregation! A 'practical', and supposedly 'courageous', study of the evils of gossip, the cruelties of slander, which in the last sentence or two is related to something the preacher has heard is being said about himself—or about his wife! To the preacher, in his hurt indignation, this will seem for a while to be effective, relevant, 'about time it was said'. To his hearers it will be clear that he has used the pulpit to 'get something off his chest': some will say it humorously, not really expecting their preacher to be above that kind of thing; others will say it resentfully. Everybody will know, including the preacher presently, that he was not preaching.

Other snares to avoid include introducing into the conclusion some striking new thought, which may easily eclipse all else that you have said. Then the ending ceases to be a conclusion, and becomes a tangent—or even the beginning of a different sermon! A new and striking way of saying what you have been saying all along, may be excellent—a last blow that drives *the same nail* right home. But a new idea, if relevant at all, should be tucked in elsewhere in the sermon. The same danger lurks in a striking story, unless it is so perfectly appropriate to the whole message that it does not sidetrack the mind, or erase all earlier impressions.

Avoid, too, the temptation to retrieve a poor sermon by repeating its main points in a higher key, with more noise and emphasis. Getting worked up is not in itself an effective conclusion: it may descend to mere bullying. Recalling the headings and a telling phrase or two can be emphasis in itself—but beware re-preaching!

Avoid, most of all, the apology. All preachers know occasions when it seems to be due; when the sermon has not gone well, when the preacher himself lost confidence in it—or even lost the place! But what possible good can an apology do? It can only make the situation worse. It will undermine any effect the sermon has had on some soul who found in it a word from God; and it will embarrass everyone else. Let it stand. An apology, at any rate, is no sermon-conclusion. If quite in despair, announce the hymn, with dignity.

Among things to seek, on the other hand, in framing a conclusion, perhaps the first is *brevity*. Conclusions lose all their point if they wander: they should thrust, not waver. Three sentences are often enough—never use more than six or so. Seek, also, to be *personal*. All the wide-ranging examples, the biblical illustrations, the historical arguments, the general principles, belong in the body of the sermon: the conclusion should fall into the lap of the individual listener.

Do not avoid *emotion*. It would be misleading to say 'Seek an emotional ending', but certainly do not evade it. A truth genuinely felt, a duty carefully expounded, a vision sincerely kindled, must touch the heart and move the affections, if the listener has any faith or love at all. If the sermon is to accomplish anything, it must move the will, and all the motive-powers of personality reside in the feelings. No man is moved only by thinking: and no Christian sermon can end 'dead cold'.

Most of all, seek to *touch the conscience*. We have already seen the importance of 'manifesting the truth to every man's conscience in the sight of God', and have noted that conscience can only be addressed through mind, feeling, imagination, will. The concluding sentences of the sermon are the appropriate moments for pressing this home, though the whole sermon must of course reinforce that appeal.

To end with a question demanding a serious answer is to approach conscience through the mind. To appeal to gratitude, regret, shame, admiration, hero-worship, idealism—so long as sentimentalism is avoided—is to approach conscience through feeling. Vision, insight, examples, attractiveness or warning ply the imagination; to lead towards some action, signature, decision, commitment of membership or loyalty, is to seek conscience through the will. But in each case, the inner witness to the human spirit by the Spirit of God, the appeal to the ally of truth within the soul, lends strength to the final words. Our *last* argument is not 'You know it makes sense', but 'you know that this is true . . . and right . . . and unanswerable: you must respond—or simply run away!'

Very occasionally, the best conclusion may be *a word of prayer*. This too can be so artificial as to become dishonest: and—in the case of prayer more than of any other utterance in the pulpit —to be artificial, ostentatious, theatrical, is to be irreverent. Far better to use this method of ending very rarely, never preparing for it, but so responding when the theme, and the occasion, prompt it. Your people will then realise how moved you are, at that moment— and will pray with you. To 'end with prayer' must never be allowed to become an evangelical gimmick.

Where, then, should the conclusion come? The suggestion that the last sentence and the first should be as close together as possible reflects again the modern incapacity for concentrated, or prolonged, listening. But the question of sermon-length is important, not only to a preacher's popularity but to his efficiency. Time is subjective and relative: it flies or it drags according to the experience, the interest, the anticipation or fears, the concentration or idleness, of the mind observing it. Hence the real length of a sermon depends upon its interest, content and effectiveness, not upon the number of minutes it takes to deliver.

James Black counsels that we should finish when the thought ends: which could make some sermons very short indeed. Some would say, finish when the purpose is achieved, so far as lies with us. Others again suggest that subject and material determine length, which ought not to be arbitrarily fixed by convention or habit. A congregation will certainly appreciate the preacher whose length, like everything else in his preaching, varies with his theme, and who ends always when he has done.

Perhaps the truth of the matter lies in the unarguable fact that when interest fails, communication ends. The preaching is finished when the mind stops listening and the emotions cease to respond—

however long the preacher goes on talking. Closing the sermon is simply recognising either (a) that there is no more to be said at that time, or (b) that no more will be heard, whatever is said. In either case—Stop! And if you contrive to stop while the congregation wish you still to continue, they will certainly want to hear you again.

And when you announce your intention of stopping, keep your promise. An apostle may say 'Finally, brethren . . .' and go on for two more chapters: but not you. A troubled English vicar asked a farm-labourer why he came to church only when the assistant preached. 'Well sir,' said the labourer, 'young Mr Smith, he says "in conclusion" and he do conclude. But you say "lastly" and you *do* last.'

11 EFFECTING THE INTRODUCTION

THE LAST section of the sermon to be prepared is the introduction. The theme chosen, the audience envisaged and the purpose defined, the material assembled and shaped, the conclusion written out, the preacher may turn his attention to how he is to begin. Experience shows that if he starts his thinking *from* an introduction, several things can go wrong.

The most common is to give the whole sermon-content away in the first few sentences, anticipating too much of the theme and its development. The first few minutes will then be rich, thoughtful, and promising—but the rest will be inferior, repetitive, elaborating what was better expressed at the outset. Disappointing sermons which began well are too familiar for this danger to need emphasis: but the cause is not so often understood. It is quite simply that the man sat down with his head full of the message and began right away with the first paragraph—into which it all tumbled!

Alternatively, a bright idea for an introduction can very easily overwhelm the whole message. The introductory thoughts pass into wider and wider illustration and application, until the message we finally compose is not that we intended, but something which 'flowed' unprompted from the first sentences. In which case we have not prepared an introduction for our sermon, but another, different, sermon.

An introduction prepared first can also be too long: doing it last, we know how much there is to be said, and keep the opening sentences in their place.

The deepest reason for this procedure, however, is the obvious one: until you know what the theme and development are, and what material you are going to use at each point, you cannot judge the best way to introduce it, or know what relevant thoughts and quotations will be available for use. In a well-planned sermon, for example, a somewhat sombre theme would need a light and attractive introduction; a challenging theme might well begin with divine promises. The careful exposition of a great Christian truth may need to be introduced with some explanation of the perennial moral or intellectual question which that truth intends to answer. It is difficult to see how one *can* prepare an introduction until it is clear and settled what one is introducing!

If the introduction fails, the whole sermon is usually a lost cause. It takes great courage, and considerable skill, to recapture the expectancy, the hopeful and worshipful attention, which a rambling, unclear, unconvincing, or tedious, introduction has dissipated. The opening sentences are all-important, on several counts.

(i) The introduction, to succeed, should *introduce yourself*. Cicero is often quoted, and justly, for his remark that the opening of an address is meant to 'arouse interest, secure favour, and prepare to lead'. 'To secure favour' is much more significant if we intend to persuade, to carry people with us. In an unfamiliar congregation, of course, even our voice, our manner, our habits of thought and speech, our accent, will need introduction, and the congregation may well be adjusting to these during our carefully prepared opening. If they cannot hear the introduction without strain, they may well not listen further.

Nor will they listen attentively if, from the opening sentences, they sum you up as arrogant, conceited, cross, contentious, 'too clever by half', or showing-off. Thus the introduction will best be in characteristic vein—something manifestly your own—direct, personal and unpretentious. Keep the fireworks until they have learned to trust your taper. By the introduction, take the congregation into your confidence and start a conversation on the things of God: the whole sermon, and the whole service, will benefit.

(ii) The introduction, to succeed, should also *introduce the subject*. This may be done formally—'It is time we turned our attention to . . .' or 'What the apostle is concerned about in this passage is . . .' or 'This is Advent Sunday, when the whole church is thinking about . . .' It may be done methodically, letting the introduction outline the sermon by announcing the divisions as well as the theme; or by so focussing the text as to suggest the way the sermon will go.

John 12: 29,30—'The people therefore, that stood by, and heard it, said that it thundered: others said, An angel spake to him. Jesus answered and said, This voice . . . So, we have three levels of spiritual perception playing upon a single event. Some can perceive nothing but the natural world about them—they say merely that it thundered. Others, however, have a dim and uncertain awareness of things not wholly of this world—they speak of angels. But Jesus sees beyond the thunder and the angels, and hears the voice of the divine Father . . .' So subject and pattern are established right away, for a sermon exploring differing levels of awareness of the spiritual world.

Much more often, introduction of the theme will be achieved informally, by any appropriate method, but taking care that when the introduction is through there is left no doubt what the subject is, or why it has been chosen. The mood and tone of the sermon will likewise be set by the opening paragraph. A quiet meditation on a devotional theme ought not to begin with a provocative argument about text or translation. A careful and painstaking exposition of a difficult passage, or a vital doctrine, will not be helped by a very emotional beginning. The whole success of the introduction lies in having the congregation 'with' you, in thought, in mood, and in interest, as you come to the main burden of the message.

(iii) The introduction, to succeed, has often to *set the scene* from which the subject arises, and *to get out of the way any necessary explanations,* of unusual or archaic words, or of details in the story which are unclear. The more briefly this can be done the better: but much is gained by removing such material from the body of the message, where it inevitably interrupts the argument, side-tracks the theme, and lowers the emotional temperature.

Matthew 27: 36 'And sitting down they watched him there' suggests a study of different types of people near to the central event of history yet unmoved—'Unblest at the Cross': a message for Good Friday. But the story has to be recalled, the scene set. The introduction might well begin abruptly: 'The ghastly job is done. Three crosses rise stark and gruesome against the darkening sky. The excited milling mob, so lately shouting after Jesus, have fallen silent, and in the eerie light on that awful hillside, groups linger to see what will happen in the end. All humanity seems represented in the different knots of onlookers—the sobered crowd, the weeping friends, the gambling soldiers, the disturbed, impressed centurion, that one man hanging beside Jesus who has found salvation. This Good Friday, all are there again, in memory and imagination—and we among them, blest or unblest, it is for us to say . . . .' So scene and theme are set, and the message proceeds to look at one group after another.

Acts 16: 10 'After he had seen the vision, immediately we endeavoured to go into Macedonia, assuredly gathering that the Lord had called us for to preach the gospel unto them' suggests a sermon on the varied steps by which God leads toward a significant forward move in world mission. But all is involved in the total story of the journey from Galatia, with its frustrations and disappointments. The introduction therefore can hardly do other than rehearse this story: 'Paul had been travelling under immense and bewildering difficulties, in which—it might seem—the guiding hand of God had had no part . . .'

Acts 9: 26 in KJV reads: 'And when Saul was come to Jerusalem, he assayed to join himself to the disciples: but they were all afraid of him, and believed not that he was a disciple.' The reasons why the church suspected Saul; whether the church ought ever to reject applications for membership; the narrowly avoided tragedy of excluding her greatest apostle; the one condition of church membership—all such ideas suggest sermons. But the central emphasis falls upon Saul's persistence, and the motives which made him—with his gifts and great experience at Damascus—*insist* upon joining the church. Such a message almost *has* to begin with: 'That old word "assayed" means' attempted": it stands for a word which Luke uses three times, always of an attempting that met difficulties, and had to be sustained, pressed hard. Luke means that Paul *persisted* in trying to join the church, would not take *No* for an answer. Even when the church left him standing on the threshold, still he insisted, he did not go away. Now why . . . ?' By so beginning, explanation, theme and story are all accomplished at once.

Similarly with 2 Corinthians 4: 4 'Christ, who is the image of God'. The meaning of the word, and the somewhat abstract air of the text, are alike dealt with if we begin in some such fashion as—'Jews were forbidden by their second great commandment to make any graven image. Throughout their history, sculptured art was forbidden, and even painting of the human figure, or of beasts, and birds. Within the great Temple the Holy of Holies stood empty of any effigy, or idol, or representation of God. It puzzled the gentiles, and especially the Greek and Roman invaders, to find no images of God in Jewish shrines. For pagans had images everywhere—the city of Corinth abounded in shrines each clustered with idols. That Corinthian congregation, part Jewish and part gentile, would know well what Paul meant when he claimed this about Christ—He, He and no less than He, is the image of God . . .'

More often than not the illumination and background of the very words of a text, in this way, are sufficient introduction of a theme, and have an interest for most worshippers.

(iv) In some cases, the introduction ought also to *redress the balance of truth*. It should set the message in a right perspective so that the place of its particular truth in the total spectrum of the gospel is not forgotten. This is, of course, dangerous counsel, for there are preachers who cannot take up any subject without beginning with the whole circle of Christian doctrine, and some men approach every text via Genesis 1: 1. Nevertheless, the point should be made: many an earnest and forceful sermon, entirely true so far as it goes, has been spoiled for thoughtful and mature hearers because the preacher has forgotten, in his zeal, that there is another side to the matter.

A message on God's wonderful providence should find a sentence or two to acknowledge that sometimes the saints suffer bewildering tragedies. A searching, and stern presentation of the demands and tribulations of a faithful Christian life ought not to omit entirely the compensations and the inner joy. If the sermon is to youth, need everyone over thirty be totally ignored? And if the plea is that the inner life of prayer and devotion needs increased attention, some admission that Christian discipleship has also public duties will add strength to the plea, and not weaken it.

Often, therefore, the introduction to a sermon will be, either explicitly or implicitly, of the pattern 'I know, and acknowledge that . . . but this too needs saying . . .' And those who observe exactly what the Bible says will, far more often than not, find that the truth they have selected to preach upon is already set, within its biblical context, against a complementary truth, which needs some brief mention.

2 Corinthians 10: 1 has the enticing phrase 'the meekness and gentleness of Christ', which could so easily start a one-sided sentimental sermon. To invite the congregation to notice, that within two verses Paul is speaking of war, then of the weapons of our warfare, the pulling down of strongholds, captivity, and revenge, will afford sufficient reminder that to be Christ-like is not all meekness and gentleness—But it demands that too . . . The proportion of truth is thus preserved, as Paul intended.

Romans 8 has its wonderful flourish of Christian trumpets, sounding out the absolute assurance of the believing heart that nothing shall separate us from the love of God. Yet note the tribulation, distress, persecution, nakedness, peril, sword, being killed all the day long! We are more than conquerors when we are *not separated* from God's love—not when all goes easily for us.

Psalm 91 has a marvellous flight of faith—'He shall deliver thee . . . He shall cover thee . . . Thou shalt not be afraid . . . A thousand shall fall at thy side and ten thousand at thy right hand, but it shall not come nigh thee . . . There shall no evil befall thee . . .' Older Christians in the congregation begin to wonder if the preacher, or the Psalmist know anything about life as it is! But read on to the answer of God to this over-exuberant faith: 'Because he hath set his love upon me, therefore will I deliver him . . . I will be *with him in trouble* . . .' Any sermon on confidence should have that balancing truth at least conceded in its introduction.

1 Corinthians 15: 13–19 is an intense argument: To begin, therefore, with something like: 'Paul was first and above all else a pastor-evangelist. He comes down to us as a master theologian, a teacher of the Christian centuries, our highest authority in expounding the fact of Christ. Yet he was not a bit like that. He never sat long in a study, once he was converted—he sat oftener in prison! He wrote no books, gave no lectures . . . He was eager, passionate, practical; concerned for all men, worn with travel, liable to tears, spending life and strength in preaching, visiting, befriending folk, agonising over men, striving and suffering. The last man, you would say if you met him, the last man to be interested in argument for argument's sake. He was an apostle, not a debater or a don. Yet here he is arguing like a trained logician! He knew in his bones that however practical and passionate and down-to-earth you intend to be, you will never live the Christian life competently, and enduringly, unless you get certain

things straight from the start. And this is one—one he is prepared to argue about as long as need be: that Jesus is alive!'—to begin thus is not only to redress the picture of Paul himself, but to set the whole theme in intensely practical light, as Paul himself does in the last sentence of the chapter.

If the introduction to a sermon ought to attempt all this, beside the over-riding necessity of kindling interest, it is hardly surprising that it needs some care and thought. The first idea for an introduction is rarely right: some casting about, some trial of this one and of that, is usually necessary. And also some understanding of where we may go wrong.

Failure may arise from *too great length*, the congregation wishing you would come to the point. An abrupt 'Oi, you!' may not be the politest way to begin a sermon, but it has the double effectiveness of surprise and attention, and—intolerable though it would be— it is preferable to the tedious, rambling, time-filling and time-wasting paragraphs that pad out a thin sermon with goose-feathers.

Failure may arise from *too great width*, as the first sentences roam the contemporary scene, the current press, the trends of modern behaviour, the problems of world conflict, the bankruptcy of world statesmanship, and all the rest, before homing at last on some text like 'Follow me'. Such an introduction could serve (and probably has served) for a dozen different sermons. One cannot say worse of it than that: though the hearers' comments might be more expressive.

Failure arises sometimes from an introduction's being *too obvious*, and consequently dull. 'We are gathered here together to consider the word of God, and I feel led to speak to you on this great verse from the greatest of all books, namely . . .'—thirty entirely wasted words, saying the obvious. By the end only the deaf will be even trying to listen. The rest will have divined already that this man has nothing to say, and he knows it.

Introductions fail if they are *too predictable*. Some men *always* begin with the context, or with a problem, or by arguing with some recent public statement, or by mentioning the name of the book that prompted the theme. As soon as the text is announced, or even the hymn before the sermon, habitual listeners can foresee how the preacher will begin: 'Not that again!' is a devastating comment. Our people will often grow fond of our mannerisms: but never of our lazy-mindedness.

And introductions invariably fail if they affect some kind of *superiority*, assuming that the congregation knows what the intellectuals have been saying, or what some technical jargon means. 'Of course, as everyone knows . . .' followed by a reference to the latest intellectual craze, is a fatal beginning, creating barriers, arousing resentment, leaving the worthy old soul in the back row bewildered and humbled. So, too, a *flippant*, careless, off-hand, or over-clever opening can repel the soul who is trying to catch the voice of God in a service of worship. Such approaches are weaknesses of character more than of technique.

Finally, there is the introduction that fails because it is altogether *too remote* and irrelevant to awaken interest. A question is started, but it is a manufactured question, framed only in order that the sermon may answer it. A problem is posed, but it is an artificial, academic problem which no hearer ever thought of. The assertion which is to be proved, the duty to be illustrated and enforced, touches the lives of the hearers at no sensitive spot, and it will make little difference whether the proof be cogent, the illustration adequate, or not. The majority stop listening and think of something else.

Jesse Jai McNeil defines three basic urges to which the gospel must appeal in modern society. One is the urge to do, the impulse to achieve. A second is the urge to belong, which we may recognise as the innate need for community. And the third is the urge to be— which is usually understood as the impulse to discover authentic, real-life, experience. We ought to add the urge to know, the impulse to find meaning, to understand, and so to believe. For many, an equally clamant need is the hunger for what case-workers call 'support', the moral and emotional 'comforting', in faith and friendship, that lends men strength to attempt and to endure. Perhaps, too, the basic urge towards peace, integration, assured forgiveness, inner harmony, is more widely felt than we realise.

Every preacher will have his own list of things that people are deeply, compulsively, concerned about. And every wise preacher will often ask himself to which basic need his opening words should be addressed, in the light of the message which is to follow. A man has learned much when he can tear himself away from his own interest in a subject, and think of the needs of those who listen. Only so will he take his listeners by the hand, and lay hold of the inner ear.

The prophet Isaiah well understood how to gain attention by speaking to a present, conscious need. Isaiah 55 has a model introduction, from this point of view—'Ho, every one that thirsteth . . . he that hath no money . . . buy . . . eat . . . why spend . . . why labour for nothing . . .?' Isaiah 40 has so, too, when the condition of the Babylonian exiles is remembered; the opening of chapters 60, 61, and even 54 shows the same skill. All begin, not with what the prophet is bursting to say, but with what he knows the people deeply want—and so he catches at their attention, almost against their will. (See also Chapter 16, below.)

Ringing the Changes

Introduction-patterns, even more than sermon-outlines, need to be constantly varied, no method being repeated in any three or four sermons. Just how various the approach may be, and to what different uses the introduction may be put, is best illustrated by brief examples.

(i) The *textual introduction* seizes at once (as we have seen) on some word or thought in the text and by focussing upon it announces the theme, and perhaps the pattern, of the whole message.

> Every schoolboy knows that the Samaritan was 'good', and why. The real question is not about him, but about the others: how did a priest and a levite get into the story at all. In answer to the lawyer's question about Who is my neighbour, they are wholly unnecessary—interlopers, gate-crashers. And not very welcome ones at that. What then are they dragged in for? and for a second and related question, Why is the only attractive character in the tale a foreigner? This may introduce a study of the parable's main point, the real meaning of *neighbour*, as it overleaps religion, class and race. The theme is suggested, and some curiosity aroused, merely by asking questions of the text.

> 'Follow me' said Jesus, but He did not say where. The first of all gospel invitations, the fundamental confrontation out of which the whole, world-transforming Christian movement was to spring, was entirely open-ended. Jesus called to adventure—without indicating either cost or reward. He found men where they were, and challenged them to change—but where it would lead, where it might end—that they had to leave to Him . . . Again, without leaving the text for a moment, a significant uncertainty in every gospel commitment is spotlighted, and the faith involved in following Christ is brought to the surface. A theme, and its relevance, are before us at once, with probably some interest in so disturbing a presentation.

(ii) The *contextual introduction* places the gem back in its setting for a few moments, to catch the light so afforded, before proceeding with detailed examination. How the sentence lies in the argument of the passage; how the question came to be asked; why the apostle takes up this topic just where he does, and for those original readers; why it should be Peter who makes that remark; to what experience of Israel do we owe this particular insight, or prophecy? In the preparation of the message, we have emphasized, such questions are imperative: without them, the *true* meaning of the passage, the word of God that was given through it, cannot be discovered. Sometimes, however, instead of leaving the questions and their answers on the study desk, we may carry them into the sermon, sharing with our people the steps by which we ourselves came to interpret the words before us.

1 Corinthians 1: 19—'The Son of God, Jesus Christ . . . was not yea and nay, but in him was yea.' That is an odd remark to come up with suddenly. Especially in a passage where Paul has been explaining patiently his comings and goings between Corinth and Macedonia and Judea. 'Christ was never yes and no, but in Him was the Yes!' —And all the promises of God are yes in Him, the apostle goes on. What brought that to his mind? It was criticism of himself and his companions, whispered about in the church at Corinth, and then reported to Paul: the charge that no one could rely upon his word. He said he would come, and then he changed his plans. That is the inconsequent, unreliable impulsive sort of man he is: yes and no, I will, I will not. At first Paul begins to explain, to give reason for not coming when he promised: then, suddenly impatient with self-defence, he comes to the point: whatever they think of him does not much matter—it is no excuse for their own fickleness! Christ was not yes and no: the Christ they had preached, whom the Corinthians had believed—He was not inconstant. He is ever YES—and all God's promises find their steadfast, unchanging YES in Him. Christ is God's everlasting YES to all the finest insights of humanity. The somewhat pedestrian context starts us on a story, rather than an abstract idea; at the same time bringing some light to the unusual expression here used of Christ.

Mark 13: 10—'The gospel must first be published among all nations' suggests a sermon on missionary obligation. 'Must' you notice: this is no personal option—but a categorical imperative: 'first' you notice: this is not one obligation which must find its place among many others—but top priority. Surely, someone says, it depends upon circumstances! Well, look at the circumstances which surround the command—and the context supplies deceivers, wars, rumours of wars, persecution, betrayal, blasphemy, flight, apostasy . . . Once again we have not strayed from the surrounding verses, yet a theme is set, possible objections to the theme are met from the outset, the whole context of missionary demand in the modern world is suggested, and the passage speaks across the centuries.

(iii) The *topical introduction* begins where the hearers are, with something contemporary, something present to the listener's mind, to which the text, and eventually the sermon, is at once attached. A world event, the death of a great man, an anniversary, or a public tragedy; a public debate and current topic of conversation, a Christian festival—scores of items of living, ready-made interest, may provide the springboard from the pulpit to the listener's mind.

Two cautions are here in place. Great care is necessary if the sermon is not to descend to mere comment on the contemporary scene. However it started in the preacher's mind, the sermon should in the end be seen to be a word of God, scripture-based and timeless. References to the topical event should not therefore be allowed to overflow the introduction and dominate the sermon. There is a world of difference between a Christian sermon which has topical relevance, and a string of comments upon some thing everyone has been discussing all the week.

The other caution concerns the way the topicality is mentioned. *To allude is always more telling than to connect.* To tell your people that a great murder trial has been going on during recent weeks, reminding all of the solemn commandment, Thou shalt not kill . . . is banal, so painfully obvious as to throw away at once whatever interest was aimed at. To preach on that commandment, without mentioning the trial, or with at most a late and passing reference to a phrase uttered, or a legal decision, so that the listener perceives for himself, with some surprise and pleasure, the connection with current events—is far more effective.

'To live as free men' is a fitting subject for Independence Day: but there is no need to say so. Just preach upon it, on or near the Day, and perhaps make reference, quite incidentally, to the Declaration.

'Exercise thyself unto godliness' is a promising text for the World Olympics season, especially when linked with the New Testament's many references to running, boxing, relay-racing, wrestling, the prize, the crown, the stadium and all the rest. But the topical connection is too obvious to mention. Begin with the small Jewish lad growing up in Tarsus (which had its own Stadium and Games), forbidden to attend the heathen athletics, envious, curious, unhappy probably—but learning much about the language and the contests from his friends, and often seeing the athletes at their exercises in the streets: then the later memories, as he visited great Games centres like Corinth . . . and coveted for Christian hearts the same eagerness, and striving, and pressing toward the mark.

(iv) The *thesis introduction* likewise needs to be handled carefully, for it has an academic, intellectualist, flavour and can reduce the sermon to a lecture. Nevertheless it is sometimes useful, and takes its place among the changes to be rung. In addressing specialist audiences, on any subject, it is possible to begin with a formal statement of what you intend to prove, or illustrate, or explain, and then to proceed in logical order to do so. Non-specialist audiences would

E

hardly respond to this approach, unless the thesis was invested with more popular interest.

But variations of this method of beginning are possible to the preacher. A favourite version of it is the diagnosis, to which some cure or antidote will be prescribed in the following sermon. 'Everyone knows how the modern church needs revival. It is lifeless, divided, dead . . .' and there follows the preacher's idea of how the condition can be met—probably as facile, sweeping, and useless as his diagnosis! Or: 'An old problem seems to be raising its head once more, as it did in ancient Israel, in the time of our Lord, and in the early church—the perennial problem of the relation of reform and progress to tradition and loyalty to the past'. Such a statement of thesis could effectively introduce a fairly abstract theme, provided that historical illustrations make it concrete and interesting.

If the statement of theme can be thrown into controversial form, its academic flavour disappears. 'Not everyone agrees that it is better to give than to receive. The child does not usually believe it—but it soon learns. The thief does not believe it, obviously. A whole class or type of people, who in temperament and outlook are society's claimants, dependents, asserters of their rights, people to whom, in their own eyes, the world owes a living and all else beside—they do not believe it. Nor does the Christian who boasts to himself of his generosity to charitable causes, or complains of the demands made upon him, or talks of 'sacrifice'. For all that is impossible to the man who really believes that giving things away is a benefit to the giver. Yet that seems to be what Jesus said . . .'

Another form of the thesis-statement is the brisk summarising sentence, which the sermon then unfolds in detail. 'Freedom is at once the demand of youth, the fear of parents, a menace to Authority, a necessity of the mature, the despair of thinkers, and the gift of Christ.' That is not as brisk as it might be, but its compactness and range arouse interest. 'The apostolic church was not only amazingly flexible, and incredibly tough, it was joyously irrepressible: that is the meaning of the gift of the Spirit.' Such one-sentence introductions can be arresting, and sufficient, though they need a somewhat rare quality of attention.

Yet another form of thesis-statement may simply define a difficulty to be discussed.

Everyone wishes that he could look into the future; not only the spiritists, the racing tipsters, the self-appointed prophets, the fairground charlatans, but ordinary people consulting 'What the Stars Foretell', or having their destiny read from tea leaves or from their palms. We all believe we would be so much wiser, and happier, and avoid many mistakes, if we could see forward. It may be doubted—but at any rate, we cannot. And Paul seems to think it is better that we cannot: Eye hath not seen, nor ear heard, neither have entered into the heart of man, the things which God hath prepared for them that love him. Is it really better not to know? How should we handle the hidden future?

If it be true, as Paul declares, that we are saved in hope, why are there so many despondent Christians about? Is there perhaps something about our time which justifies, or at least explains, Christians' discouragement and concern? Is it perhaps that Christianity is essentially pessimistic in some respects, with its doctrine of a cross to be believed in and a cross to be borne? Or are we just failing to be truly Christian? This type of introduction can be very effective for the more studious congregation; one danger is that too many questions may be raised; another, that the sermon concentrates on questions and fails to press to basic truth and principles. But well controlled, the pattern attracts many.

(v) The *startling introduction*, and its younger brothers the surprise and the puzzle, can be useful ways of leading into an already prepared sermon. Where the whole sermon depends upon the arresting beginning, the total performance is likely to descend to a gimmick. Once more, the *message* should be settled, an earnest and well-considered, thoroughly prepared line of truth, with a serious purpose and a persuasive approach: *then*, when one is casting about for the best way to begin, it is safe enough to be bright and provocative, raising astonishing questions, propounding conundrums, emphasizing the ridiculous, or setting the congregation laughing.

But where it becomes all too clear that the whole sermon began in the preacher's mind with some such whimsical, provocative, original, or ridiculous idea, the only response will be impatience. Examples are hard to invent, for this method needs a rare sparkle in the mind: but a few more sober ones may suggest others—especially to beginners!

'It is hard to take Jesus seriously, sometimes. He says ridiculous things: Blessed are the meek! and It is more blessed to give than to receive! He asks the impossible: If a man smite thee on the one cheek, turn to him the other! and Sell all you have and give to the poor, and come, follow me! He says positively dangerous things, too: about the supposed duty to hate your father and mother, and the advice to sell your shirt and buy a sword. He solemnly pronounces the incredible as if it were literally true: If ye shall ask anything in my name, it shall be done for you! And sometimes He voices downright rebellion against authority: The scribes and the Pharisees sit on Moses' seat . . . do not practice what they do . . . How can you take such a teacher, such a leader, seriously?' This would lead into a sermon carefully distinguishing what it means to take Jesus literally from what it means to take Him seriously; and showing that He always challenges our own insight and demands our own moral judgement.

A few eyebrows will rise if a sermon begins: 'The rabbis, and many of the listening crowd, might well have burst out laughing at Jesus' odd idea of a *good* shepherd. It was common opinion among religious experts that to be a shepherd was next door to being a heathen. Others spoke of "the homely, slighted shepherds' trade". The shepherds at Bethlehem represent the sinners, the unchurched, the people of the land who know not the law . . .

Macaulay begins an essay with a most discouraging remark: 'We doubt whether any name in literary history be so grievously odious as that of the man whose character . . . we now propose to consider . . .' But Macaulay defers naming his subject, leaving us curious and his own gentle reader apprehensive. We might similarly begin a study of Jacob: 'He was a thoroughly nasty piece of work, if you like! A sneak, a liar, a runaway coward, as mean a scoundrel as ever brewed porridge; his unscrupulousness made his brother see red, and his duplicity made his blind father grieve to his grave. Typical youthful selfishness doing its own thing and letting the rest go rot . . .' At least the young people will follow so far, and presently find themselves caught up in the story of Jacob.

(vi) The *crab-like introduction* seeks to lend interest to an otherwise pedestrian theme by coming at it 'sideways'.

Zechariah 4: 6—'Not by might, nor by power, but by my spirit, saith the Lord of hosts.' Best known, and best loved, of all Old Testament stories is that of David and Goliath—the brute and the boy, the bully and the shepherd lad, might versus innocence, ruthless strength faced by little Jack the giant-killer. Every nation has its parallel to five smooth stones, effective against thick armour and hopeless odds, when wisdom, courage, and patriotism, aim them. But in a special way, the David-Goliath story is Israel's story, a symbol of the faith by which she has survived amid the great empires of the world. She has always been David, defying Goliath in the person of Babylon, or Persia, or Greece, or Rome: she has always believed in forces beyond brute strength and armour. So this is Israel's text, and Israel's experience . . . The battle is not to the swift, nor victory to the strong: it is not by might, nor by power, but by my spirit, saith the Lord . . . In this instance, the side-approach serves also to give depth and range, and some historical argument, to the meaning of the chosen words.

The climax of the story in John 4 is the announcement 'I that speak unto thee, am He'—in the original, simply 'I am'. So the approach may be indirect, yet relevant and illuminating: Among scenes of Israel's history which no Jew could ever forget, is that of Moses in the desert standing before the bush that burned and was not consumed. There the great leader was called, and commissioned, to one of the greatest tasks in history. There he argued with God, seeking release from the assignment; and there he learned God's Name, in the moment of his surrender. 'Who shall I say sent me?' he asks. 'I am' said Yahweh—'say that I AM hath sent you!' Such was the sacred Name, to be pronounced only with bated breath and awe and fear: later never to be pronounced at all, the unspeakably holy word. And that is the Name which on the lips of Jesus echoes through this gospel—I am the Way, I am the Bread of life, I am the light of the world, I am the resurrection; and to this half-heathen woman in her deep need, the sacred word again—'I, that speak unto thee, I AM.' Here again we approach the text sideways, but bringing real illumination.

(vii) The *far-out introduction* carries the same technique still further, deliberately coming at the theme from as far afield as possible. Attention is caught by 'keeping them guessing'. Yet it is important, if the process is not to become trivial, that there should be some underlying connection, perceived before the sermon is through, between the far-out beginning and the message itself. It should not be a mere trick of approach, but *in addition* make some contribution to the overall purpose.

'Cast thy burden upon the Lord . . . Take up thy cross and follow' suggests a message upon the burden we lose, and the new obligations we accept, in Christ. The source of the suggestion, provided also the introduction, beginning in inland China, in days of extreme stress and danger, when it was expedient for western missionaries to leave for the sake of Chinese Christians. Weary and discouraged, one made her way toward the frontier, but found rest and hospitality at a lovely house high upon a hillside, where for a few days she could recuperate, pray and plan. Exploring the grounds alone she found a small place of retreat, a tiny chapel of quiet. Entering, she found one small window only, which drew her eyes to the far view across a lovely valley. As she sat to gaze, she saw above the window the words —'Cast thy burden upon the Lord . . .' and deeply moved, she bowed in thankfulness. Rising to leave, renewed in heart, she stooped a little to pass the low door, and there above it was the other word she so badly needed: 'Take up thy cross . . .' The whole effect of this far-out introduction would be lost if the texts were announced beforehand: the introduction itself should lead to them.

Similarly, a sermon for young people might emphasize the endless opportunities, the fresh beginnings, the splendid adventure in faith and experience to which Christ beckons us. A formal text announcement would be tame. Begin with: A great stone lay before the mouth of a vast cave in a high hillside. The stone had the shape, and the fastenings of a mighty door—yet there was no handle, or key, or latch, and it remained fast shut, immovable, impregnable, until someone stood before it to say the magic word 'Open, sesame!'—

and it flew wide. A long high wall surrounded a fine garden, in which a lovely princess sat, lonely and sad, until with infinite patience a handsome prince probing every stone and crevice of the wall found the secret spring which set her free. A small door low down in the wide, over-shadowing tree let Alice into Wonderland, while in far Hamelin,

> When, lo, as they reached the mountain's side,
> A wondrous portal opened wide,

and the children followed the piper to a joyous land

> Where waters gushed and fruit-trees grew
> And flowers put forth a fairer hue,
> And everything was strange and new;
> The sparrows were brighter than peacocks here,
> And their dogs outran our fallow deer,
> And honey-bees had lost their stings,
> And horses were born with eagles' wings . . .

Why do you suppose there are so many doors and gates and hidden cave-mouths, and wide portals in so many stories? Is it because stories are for young people, and youth is a time of opening doors—when all life swings open before you, full of surprises and full of invitations to discovery, and adventure, to find treasure, and romance and happiness? Youth is the time for open doors—and Jesus knew it. He said to young people around Him, I am the door: by me if any man enter in he shall be saved, and shall go in and out, and find pasture.

The danger of taking a long way round is that it is easy to get lost; equally easy to take too long. It is imperative to arrive at last at the subject intended. A great deal is gained, also, if in the interest-catching promenade some ideas have been struck out, and a few points made, which will add illumination to the text, and the sermon, when it comes.

(viii) At the opposite extreme to the far-out beginning is that which plunges immediately into the middle of the theme, and works from there both backwards and forwards. Some of the greatest stories in the world are so presented, from Homer's *Odyssey* to Milton's *Paradise Lost* and Dickens' *Tale of Two Cities*. A. C. Bradley shows Shakespeare's skill with this device: from the beginning of the play things are happening which in some degree arrest, startle, and excite; but a certain amount of information has to be imparted, and this is usually dull and undramatic. So Prospero's long explanation of years gone by is given to Miranda in the second scene of *Tempest*; while in the tragedies Shakespeare usually begins with a scene, or part-scene, full of life and stir, and having secured a hearing he proceeds to conversations at a lower pitch conveying much information. This happens in *Romeo and Juliet, Julius*

Caesar, Coriolanus, Hamlet and *Macbeth.* The modern detective story consists, of course, of a climax (the crime) from which the detective and the reader work backwards through causes and motives to the origin. In the cinema, this is the familiar construction of the 'flashback'.

The gospel of Mark uses this method, somewhat unexpectedly. It begins with Jesus being baptised by John and, when John is imprisoned, appearing in Galilee with His message of the kingdom. We wait until chapter six to hear how John came to be put in prison, and the circumstances in which Jesus began to preach. Luke is even more successful in using this construction. Writing the early story of the church, mainly for gentiles, Luke begins with Pentecost and the excitements in Jerusalem that followed, holding back the necessary Old Testament preparation until chapter seven, where Stephen's long speech puts the readers in possession of all the background and introduction to Christianity.

This pattern is extremely useful in preaching when the matter which has to be presented, in order to make sense of the message, is either too familiar or too pedestrian to capture attention at the outset. To trace a biography from a life's beginning through youth, manhood, age to death may be logical and obvious—but that is its fault. To present the man in some crisis of experience, some vital decision, some tragic outcome of his choice, and then to trace backwards to its origin, and onwards to its consequence, is to lend new vividness even to the familiar. So with a well-known historical event, such as the defeat of Israel at Ai, the death of Jezebel, the dedication of Nehemiah's wall, the death of John the Baptist, to begin in the middle of the story is almost inevitable.

For a study of Mark's career, begin with Paul's commendation of him (Colossians 4: 10); work back to the *need* for that, in the quarrel over Mark between Paul and Barnabas; to our natural sympathy with the young man, until we remember his fine beginning and great privileges (the Jerusalem home and presence at Christ's arrest). Then show how in spite of mistake and failure, that early start bore fruit at the end, not only in Paul's sight but in Peter's (1 Peter 5: 13) and in the immense debt of the whole church for the gospel he wrote. This presents the familiar material more interestingly— though, of course, more analysis than this is required.

David's great sin, conviction, and forgiveness, could hardly be made dull, by even the most prosaic preacher, in whatever order he chose to present it. But it gains dramatic impact to begin with Nathan's 'Thou art the man!'—and thereafter to see David's beginnings, temptation, sin, and penitence, through Nathan's eyes; and to close with the clear echoes in Psalm 51 of Nathan's courageous accusation

Sometimes this construction serves for a doctrinal or argumentative theme. A sermon on the Ascension, for example might well start the question if its *credibility*, and then turn back upon the whole life and ministry of Jesus to show who it was that ascended—suggesting that, with Him in mind, what seemed incredible becomes in fact inevitable. (Peter does this with the resurrection, Acts 2: 24.) Instead, then of beginning with the story of Jesus, leading up to ascension, one might begin with the Eleven listening, watching, wondering, and then overjoyed, at Bethany: and only then ask, how came they there? The answer lay, or at least began, some five miles away, at Bethlehem—what an enormous spiritual distance is covered by those five miles between Bethlehem and Bethany!—So the incarnation, the baptism, the lakeside where He called them, the miracles (like that at Bethany) the homes He changes (as that of Mary and Martha), the cross for which He was there anointed . . . all can be drawn upon by 'flashback' from Bethany to suggest how fitting was the glorious end and promise.

Those who feel that far too much labour is here being expended on 'the mere introduction' to the real message, should recall once more how much the introduction is expected to accomplish, and also our stress upon leaving its preparation until the body of the sermon is complete. One reason for this, we said, was to keep the introduction in its place. That place is small, but vital. The sermon will succeed, or fail, very largely as the opening sentences do, or do not, sieze the congregation. A painter may, if he so chooses, fling a pot of paint in the face of the public, despising those who turn away. The preacher bearing the word of God can affect no such indifference to the reception he may get: he will count no labour lost which gains an entrance in any mind for the precious truth God has given him to proclaim.

12 EVANGELISTIC ADJUSTMENTS

THE DISTINCTION often drawn between pastoral and evangelistic preaching is convenient, but it is not absolute. No congregation consists wholly of saints, nor wholly of sinners; it may be doubted if any individual who attends Christian worship is ever all saint or all sinner!

The pastor will often find that sermons lead to saving decisions over a period, so that no one message can be pointed to as the effective one. When it can, the pastor may be surprised to find that it was not a sermon which he would have classified as 'evangelistic'. On the other hand it will often happen that a sermon intended for non-believers helps someone for the first time towards a clarity and confidence of faith which he, as that person's pastor, assumed was already possessed.

For all that, the distinction is useful. It helps to pinpoint differences of assumption and approach. So far we have considered preaching mainly within a congregation at least religious enough to be present for worship: when the preacher faces a largely non-religious audience, certain adjustments of attitude, and of method, are necessary. The task of evangelism is so important in our time that some consideration of these adjustments is demanded, if the student-preacher is to be even partially prepared for an all-round ministry.

The Pastoral Situation

A man preaching in a pastoral context can assume that he will have other opportunities—or that other preachers will have opportunity—to emphasize other sides of truth. He need not aim at delivering his whole soul on each occasion! Indeed, he will practice a little judicious husbanding of resources, not pouring out all that he has within reach, but remembering that other Sundays are coming, and other sermons. That reflection will often help him to prune his material without a sense of loss. The evangelist has more limited opportunity.

Within a pastoral situation, too, a man can rely upon considerable knowledge of his people, and upon their interest and concern for his ministry to them. He can assume acceptance of his role as a proclaimer of the word of God, one whose utterances draw acknowledged authority from their consistency with scripture. No outsider would grant him that authority, without controversy. Again the pastor can be more personal, without indulging in personalities, and often a sense of friendship will lend quality to his preaching, and much encouragement. The evangelist must usually present his message amidst indifference, and to strangers.

If the great danger of pastoral preaching is repetitiveness, and its great demand variety, so its great advantage is the opportunity to grow with your people, to explore the word of God and the Christian life, together. The man who speaks often to the same people can attempt a truly educative, maturing ministry, and see those who have already come to Christ grow in grace and in their knowledge of Him. If this demands greater maturity and progress in the preaching, it also offers richer rewards, tempting some pastors to neglect altogether 'the work of an evangelist'. But what is a pastor (or any regular visitor to the same fellowship) to do about evangelism?

He may determine to preach an evangelistic sermon once every Sunday, because that is the pattern he has taught himself to consider *right*, although his congregation is invariably of committed Christians. That is scarcely bringing men the word of God in all its relevance and appropriateness. Such preaching is purposeless and boring, except for those Christians so determinedly 'evangelical' that they refuse ever to move on from the first principles of the doctrine of Christ to something more mature, more searching, and more demanding.

What is worse, such a man is *pretending*. The whole 'evangelistic' performance of appealing for decisions to the already decided is insincere, a dishonest pose, neither beloved by listeners with any integrity, nor blessed by God.

But this raises the difficult question of our evangelistic approach to fellow-worshippers. Not all who worship regularly will be fully committed to Christ in saving faith and new life. Nevertheless, in our hymns and prayers (and in the monetary offering) we assume their Christian standing and faith. Then, as we rise to preach, we may mentally change gear, and attack these same fellow-worshippers as 'miserable sinners'. This again would be insincere. One remedy is, not to avoid the call to decision and commitment in public worship-services, but to present it as to *half*-believers, men and women with partial insights and elementary loyalties, upon which you would build more.

Dr. G. R. Beasley-Murray, in an address concerning 'Evangelising the Post-Christian Man' suggests we ought to consider whether our traditional religious services are the right context for evangelism. 'It is my conviction that, while Christian worship may appeal to some people who do not share the Christian faith, it is a mistake to order services with them in mind. The primary object in Christian worship is the offering of praise and adoration by those who have responded to the good news of God's redemption in Christ . . . In such a circumstance the non-Christian can at best only be an on-looker, not a participator. When a service is so adapted that Christians and non-Christians can feel equally at home, we merely flatten the service, making it neither Christian nor a fit vehicle for the gospel; and when we arrange a service to serve as a context for the proclama-tion of the gospel, we unnecessarily introduce non-Christian people to a setting in which they are not at home . . . I would plead for attempts to be made to present the gospel to contemporaries of ours who think that Christianity is dead and ought to be buried, who never sing hymns and never intend to do so, and who never want to hear anyone else sing them either, but who would be prepared to enter a meeting that had no frills but was arranged for the sole purpose of presenting the belief that Christianity works in twentieth century everyday life; such a meeting would include testimony and pro-clamation and perhaps provide opportunity for questions and dis-cussion.'

The evangelistic pastor will not cease to remind his people that evangelism is the task of the church, not simply of the pulpit. The kind of spiritual power that saves men is not to be generated by pulpit eloquence, publicist's expertise, or highly organised church machinery. It flows through truth spoken by the earnest and the wise; it kindles through the radiance of godly living; it illumines, warns, awakens, through the fellowship of caring souls, where spirit meets spirit and God changes men.

That kind of power within the church will foster a pastoral evangelism of a high order. But it depends upon a number of things—a high tradition of great souls, a high reputation in the neighbourhood for true character and genuine helpfulness, a high conception of the church's task, a high temperature of devotion in which talk of spiritual things is free and natural—not glib but filled with gladness. Such a fellowship will pray souls in, love them in, and what is equally important, never easily let them go.

So the evangelistic pastor will seek as eagerly to develop an evangelistic church as to prepare evangelistic sermons. Some churches that demand most loudly that preachers should 'stick to the old gospel' never get within sight of the truth that the church also must embody that gospel in her life and ways. It is in the corporate experience of the church that the living truth is grounded and confirmed; in her corporate activity it is enshrined and expressed. Men must see the gospel in the church, as well as hear it: in the homeliness of the church, the fellowship of the gospel; in the attitude of the church to people, the forgiveness of the gospel; in the conduct of church affairs, the reality of divine guidance; in the radiance and joy of her common life, the sufficiency of Christ to satisfy; in the character of her people, the power of grace to transform and refine life. Such a gospel church the evangelistic pastor will regard as his first and most essential instrument in winning men for Christ, the essential sounding-board for gospel sermons.

The church's programme of service and methods of outreach carry us far beyond the work of preaching. We may leave that wider theme with the observation that the pastor who watches for the souls God has placed within his reach will, by being the man he is, more than by any wisdom of technique, find ways to use not only the worship-services, but marriage, bereavement, illness, the arrival of the baby, family crises, and many other soul-disturbing moments, as avenues to new faith and commitment. But still, behind all that he says and does in these more intimate occasions, will stand his pulpit ministry among these people: a ministry in which a clear gospel is proclaimed, and a clear personal faith and commitment towards Christ is expected.

The Evangelistic Situation

Dr James Denney, who 'to a scholarship of outstanding worth added the glow and passion of an evangelist' was known to have castigated with biting words a preacher who prefaced a speech by apologising for giving what he called a simple, evangelistic address, on the ground that he had not had time to prepare 'a proper sermon'. Said Denney: 'No task can so tax the strength of the preacher as to preach the love of God, and so to preach it that men are persuaded to commit themselves to it.' Today, as Denney would be first to concede, it taxes not only his strength, but his wit and all his wisdom. Evangelistic preaching demands so much.

(i) The catching and holding of *interest*, and (ii) the concern that the message shall be pertinently *relevant* to daily life and personal need, required in all effective preaching, are pre-eminently necessary in the kind of sermon which can presume upon neither attentiveness nor belief. (iii) *Sympathy*, is even more necessary here than in 'ordinary' preaching, but here it is much more difficult.

For the preacher has a fundamental, almost unconscious, understanding with his fellow-worshippers. They live largely in the same thought-world, and aim at very similar goals. The non-believer belongs, quite literally, to another life, and much about his thinking, behaviour, manner, attitude, language, and even his appearance, may be unattractive. The obvious temptations are to denounce, to affect superiority, or just to remain aloof—each an opposite of sympathy.

Pulpit denunciation is pointless, irrelevant, ill-mannered, cowardly, and wholly unauthorised. Christ came not to condemn the world, but that the world might be saved. Whatever we may say about the sins of men by way of illustrating human need, to the sinner we can say in Christ's name only 'Neither do I condemn thee, go, and sin no more'. An implied claim that sensible people (like ourselves!) believe and are saved; a testimony that seems to suggest that we know all the answers, or that we have explored all the height and depth of Christian living; the spiritual assurance that rises into unspiritual arrogance and talks to men across a gulf of folly and wilful unbelief—all comprise bad psychology, hopeless salesmanship, and very poor Christianity.

The evangelist may never *preach down* to people, never be irritated, scolding, argumentative, or aloof. He must first, like Ezekiel, in mind and spirit 'sit where they sit'; like Paul he must become all things to all men; like the Master, he must be willing to be numbered among transgressors, and in some sense bear the sin of many. His task is to build a bridge from his own side of every gulf, to stretch a hand of invitation and of help, and keep it stretched until it tires and falls.

Related to sympathy is (iv) *conciliation*. In evangelism especially, the preacher offers his wares in a buyers' market. Within his own congregation, the preacher is assured of a hearing, but in his evangelistic outreach the same man has to win his right to speak at all, and dare not presume upon any inherent authority. It is true that in New Testament terms he is a *herald*, needing but to declare his true tidings, about which there can be no argument. On some points, that will be his stance, before everyone.

But, also in New Testament terms, the gospel preacher is an *ambassador*, needing to persuade, to negotiate, to conciliate (so 2 Corinthians 5: 18–20). As such, he cannot assume the privileged position which his fellow-Christians gladly afford him, but must begin simply as a fellow-man, with a faith, a testimony, and some evidence, to offer. The difference in approach is considerable, affecting not only presentation but preparation. It prunes what we would say of its habitual dogmatism, its assumed self-evidence, its reliance upon the quoted words of scripture as sufficient proof of any point, and its love of academic theological logic for its own sake. Nothing of this has any value in evangelism. We have to persuade the outsider first to listen, before we can persuade him to believe. Without a winsome, reasonable, conciliatory spirit, we shall never do either.

(v) Caution against dogmatism and assumed superiority in no way implies that the evangelistic sermon cannot be confident, assured, even assertive: it must have *certainty*. To quote Dr Denney again, 'Nobody has any right to preach who has not mighty affirmations to make concerning God's Son, Jesus Christ—affirmations in which there is no ambiguity and which no questions can reach.' The words of Peter at the Gate Beautiful set the absolute limit of our ministry to the lame and needy world: 'Such as I have give I thee.' Like Elijah, stretching himself upon the dead to re-awaken the spirit, we can only kindle by warmth and impart salvation by a 'kiss of life'.

But the honest thinker, eager to persuade, will not profess a certainty he does not possess, nor about things beyond the range of his experience. A man can be unshakably sure of what God has done for him, of what Christ means to him, how his life has been transformed by the gospel. About all else, outside the range of personal experience, he can have only opinions, well-informed or otherwise, and he will do well to remember the distinction. So, the evangelistic preacher will keep close to the central certainties of the gospel, confirmed by his own testimony into personal convictions—and refuse to be dogmatic about *anything else*.

In this way, the evangelist will observe also (vi) the *strategy* of persuasion. He will deliberately avoid raising unnecessary obstacles to his own purpose, or providing escape-routes for the evasive. The wise evangelist will not obscure the central question—What think ye of Christ?—with supplementary questions about the fall of Adam, evolution, where Cain got his wife, Jonah's whale, Calvinist theology, or the programme of the second advent of Christ. A preacher must have a sound theology as his reserve capital, not his spending money. Without it, his sermons will be thin: putting it into his sermons will only ensure that his congregation of non-believers will get thinner. The place for exploring the Christian creed is in enquirers' classes and Bible Class, occasionally in the worship-service. But not in the evangelistic address, where everything that obscures Christ defeats its own purpose.

(vii) Related to this avoidance of unnecessary obstacles is the need to be *positive* at all times. It is an odd, but familiar, habit to state the difference Christ has made to us in a string of negatives. 'When I came to Christ, I gave up ... ... and so Christ will save you from ... this ... and this ... and this ...' Presumably this is because, for many, conversion was the end of an inner conflict, a relief from guilt-feelings associated with some moral defeat. If among our hearers anyone happens to be in that position, this formulation may meet their need—but they are then already half way home.

For most people, the negatives are meaningless. They do not want to be saved from things that they enjoy. The ever-positive approach requires some self-discipline, and the learning of a new habit of thought, but it alone is worthy of the Christ who is the Great Giver, not the Taker-away. He is the precious Lord, who so fills life with new interest, so captivates the heart and will by His infusion of purpose, faith, and joy, as to *crowd out* the insipid, the futile, the vicious.

Jesus is the Leader who calls to endless discovery. If our beloved negatives really imply that what Christ bestows is infinitely better than anything the world offers—then let us say just that, and leave to Him to expel all alien things. 'I am come that they might have life ... more abundantly; Come unto me, and rest ... Come and see ... Come and dine ... Come, for all things are now ready ... Let him that is athirst come!'—always the New Testament message is positive. Let the glorious things Christ gives devalue the things unworthy of His name. He purifies men, not by purging but—as Chalmers used to say—by the exclusive power of a new and positive affection.

Evangelistic preaching needs to pay very special attention to (viii) *intelligibility*, and this can cause the preacher both labour and hostility. The need arises largely from the wide gulf—of language, thought, assumptions and attitudes—that has to be passed. Dr G. R. Beasley-Murray, in the address already referred to, has retold the story of Joseph Parker's remark to a disappointed young preacher, after hearing him preach: 'Young man, I think I can tell you what is wrong. For the last half hour you have been trying to get something out of your head instead of trying to get something into mine.' And Dr Beasley-Murray adds:

Our problem as witnesses for Christ is to speak so as to be understood —not merely in the sense of using simple words, but of speaking compelling words that reveal to our hearers the relevance of the gospel and its power to save them. That is to say, we have to speak into the situation of our contemporaries, or more accurately into their situations, for not all have identical needs.

Nor, we have to add, have we all identical language, or give the same meanings to identical words.

There are still some for whom the classical forms of evangelistic preaching may be effective. They retain something of Christian thought, information, feeling, from home, church and school training: and the task of the evangelist is to re-awaken such memories and bring to life such buried thoughts and motives.

But for the great majority today, this is not the situation, nor the type of evangelism most likely to succeed. For them, the basic information is lacking, the religious terms are strange. Conversion, salvation, spirit, regeneration, redemption, blood, atonement, sacrifice, consecration, faith—all such, in their Christian meaning, constitute a foreign language outside the enclave of the church: not one of them would normally crop up in a comic strip, film, or newspaper. What is worse, the basic religious assumptions are unintelligible—the personality of God, the absolute distinction between right and wrong, the imperative moral law, the continuity of history, and the idea of purpose in history (as against fate, astrology, superstition) the notion of prayer, personal responsibility,— all are meaningless to thousands whose education and home life have been within Christendom yet shaped by a non-Christian type of culture.

Trying to preach the gospel in an alien tongue is exceedingly demanding. Yet to preach to the modern outsider in our Christian language is like trying to do modern business with an ancient coinage. We have to say all that our language *means*, with centuries of Christian thought and immeasurable tracts of Christian experience behind it, but express it in the *talk* of the town. We must say all that these great words and their assumptions convey, or we have no gospel. But we must not use them, or we shall not be understood. We must translate, both into the words familiar to the hearers, and so far as possible in the light of the alien assumptions that direct their thinking.

If on the content of our message we are clear, uncompromising, convinced, on its language and expression we must be as nimble and as flexible as our minds will allow, to convey yesterday's truth in the terms of today, and of the unbeliever. If communication is to be effective, it *must* be made in the receiver's language. To require men to learn our terms before we will speak to them is the denial alike of all evangelism and of Christian love. What possible use is an unintelligible advertisement?

The process of re-learning a Christian way of thinking, in Christian terms, will follow later, after conversion. We have to lead the listener to Christ in the listener's own tongue, then teach the young Christian to speak properly, when his new experience gives meaning to the new language.

Unfortunately, the effort this requires, especially of the beginner at preaching, is not the whole price to be paid for getting beside the modern unbeliever. Some earnest Christians do not know the gospel well enough to recognise it in modern dress: they fail to catch the old profound meanings beneath the new words and fresh metaphors. They will therefore question if the gospel is being preached at all. To evade this well-meant but superficial hostility by adhering to unintelligible terms supposed to be 'hallowed', and 'fundamental', is lazy, sometimes cowardly, and completely unevangelistic in a spiritually illiterate generation.

It is well, here, to notice the test which Paul proposes, by which to assess the validity and fruitfulness of church life in Corinth. Unexpectedly, he asks what the *outsider* will think of it, the ignorant and unbelieving visitor to the service. Will he find everything chaotic, meaningless, unintelligible, and say you are mad? Or will he be converted, the secrets of his heart being exposed, and fall down and confess that God is in truth among you? The test is as relevant now, and as authoritative, as it was then. Moreover, it is fascinating to watch how, as the church moved out from Palestine of the gospels to the pagan society of the epistles, the vocabulary of the church changed. 'Lord' replaced 'King, Messiah'; 'salvation' replaced the 'blessedness' of the gospels; 'church' replaced 'kingdom'; faith-union with an ascended Lord replaced 'follow me'. And then to watch the idiom change again, as John addresses the Greek world. The apostolic church was no slave to traditional terminology: they were too much in earnest about their mission to care in what language men expressed the eternal, universal truth.

This leads to a deeper concern yet about evangelistic preaching: the need for (ix) *clarity of aim*. What, in essence, is an evangelistic sermon? Is a sermon on Joshua—his commission, his courage, and his confidence in God, closed with an appeal to commit oneself 'likewise' to confidence in Christ—an evangelistic sermon? Is a series of dramatic stories, strung on a slender thread of thought, followed by exhortations to hold up the hand, to be baptised, to join the church, sign a card, or see a counsellor, an evangelistic sermon? Or is it a gush of feeling in a rush of words, leaving no truth, no declaration that certain things are so, to linger in the mind when 'the feeling of the meeting' has passed, and the young convert is alone, tempted, and feeling vaguely let down by his emotions? Reading a famous sermon said to have converted above five hundred people, and finding it to be a study of Naboth—perhaps even more, of Jezebel—one is simply bewildered.

The theology of evangelism is not our present topic, but it would seem self-evident that an evangelistic sermon should contain at least a minimum exposition of the way of salvation, an outline of the first steps to Christian life, some idea of what faith and decision *mean*. Certainly the pattern of conversion cannot be rigidly defined: you cannot stereotype experience of the Spirit who blows where He lists. Everyone must begin where he is and proceed by the way God appoints *for him*. Confession, tears, conflict, surrender, is not the invariable path to Christ. Nor, it would seem, is a sense of over-whelming guilt, followed by the relief of forgiveness and the joy of assurance, the most frequent form of conversion among our contemporaries. The deliberate creation of a sense of guilt in order to relieve it with the message of the cross, seems a psychologically dangerous procedure, as well as very doubtfully effective in producing saints.

This is, for many keenly evangelistic preachers, the chief problem. There is no one infallible and universal formula of salvation. Certain basic facts, interpreted in the light of fundamental Christian insights about God, love, judgement, sin, forgiveness, freedom, ethics, the Saviourhood of Christ, have kindled in many people a spiritual experience of redemptive and creative quality. But every Christian life is new, and every Christian testimony is fresh, original, and individual. Christian faith is *always* a new discovery, a fresh revelation that comes privately from the Father, as to Peter at Caesarea and to Paul at Damascus.

Our task, therefore, is not indoctrination, but the initiation of a new experiment, the invitation to a new experience. What we are after is not conformity to an inherited pattern, but rediscovery of the inherent truth. And so all evangelistic invitations will be to 'Come and see', to trust Christ and discover who He is, to respond to Him and see what happens.

The positive, many-sided appeal of Jesus, and His invitation to fullness of life; the individual and varied nature of the approach to spiritual experience, culminating in all cases in deliberate and confessed faith, obedience, and fellowship with Him; the acceptance of His Lordship and Saviourhood as the determining factors in the new life being entered upon; with some elementary understanding of the basic standards of the behaviour required of the Christian—such would seem to be essential key-notes in an evangelistic ministry. Most would expect some expression from converts of loyalty to the Christian fellowship, and acceptance of the general obligation to engage in Christian service.

But the presentation of the gospel as challenge, demand, duty, or decision, as something which we do for Christ, is not primary, and is sometimes greatly over-stressed. What Christ did for us at Bethlehem and Calvary, does for us now in glory, and will do for us in the Last Day—this is primary. The appeal should be to trust, rather than to try; to accept rather than to decide; to rest in Him rather than to resolve to be better; to be saved rather than to serve. Trust precedes obedience, in time and in priority. It is still the essence of the gospel that we are redeemed not by anything we do, but by what God has already done for us in Christ. The aim of bringing men to *faith* in Christ as Saviour and Lord, should be made clear, and kept clear, in all evangelistic preaching.

Finally, such preaching must (x) *come to the point*. Where the individual listener may start his spiritual discoveries; what difference decision to trust Christ will make to him immediately, should be made crystal clear before the sermon closes. Something that he can accept, do, realise, try out, act upon, or remember, should be plainly indicated. Many good addresses fail here: we leave an indistinct idea of what is to be done next. We carry a listener with us, interested, curious, disturbed, a little persuaded; we say 'Come . . .'—and we close.

He should be asked for a clear *Yes* or *No* to the truth presented. He should be made to search his own heart as to why the experience described has not happened to him. He should be led to name to himself the obstacles in his life that hinder his following Christ, and to decide what he will do about them. He may be asked to take away with him a copy of a Gospel, with a promise to read it through. Whatever point of reaction we devise, it should focus the message we have presented upon the listener's will, and provoke response.

Usually, the crux of the matter will lie in some single issue, some quite individual and private practical decision, upon which a whole life's response to Christ will turn. It may be some habit to be broken, some restitution to be made, some decision to be reached, or revoked, some relationship to be ended, some truth or fact to be accepted and relied upon. The *particularity* of the claim of Christ should be made as clear as preaching can make it, and the listener left in no doubt what Christ requires him to do in his immediate situation. The very first time a soul reacts to some practical problem in deliberate faith-obedience towards Jesus, is the turning point in every life. To that 'conversion point' every evangelistic sermon should eventually lead.

And with some *urgency*, which is not the same as emotional pressure, frantic appeal, or attempting to frighten into commitment, but something deeper and more lasting. Robert Menzies well describes the true urgency needed in evangelism: 'once for all, all or nothing, now or never, either—or.' That fourfold chord will sound in all earnest preaching intended to bring men and women to faith in Christ.

Evangelistic Themes

While the process of gathering materials, defining the purpose, envisaging the audience, and shaping the message, will be the same for all sermons, there will of course be some difference of approach when the aim is evangelistic. Essentially, the message will still *be* the word of God: but the methodical exposition of an announced text will rarely serve for evangelism—though a master in scripture exposition may still make even the unbeliever listen. Generally, a theme revolving around, or returning to a passage, is more useful.

One way of getting started is to sit thinking of someone you know well, who is not a Christian. Consider his background, his character, and needs. What would you say to him, if opportunity offered—what aspect of the gospel would most appeal to him? It does not matter that he might not be present when you preach, for others will be there, similar in many respects. In any case, such reflections prompt the right approach; while detailed preparation may widen the ideas that come to you, so that older, younger, or even the opposite type of person, may be included in the final sermon.

Another attractive method is to take a fairly familiar Bible story and give to it a strictly modern twist. Tell it as a contemporary incident, concealing until later the names, and date. So, you will surprise the listener into attention, with the discovery that anything so 'up-to-date' is really from the Bible.

A poor lad, born into a miserable home, into disgrace, bad heredity, father no hero, mother broken in spirit; he had no chance, no home training—criminal in the making: typical case for sociologist and forensic psychiatrist. Yet he won through, so that his name has lived, haloed simply by his moral victory, for some 2,500 years. For he came not from New York, Chicago, London or Glasgow, but ancient Israel. His one secret: when all around you threatens to destroy, lay hold of the power above you. (1 Chronicles 4: 9–10: see R. E. O. White, *They Teach Us to Pray*, pp. 32ff.).

Jesus' story of two sons, one saying *yes* and meaning *no*, the other saying *no* meaning *yes*, offers a fine theme for study of two types of modern youth who both cause concern: the conformist who lacks character and conviction of his own; the rebel who yet 'has the heart of the matter in him'. How Jesus knew youth!

A man reaches middle age to find that the real problem of his life has lain in wait for him. The struggles of youth behind him, a certain maturity bringing relative calm, he discovers suddenly that life has trapped him—in the gentlest way, yet relentlessly. For he finds himself heir to a great name, a great reputation, a fine religious piety, an enormous task and a daunting responsibility. And with it, at middle life, has come the realisation that he has not the character to match his inheritance—what a modern story that is! Yet it is Solomon, at David's death—and David's prayer for him reveals that David knew the danger.

Relevant evangelistic sermons often grow from reflection in private on some of the pressing problems of the time. Here, the danger is that the preacher will seek to deal with the problem, on its wide and far-reaching circumference, when all he is really qualified to talk about is the root-cause which he believes lies at its centre. Or, he may be betrayed into describing the problem—especially if it be a moral one—in such lurid and condemnatory terms that he loses the patience of his hearers and the thread of his message.

The method can be fruitful, but the secret lies in sharply distinguishing symptom from cause. In private reflection probe to what seems to be at the heart of the problem: then take *that* as your theme. The way the topic arose in the mind—the newspaper report, the disgraceful events on some college campus, the current discussion of African radicalism—will probably never be mentioned in the sermon; or at most only to illustrate the theme. Rarely has a Christian preacher the inside knowledge to comment upon such matters competently. In any case, to discuss a problem is not evangelism, though to present the Christian answer to its root cause may well be.

One might ponder the strange fascination of Communism. As a deliverance of oppressed peasantry, it makes some sort of sense:

as a world-wide ideology it is an enigma: diametrically opposed (despite its promises) to enriching private property, which is most men's hope; violent and repressive towards minorities—in a generation professing to demand freedom; its history patent falsehood; and its basic theory of man as economically determined plainly untrue. Yet it holds men fascinated, to the point of devotion, and martyrdom. Why? Is it that man *must* have a cause, a City of God, a hope of a new world? Or is it that the breakdown of western democracy in two world wars left such a vacancy in men's minds, hearts, and hopes, that *any* new idea would have swept the world, and the domestic Russian situation happened to throw up such an idea? Are most of our evils really traceable to the failures of our good intentions? Is the lesson that men must have gods, good or bad; must have a purpose, false or true; must have a hope, distant or near; must have a dedication to lend life dignity? From there it is a short step to what Christianity has offered men in the past. Whether one would use the 'fascination of the word *Communism* for modern minds' in this sermon is debatable—but a theme has emerged: the basic need of human nature for heroes, purpose, hope and a cause.

One might ponder the whole tragic problem of drug-addiction, not excluding nicotine and alcohol: and the strange inadequacy in man's own nature that demands some artificial stimulus to make life more exciting, interesting, enriching, tolerable. Why? Is man after all—with all his boasted modern knowledge and unparalleled power—*incompetent* for life, *incomplete*, *inadequate*? Was Augustine right, about man being innately restless and unfulfilled? What a light that throws on man!

Behind both these reflection-themes lies another possible line. The basic opportunity of communism, and the basic craving for artificial stimuli, arise alike from a vacancy in life, an emptiness in the mind, heart, and soul of the modern world. That emptiness may be traced to the rejection of a Christian way, (probably through over-hasty assumptions about the incompatibility of religion and modern science); or it may be traced to the disillusionment wrought by war. Probably *disillusionment* is a key word of our age: men had believed in Christianity, in socialism, in science, in world peace, in reasonable discussion between nations, in democracy: few believe any longer that either of these can save the world. When the house has been energetically swept and garnished by reforming endeavours, but no positive and possessive conviction enters to take charge—the *vacancy invites the devil*. If nature abhors a vacuum, the devil welcomes it. Jesus said that—as He said most things that matter!

Frustration is a common mental ailment: it lies behind most ill-temper, impatience, bitterness, rebelliousness . . . But frustration is a rather special kind of trouble. It does not afflict people who never tried—it is therefore a kind of compliment! Only those who dream, and endeavour, ever know frustration. And it never afflicts those who succeed. What makes frustration?—high ideals with low resources; worthy aspiration, combined with want of character; sometimes, indeed, a Christian conscience without a Christian faith . . .

Freedom is an obvious modern problem that can start a dozen sermons. All want it for themselves (only!). What is it? Freedom from parents, school, church, work, vows, God, yourself, your own decisions, your past, responsibility? An interesting play around all the complicated suggestions here is the story of Onesimus: in bondage as a slave, and (rightly) rebelling, wanting liberty—every man needs and should have it. Taking it—freedom of body and soul, of movement, of self-determination: why not? But taking also, freedom of other's possessions, defying social and moral restraints; and freedom from responsibility—he merely fled, to hide, instead of winning freedom (as slaves often could). Result—a new bondage, of fear, and concealment, and guilt. Out of bondage through freedom into bondage! Then he met a man in bonds—in prison, perhaps in chains, in danger of death: all because of a deeper bondage, to a cause, a conviction, a Christ—a bondage accepted for the sake of a bondage rejoiced in! That man-in-bondage set Onesimus free—to return home, unafraid, and forgiven. Freedom at last? Well, but a Christian now: free to be, like Paul, a bondslave of Christ. So—bondage, 'freedom', bondage, set free by one doubly bound, to be free, in a chosen bondage—that is the story of Onesimus—and of freedom.

Such illustrations are not here worked out to sermon-patterns for the essential reason that the reflection of each man will lead in a different direction. The method is ever the same, for all that: a modern problem, probed for its root-cause, which is then found to be adequately treated somwhere in scripture—which becomes the theme. Whether the original process of thought is revealed in the sermon is a matter for individual decision. A relevant theme in a modern setting and related to God's word, is the one desired result, from which the positive message of Christ to modern men may once again be affirmed.

Sometimes the inattentive ear may be caught by a sermon which starts from a very topical event, reflected upon in the same probing way until it yields an idea which leads straight to a passage of scripture. Some new scientific statement—'test-tube babies' for a ridiculous example—may set one thinking of the mysteries of birth, inheritance. The real question is not where a life begins but where it goes, not origin but quality . . . Once more, the wise preacher will neither assess nor comment upon the 'scientific' dogma, which is probably only a journalist's bright idea: but 'Supposing it were true . . .' leads off to the biblical assessment of life itself.

A space-satellite out of control and useless is a nice modern parable, well handled: star-struck, but lost, because out of touch with home. Man's feeling of being lost, in a universe too big for him, in a confusion of ideologies too complicated for him, in a surge of psychological impulses too strong for him, in an endless endeavour towards a goal he no longer really believes in—what a context in which to define 'lostness' as knowing not the way nor the why, neither your goal nor your home—and leading to Him who came to seek and to save that which was lost. Sheep and star-ships seem far apart, but the meaning of *feeling lost* is much the same!

A social report on the number of 'unwanted' babies (itself a provocative phrase: what then *was* wanted?) may start a brief survey of the number of children whose effective parents are the local or national authorities: 'children of society'. Yet most came into homes, wanted, waited for, welcomed, helpless, full of promise— then their infant world collapsed; the human love which made them just broke down. Individuals untrue to each other, not bound by any higher law or loyalty, destroy what they themselves create, and *inflict* the misery they cry out against when it touches themselves! From this very human line, to the necessity of some moral order to save men from themselves, and so to the pattern of life and of people which Jesus exhibits, is a short way.

Song titles can express something deeper than first-hearing suggests, especially perhaps some modern folk songs. 'I know where I'm going, and I know who goes with me'; 'River, stay away from my door'; 'It's later than you think'; 'Where are all the flowers gone?'; 'The answer, my friend, is blowing in the wind'; 'Brother Man'. To preach upon such titles or songs would be empty and over-clever. But to probe them, for 'the cry at the heart of the singer', and then to preach on the biblical answer to that cry (perhaps citing the song-phrase once or twice by the way), is to touch a chord in young minds without seeming to, and win attention.

In all these suggestions for getting started upon evangelistic themes, the principles are the same. Instead of fastening upon something familar and attractive to *Christian* minds one must fasten upon something in the *non-Christian* mind. But that must not be taken at its face value, as a mere 'text', but probed for what is implied, and struggling for expression through it. Then the biblical truth relevant to *that* idea, or want, or problem, or interest, provides the message of the sermon. It is by no means easy to plan sermons in this way. Merely to preach upon a pop song is silly. But to preach the gospel invitation in answer to the yearning which seems to find expression in the pop song, may at least make some young listener wonder what you are after!

Much else might be said about evangelism, and even about evangelistic preaching—not least to raise the question of motive. It is certain that no sermon, or other approach to the unbeliever, will win him, or deserve to win him, unless we are quite clear that we want him not for *our* sake, or the *church's*; not even for *Christ's* sake (which will not impress him, yet), but for *his own* sake. But that again would take us beyond preaching technique into personal love for men. Of one thing the earnest beginner may be quite sure: as he sets out to prepare and to preach a sermon designed to win men for Christ, the prompting and power of the Spirit of Christ are *with* him, all the way. A man may justly hope for that, in all his preaching: when he is doing the work of an evangelist, he may be absolutely sure that the Spirit is striving with him, to take of the things of Christ and reveal them unto men.

13 GETTING THE MESSAGE ACROSS

IT IS said that a play does not 'happen' until it is performed. Unless at some point the written lines are spoken by living actors to a living audience, there *is* no play. That is true at any rate of the sermon: until it is preached as a contribution to worship, there is no sharing of the word of God, no experience of the divine presence, in fact no sermon at all. The occasion transmutes the words prepared into a spiritual experience.

To that sense of a spiritual occasion, all that will be said about delivering the message must contribute. Although no spiritual effect would last if the sermon be entirely forgotten, yet—as we have said—*remembering* is not the primary response to a sermon. Acceptance and obedience towards the truth presented, is what the preacher aims at. Assuming that his preparation has been as thorough as ability and conscientiousness can make it, how may the result be persuasively preached ?

'Delivery' said Cicero 'is the management with grace of voice, countenance, and gesture.' Most preachers, however, disdain counsel on the mere mechanics of preaching, preferring to trust 'mother nature'. Let us then dismiss in phrases the practical hints—

Power of voice lies in deep breathing, not throat squeezing;
Clearness is better than loudness if you want to be heard
  (though a little extra volume and energy *as well* will help those
  hard of hearing in a large auditorium);
Talking through your top front teeth will relieve your vocal chords—
  and your hearers;
  (In the open air, always speak down-wind, with a solid wall behind
  you).

As to speed of speech, habit and temperament will have more influence than any advice, but two points deserve mention. (i) A *variation of speed* according to meaning is both the natural rhythm of speech and a great help to sustained listening. Slowness always lends emphasis and solemnity; speed quickens excitement and expectancy, but lessens the depth of impression. Such effects, however, depend upon variation—a constant speed, either slow or fast, is merely monotonous.

(ii) The psychological order of communication is relevant, and should be kept in mind. First come the speaker's own thoughts, then the words which utter them; next the listener's hearing of the sounds, dividing them into words, and lastly the listener's interpretation of the words in his own thought, reproducing the thought of the speaker. This is so obvious as often to be missed. The speaker can utter quickly because for him thoughts precede words; the hearer finds it hard to keep up because for him thoughts follow the spoken words. There is always some time-lag; probably because of this, slow speech is more impressive—words and thoughts being more nearly simultaneous. In exposition and explanation, slower speech will be appropriate; once the idea is caught, an interested hearer can of course think very swiftly, and illustrations, examples, and applications may be presented more quickly.

A surprising amount of what we call 'personality' in a speaker lies in one simple characteristic. He manifestly *expects* to be listened to. Whether he deserves to be, the audience will decide for themselves; but something in his manner, his eyes, his stillness, communicates his expectation to them. And most of all, perhaps, in his waiting. If he rushes into his sermon before the congregation are comfortable and have their breath, they will surely suspect that he does not really expect attention—and he will have to work for it.

This is especially clear in speaking to children. To refuse to talk while others are whispering enormously enhances the speaker in the children's eyes. And a preacher who at the beginning of the service and again at the beginning of the sermon, *waits for attention* will get it. But, silence is enough: the chiding, impatient look is out of place.

Most manuals of preaching, following Spurgeon's *Lectures to My Students*, used to give much attention to gesture, the right facial expressions to convey emotion, the demonstrative use of the hands, arms, and body, and so on. The rural lad suddenly promoted to oversight of a great city pulpit probably felt a quite desperate need for guidance in polite deportment: he must often have felt boorish and clumsy in London society. Fewer would be so concerned today, and in any case the best counsel is—Be yourself. As to hands, it is best not to pretend you have not any—try to forget them; but *never* address an audience with hands in your pockets. Nor, for that matter, ever cough or sneeze in the face of assembled worshippers—at least be seated. The only sound principle is to behave always as you would in the 'best' houses you have ever visited.

Gesture, voice, and facial expression are problems for the beginner only because great nervousness makes him tense and unnatural. To many, this seems an almost insurmountable barrier to all effectiveness, and pleasure, in preaching. Yet 'expert' and confident preachers are by no means the most persuasive. The least experienced preacher can count upon a certain sympathy with himself and with his purpose, and even a certain suggestibility, in a Christian congregation which has invited him to conduct their worship—and he should ever remember that.

Moreover, diffidence and nervousness are not wholly disadvantages: over-confidence certainly is. Most Christian speakers may well be grateful to Mr P. E. Sangster (*Speech in the Pulpit*) for distinguishing nervousness from fright. Nervousness keys us up, fright paralyses; nervousness ensures our best, fright our worst; nervousness arises from the realisation that God has given us a great task, fright from a suspicion that we are not 'good enough' for it.

If by 'good enough' we really mean not well enough equipped or prepared, the cure lies in greater thoroughness, honesty of study, and dedication—with the resolution, as Bishop Henson advises, 'to do our work unworrying, and leave the issues with God'. If however we really mean 'not worthy to attempt to preach to others', the cure lies in a truer relation to God. The cure of nervousness assuredly never lies in any bolstered conceit of 'prowess'.

No Christian congregation will reject the nervous preacher who is doing his best for God. William Blake worked in a state of white-hot emotion, fearing to miss any detail of what God required him to do with perfection. To a young friend, Palmer, Blake once said, 'Do you ever work with fear and with trembling?' 'Yes, always,' was the reply. Thenceforth (says the historian) Blake loved him. So, very often, the Christian worshipper will find all the more winsome and persuasive the preacher whose earnestness is struggling with his want of self-confidence, and his awareness of his own frailties. Probably we should never pray that God will make us less nervous, but only more dependent.

One troublesome expression of nervousness that does need vigilance is a tendency to become facetious. Says Thomas Fuller, 'Some, for fear their orations should giggle, will not let them smile.' This is to avoid indigestion by starvation! Flippancy, and the retailing of hackneyed jokes, or of any jokes at all, must always detract from worship: but humour is a precious gift, and well used, a powerful one. We ought not to be entirely afraid of what Stevenson calls 'a little judicious levity'.

Jesus used humour with devastating effect on occasion. Dr T. R.

Glover calls attention to the description of the Pharisees, carefully drawing the fringe of their prayer-shawl across the surface of their drinking-water to strain out the unclean gnat, while nonchalantly swallowing whole camels unnoticed—head, horns, long hairy neck, one hump, two humps, knobbly knees and all! Sayings which come down to us with the solemnity of centuries must have made their original hearers smile, sometimes uncertainly, often with great enjoyment.

The careful removal of a speck of dust from a friend's eye by an operator squinting around a plank jutting from his own eye; the nice irony of the remark about food, clothes, riches, that 'after all these things do the *gentiles* seek'; the laughter in 'Why worry for tomorrow—today has trouble enough!' are all humorous. The last is dreadfully pessimistic, if taken seriously. And surely the instruction to Peter on how to find money for taxes when you live beside a lake, must have made Peter blush and twinkle at the same time!

Nevertheless, the beginner must be careful, and the experienced preacher scarcely less so. A natural wit should certainly not be suppressed. When subject, speaker, the progress of thought, and the friendly rapport of speaker and hearers, are all in accord. then humour can be disarming and persuasive. But it can be seriously weakening, even annoying, when the occasion is inopportune, the subject solemn, or the wit is weak.

Another effect of nervousness is to tie the preacher slavishly to his notes, or sermon pages. The effect of this upon his power of persuasion has already been noted: it is needful now to add only that by some curious psychological mechanism, while nervousness tends to make a man note-tied, dispensing with notes can cure nervousness altogether.

Dr Harold Ford pertinently remarks of extempore preaching— by which he means well-prepared matter delivered in words and phrases prompted by 'the spur of the moment'—that it is the 'more apostolic way of preaching. We cannot conceive of St. Paul taking out a Greek manuscript when he addressed the cultured and critical Athenians on Mar's Hill.' To the objection, that Paul was inspired, Dr Ford replies forthrightly 'So is every true preacher of the gospel . . . That selfsame Spirit which inspired Paul operates in and through every man who has at heart the salvation of human souls and the passionate desire to preach the Living Christ.'

Dr Ford cites the eloquent Fénelon: 'A man who is well instructed and who has a great facility of expressing himself; a man who has meditated deeply in all their bearings the principles of the subject which he is to treat; who has conceived that subject in his intellect, and arranged his arguments in the clearest manner, who has prepared a certain number of striking figures and of touching sentiments which may render it sensible and bring it home to his hearers; who knows perfectly all that he ought to say, and the precise place in which to say it, so that nothing remains at the moment of delivery but to find words in which to express himself'—such is the extempore speaker. An excellent analysis of the process of preparation for effective extempore delivery.

The secret of such freedom and power lies in memorising *ideas* and not *words*. Write out what you mean to say; condense that material into the briefest, barest outline possible; mentally review this summary, again and again, until its content, order, and connecting-links, are easily recalled without reference to notes—until you can 'see your ideas'. Then get up and say what is in mind, in the words that come to the tongue as you look into the faces of the people before you, in the phrases and tone that the occasion demands. The liberation so afforded, the opportunity for personal communication, the sense of being carried along, preacher and congregation together, by the inner power of truth, has to be experienced to be believed.

Some loss of style, of precision of phrasing, even of cherished thoughts, is the price paid for that directness of communication. Many will want to delay the experiment of unscripted preaching until experience has conferred confidence: but some put it off too long, and habit reinforces nervousness to make the attempt impossible. On the other hand, some men gain such skill in the unfettered use of notes that for them the experiment is unnecessary. Every man will make his own decision. He will soon discover, too, that the sermon which *depends* upon keeping to one's notes probably owes too much to form and phrasing. Its content is too thin to stand up in everyday clothes.

'I fear,' said a disconsolate minister to one of his most loyal hearers, 'that most of our best work, long studied and prayerfully prepared, is quite forgotten before the week is out.' 'Well, minister,' she hesitantly replied, 'if you cannot remember it yourself, even while you are preaching it, you must not be too hard on us, who never thought of it till then.'

One circumstance which can make even experienced men nervous is the totally unexpected event—an emergency in the life of the congregation, a sudden death, some local tragedy—unforeseeable when the service was planned. To omit all reference to such a matter might be misunderstood, but impetuous comments and hasty adjustments to the sermon are better avoided. The safest reaction for beginners is to adhere to the pattern of worship and the message as prepared, inserting a few words of explanation or of prayer, and mentioning the unexpected nature of the occurrence as reason for no more extended reference.

The responsible preacher will not confuse his sermon with the congregation's total worship. For all that, in a well-planned service the sermon will tend to determine the theme and mood of the whole. The scripture reading will provide the background to the message, by recalling the whole passage from which text and theme are taken, by rehearsing some parallel or preparatory passage, or one affirming a similar truth. Sometimes it is interesting to let the scripture lesson illustrate the complementary truth, or even its opposite—though this needs care, for some listeners will find the result confusing.

A conscientious syllabus of scripture readings, designed to introduce the congregation to balanced knowledge of the whole word of God, will often of itself suggest areas of truth to be explored in preaching. A congregation's knowledge and use of the Bible will rarely exceed that of their habitual preachers: when they notice how often biblical conceptions control the pattern and the thought of worship, a new reverence and understanding of scripture will result.

To a lesser extent, the choice of hymns may likewise reflect the theme of the sermon, either by setting an appropriate mood, or by voicing a fitting response, sometimes by illustrating how others have illumined the theme in poetry, occasionally by provoking thought, through an unfamiliar hymn, on the question which the sermon will try to answer. Considered planning of the service as a whole, and deliberate departure from the lazy, habitual use of the familiar to explore the whole treasury of devotion, are the most needed principles. An indifferent gem is often enhanced by a careful setting. So is many an indifferent sermon.

Other values have to be considered, however, in relation to worship-song, than its connection with the sermon. Whether we approve or deplore the fact, many Christians learn more of Christian doctrine, sentiment, and feeling from the hymns they sing than from sermons or scripture lessons, and the singing is for some the most moving and best remembered part of every service. The preacher must reckon with this, and make use of it. Yet he will remember that while he is concerned mainly with the words, others are involved with the tune and the mood: and he will make his choice in consultation, often letting others select part of the congregation's praise.

The diligent preacher will *explore* fully whatever hymnbook is in use, will *record* the usage to avoid too frequent repetition, and will *vary* the metres and the mood in each service. He will generally keep to a considered *pattern of hymns*—adoration, prayer, meditation, response, with sometimes testimony or affirmation of faith interposed—or whatever is the pattern he favours. Haphazard selection is irreverent. But even so, the theme of the service as a whole will harmonise so far as he can make it do, with the message God has given for that occasion.

Prayer-time in public worship is less fittingly dominated by the sermon's theme, but a reference to the coming reflection together on God's word is as appropriate as a prayer following the preaching. It can help to create a sense that preacher and people are waiting together for the illumination of the Spirit upon the written page, that prepared thoughts may 'come alive' as the word of God spoken in power.

Of the preacher's private preparation for the pulpit little need be said. Most men find they must have opportunity before every service for quiet prayer, recollection, and mental rehearsal. Some use the hymnbook, or a book of devotion, reserved for just these moments. Only the careless and the insensitive would rush into the pulpit, even from a last-minute conference with church office-bearers about church affairs. Courteously, but firmly, a man should make it clear that such is not his way. If for no other reason, he will want to recapture a quiet spirit, and the inner reassurance that it is God's work he is about.

It is important that a man should approach the moment of preaching with a mind looking outward to others, and to God, and not inward to his own misgivings, unworthiness, or 'nerves'. He *is* doing God's work. With what assurance should be coupled the sustaining insights of Jesus and the strong confidence of Paul. In the parable of the sower, Jesus is astonishingly realistic and sure. Reviewing His own preaching in Galilee as the winds of hostility rise against Him, Jesus describes the varied reception of the word among the crowds. Only twenty-five per cent response is expected—and of that, some is no more than thirtyfold, some sixtyfold, and some a hundred.

This, from the chief Sower Himself! Yet He has no doubt at

all that the seed is the word of God: there is nothing wrong with the message. Nor does Jesus doubt that good soil will show a harvest: the earth, given the seed, 'bringeth forth fruit of itself'. This faith in the seed, and in the unhindered soil, must underlie our own work, plus the certainty that in all our own scattering of the seeds of truth, the Sower Himself is still at work.

Paul expresses similar faith, in the succinct but tremendous affirmation 'We can do nothing against the truth, but for the truth'. Paul may have learned this from Isaiah—'All flesh is as grass, and all the glory of man as the flower of grass: the grass withereth, and the flower thereof falleth away, BUT the word of the Lord endureth for ever'—*truth is immortal*. Paul may have caught this confidence from his old teacher, Gamaliel: 'If this counsel or this work be of men, it will come to nought: but if it be of God, ye cannot overthrow it'—*truth is invincible*.

Paul may even have learned it from his comrade and beloved physician, Luke, who three times in Acts describes attempts of enemies of the gospel to frustrate its work, and three times declares 'The word grew, and was multiplied, or prevailed'—*truth is invulnerable*. Or Paul may have realised this fact at the gates of Damascus, where at last the gospel caught up with him and unhorsed him—for *truth*, in the end, *is inescapable*.

Wherever he learned it, this is Paul's confidence and ours, as preachers: that men can do nothing against the truth, but for the truth. In that faith we preach, and leave the rest with God.

THE CONTINUING DISCIPLINES

14 THE DISCIPLINE OF IMAGINATION

LENGTHENING EXPERIENCE can either deepen insight and develop maturer skills, or it can harden habit and perpetuate mistakes. It cannot be said too plainly, or too often, that in preaching a man has never done learning, nor does he ever get beyond the need for watchfulness. A first manual of elementary counsel will do real disservice to a man if it leaves the impression that, with a few basic techniques understood, all he needs now is to go ahead and preach often, growing automatically more effective as the years pass.

For he will not. While some good things will come to him more easily with use, some bad things also will creep into his practice unawares. While at the beginning he is willing to learn, even (rarely) to accept criticism and benefit from it, in time he comes to think either that he knows it all, or that he is too experienced to change. That spells stagnation. A man is found preaching at forty, and at sixty, much as he did at thirty—only more carelessly; which is a waste of experience, a failure in maturity.

To remain effective, and to become more useful as life enriches his experience and his knowledge of God, a preacher *must accept a continuing discipline*. He should expect to improve, and take steps towards improvement, in matters more basic than technique: in power of imagination, in facility with words, in ability to touch the springs of human interest, in self-assessment and self-criticism. To these main elements of this continuing discipline we now turn.

Of all human gifts and capacities that contribute to fine preaching, the greatest is the power of imagination. Imagination is 'the eye of the soul', the capacity to make images in your own mind and transfer them, or kindle them, in other minds. Two serious mistakes are commonly made about it. One assumes that the only purpose of imagination in preaching is to *decorate* the message with embellishments of story or poetry that tickle the fancy but serve no spiritual purpose. The other serious mistake supposes that imagination is an innate gift which a man either has or has not, and which he can in any case do nothing to develop. Either attitude is self-impoverishing, and can be fatal to preaching power.

The Necessity of Imagination

Since the first step towards increasing imaginative facility is to be convinced of its importance, let us be clear that only by means of imagination does *any* statement of fact or truth 'come alive' in the mind of the listener or reader. Only as it kindles into memorable pictures can it move the mind to grasp or the heart to respond.

Statements of purely intellectual form, like scientific definitions, legal pronouncements, mathematical formulae, a list of dates in history, theorems governing angles and sides of a triangle, may all be presented with a minimum of imagination, though no scientist, lawyer, mathematician or logician would get far by them alone. But few statements of this kind figure in preaching, or in anything that really shapes society, enriches experience, or redeems humanity. As Einstein said (and he should know) 'Imagination is more important than knowledge.' 'The human race', said Napoleon, 'is governed by the imagination.'

Imagination lends a statement emotional and moral significance, makes it mean something to the listener, turns truth into power, adds depth and insight to knowledge, engages feeling and memory, sympathy and indignation, interest and response, on behalf of what is said.

It is true that in the sermon this manifold magic of imagination must find expression in words, helped by tone and gesture; and therefore its main pulpit use may be roughly described as 'illustration'. But that is true only if the word be given its widest possible interpretation, as meaning every use of speech that kindles images in the mind, and not —certainly not—merely the trick of thinking up dramatic stories to help out dull matter. No amount of illustrative contrivance can save a sermon which was purposeless and boring from the start, though it may serve, dishonestly, to hide the worst deficiencies.

Quiller-Couch recalls Newman's account of the way in which, in his time, young gentlemen in India went to work 'when they would engage in correspondence with the object of their affections', employing the professional letter-writer. 'The man of words, duly instructed, dips the pen of desire in the ink of devotedness and proceeds to spread it over the page of desolation. Then the nightingale of affection is heard to warble to the rose of loveliness, while the breeze of anxiety plays around the brow of expectation.' Dare one attempt a homiletic translation ? 'Provoked by a curious phrase from some obscure passage of Holy Writ, the young theologue weaves artistically his intricate, fine-spun web of tenuous ideas, upon which no positive purpose or firm conclusion dare hang, and perceiving the thinness of the result, he proceeds to accumulate adjectives, search out similes, multiply moving metaphors, and adduce appropriate anecdotes, until the gossamer thread of thought snaps under the weight of the glistening dew of ornament, and collapses in the dust.'

But freely admitting that *illustrations and imaginative flights can never take the place of divine truth earnestly expounded and applied*, it remains true that preaching is with a view to persuasion, and few people are ever persuaded by fact or logic alone. To persuade, language must touch emotion, and as Grierson says 'one great effect of emotion on language is to make it figurative, to make the writer or the speaker use words in a new and surprising manner that quickens our sense of their emotional significance'.

We are all poets when deeply moved. Words in themselves are ephemeral, vibrations in invisible air: the images they conjure in the mind are memorable, concrete, persuasive. Says James Stewart: 'Truth made concrete will find a way past many a door when abstractions knock in vain.'

For efficiency's sake, therefore, the prosy preacher must teach himself to speak in diagrams. This is an important element in the technique by which he counters that reduced capacity for listening to which reference has been made. To a visual culture, trained to absorb ideas via graphics, films, models and diagrams, the preacher must use 'visible' language. Apt illustration is the 'visual aid' for impaired concentration and memory, the pulpit's only available medium for conveying abstract thought.

Behind this plea lies psychological truth. The brain lies behind the eyes as well as between the ears. All teaching and persuasion is a matter of making mental *impressions*, including intellectual images and emotional impulses. An idea is retained in proportion to the depth with which it is first impressed, and that depends upon its vividness, clarity, repetition, and emotional charge.

The drawing, the diagram, the photograph or plan, all convey clear and vivid ideas that would take many words to impress; partly because a whole idea can be absorbed simultaneously by sight, where if it be spoken successive sentences have to build it up in stages. Repetition, too, is easier and instantaneous—a mere glance at picture or plan recalls the whole idea. While the emotional charge of a picture is likewise much more powerful when thus presented visually 'at one blow'. The picture of some African child in the last stages of starvation, with listless white eyes against dark skin, and distended stomach on stick-thin legs, is 'eloquent': that is, vivid, clear, emotionally powerful, although as a statement it could be entirely false. By such methods the mind is moved to grasp, retain, and feel the idea presented.

Then, finally on the strength of the remembered impression will depend the response awakened in the learner to whatever he has learned, in the hearer to whatever truth has been presented.

We are not then condescending to a modern trend of fashion in communication, but to the truth behind the trend, when we aim at visual aid in preaching. The maxims are clear, and imperative:

Every time you present a truth, picture it;

If you would persuade, portray;

Don't argue, imagine; don't define, depict.

Remember: no man possesses a truth until he 'sees' it for himself.

But efficiency of preaching technique is not the only issue at stake: deeper considerations must be urged.

Without imagination, the transference of truth from ages long past into today's situations, is impossible. Without imagination, the application by the speaker of the truth he has seen to the circumstances and the hearts of his hearers, is impossible. Without imagination, the logic, the clarity, the information, the truth of a sermon, are all wasted effort: the tinder remains unlit, the words are mere sounds, the ideas are intelligible, but without weight or significance or interest.

The *whole* difference between the dull sermon and the memorable one lies here. Imaginative presentation holds the attention and captures the assent of the hearer; imaginative analysis reads the motives, thoughts, defences, of the hearer and reckons with them. Imaginative application pierces indifference, making each listener feel 'he is talking to me', because it has pictured the need and the background of the listener and speaks to that. Imaginative sensitiveness saves the preacher from crudeness, cruelty, coarseness, clumsiness, because he thinks, and feels with his listeners, and shrinks from the offensive picture.

A reference to the dead as a 'corpse' will distress the newly bereaved; unthinking condemnation of erring children, of broken homes, of alcoholism, of the lack of faith that supposedly 'explains' sickness or frustration or depression,—all such insensitiveness to others' feelings and situations betrays psychologically a lack of imagination, and religiously a lack of grace. The two are very similar.

Only the imaginative can understand, or encourage. And the truth goes still further: Christian love is precisely the use of imaginative sympathy to determine another's needs and serve them. 'We sin against our dearest, not because we do not love, but because we do not imagine' (Ian MacLaren).

So Jesus said that the commandment requires we should love our neighbour as ourselves—that is, whatever we would that men should do to us, we should do to them. 'Imagine yourself in their place—and act accordingly!' Love *is* self-identification with others, an act of imaginative transference. Therefore imagination is the heart of Christian love.

It is to be feared that none of this will change the habit of the man who is convinced that souls are saved by right doctrine, and that the plain statement of the truth is all that is required of the preacher. Yet even such a preacher, prosy, unimaginative, unsympathetic, abstract, may admit that the Master preacher may have something to teach him. None of this argumentation in favour of a developing discipline of the imagination for pulpit use is necessary for anyone who has ever really listened to Jesus. The parables are by no means the only examples of the Lord's approach to the mind through the imagination. Almost every saying, question, epigram, promise, warning and prophecy illustrates the same method. It is not too much to say that Jesus' sayings, once grasped, are unforgettable: and the secret of that enduring power lies in His constant *picturing* of the truth in vivid images of almost visual clarity and impact.

Ingli James ventures to speak of Jesus as 'a popular preacher', quoting in justification 'the common people heard Him gladly'. None found Jesus boring. There is, he says, a popular preaching which is discreditable, but not because it is popular, rather because it has ceased to be preaching. What drew the crowds to Christ was that He spoke the language of the people with vivid concreteness, never in abstract terms; and that He spoke 'from their floor level'. Jesus was interested in their problems, but as His words show, He was interested also in their homes, fishing, sowing, marketing, family life, bread making, wine brewing, patching garments, shepherding—and all the rest.

Says H. H. Farmer, 'The gravest handicap (we carry) is the general suspicion that we have lost touch with the common people.' They could never accuse Jesus of that.

Beside that glorious divine example of how to preach, there can be no further argument about the *need* for imagination.

Developing Imaginative Power

Some men excuse themselves from any responsibility to handle their message with imaginative warmth by pleading that they are not 'poetic' or 'dramatic' by temperament, just plain men. They mean, or should mean, plain bores. 'Imagination', said Emerson, 'is not the talent of some men, but the health of every man.'

It is of course true that imagination varies in different men; but as a natural capacity distinctive of the human mind it is capable of development, of exercise and growth. For this reason we speak of the cultivation of imagination, and the developing facility of illustration, as part of the continuing discipline of the preacher eager to grow ever better at his task. The second step towards that end, following conviction of its necessity, is to realise how very widely the facility for picturesque speech affects sermon preparation. We can only list its main values.

(i) The simplest use of imagination in preaching is the choice of *the vivid word or phrase* to add clarity and thrust to an idea. 'Ideas have legs' says a book-title—but it is imagination which made that thought rise up and walk. 'Words are things' and imagination hurls them like thunderbolts, sharpens them like knives, polishes and sets them like gems, builds great arguments with them like solid stones, caresses them like a lover's hands.

In the gospels, scores of examples are to be found of thoughts and insights which, if shorn of their images, would remain true but no longer triumphant. The camel going through the eye of a needle: Consider the lilies . . . they toil not, neither spin; the salt of the earth; they that hunger and thirst after righteousness; This thy brother was dead and is alive; If any man will come after me, let him take up his cross and follow; I will make you fishers of men; First the blade, then the ear, then the full corn in the ear (of a social movement): we are so used to Jesus talking in filmstrips that we do not realise He is projecting on to our mental screens.

The only way to appreciate Christ's imaginative accomplishment is to try to reduce to plain literal prose the exact meaning of His phrases. 'Heavy burdens grievous to be borne, laid on men's shoulders'—of the obligation of the Torah imposed by the teaching of the rabbis. 'You shut up the kingdom of heaven against men, neither going in yourselves nor suffering them that are entering to go in'—of a doctrine of security before God so demanding that none can achieve it, while those who teach it themselves also fail to satisfy its conditions. 'Ye devour widows' houses'—of money-lending upon so harsh terms of mortage that the property is sure to fall to the money-lender in short time. 'You make clean the outside of the cup and platter but within they are full of extortion and excess'—of the law's attention to external righteousness while neglecting motive and evil desire. 'Whited sepulchres . . .'—but what a miserable exercise it is, to rob the greatest Teacher's brilliant sayings of all their life and power and yeast.

Especially plentiful are the cameo word-pictures: bursting wineskins; playing children dressed up for weddings; hidden treasure discovered by the ploughman; the empty house; the lit candle; weeds among the wheat; the breaking buds; children clamouring for bread, eggs, fish; a neighbour knocking up a friend to provide for an unexpected visitor—and the sleeping household he disturbs. If we did no more than read, and re-read, the vivid words of Jesus, we would grow more picturesque in our own speech.

John the Baptist was almost equally gifted with this vividness of mind: from so brief an account we remember the brood of vipers fleeing the scrub fire, the threshing-floor with the flail, the winnowing shovel, the burning chaff, the axe laid to the roots of trees, the baptism of fire.

The Old Testament is everywhere rich in imagination: to list only the pictures offered of God—the Potter, the Eagle, the Lion, the Refiner, the Husband, the Father, the King, the Shepherd, the Guide, the Host, the Leader in battle, the Tower, the Fortress, the Dwelling-place, the lone Warrior, the Sculptor making clay, . . . here is high doctrine in diagrams, abstract theology insinuated through visual words that throw pictures on the screen of the mind.

Dr W. E. Sangster offers two examples: a minister described a joyless Christian as one who 'telemoans me every day'; a Temperance preacher's quip 'Glasses can change one's whole personality—when emptied too often'. Of another kind: 'Faith is the bridge that links man's impotence to God's omnipotence.' Bacon's 'Counsel to which Time hath not been called, Time will not ratify'; Johnson's remark that Gray's Elegy 'abounds in images which find a mirror in every mind'; South's contention that 'An Aristotle was but the rubbish of an Adam, and Athens but the rudiments of Paradise'; Quiller-Couch's 'Whenever you feel an impulse to perpetuate a piece of exceptionally fine writing, obey it, wholeheartedly, and delete it before sending your manuscript to press—*Murder your darlings!*' the exquisite workmanship of Marion Upington's

> There's that about small sons
> That quite unpins a mother's poise;
> For even when they're quiet,
> She can hear them *thinking* noise;

and the anonymous 'a rainbow is the ribbon Nature puts on after washing her hair': 'the sharp burst of camera clicks printed a dotted line across the silence': 'Rock an' Roll—an orgy of irrational emotionalism, socially useful as a mopper-up of undirected energies;' 'Ours is a mobile society . . . (but) the perambulating Christian, even in our disrupted western society, even across the globe in almost forgotten corners of dark continents, is assured of half-made friendships, ready to be completed as he seeks out fellow-believers and finds in the Name of Jesus an already charged magnetic contact that sparks immediately into sincere interest, welcome, and comradeship.'

Over the low doorway of a church vestry, the thoughtful and courteous warning 'the height of this door is somewhat less than the average height of the human person; if therefore you are up to average, or above, in height, be especially careful how you approach and pass through, lest an accident ensue' was reduced to 'Bend or bump'.

(ii) Especially important to the preacher is the power of imagination to *present concretely what is in essence abstract* and philosophical. The preacher's subject-matter is necessarily intellectual and emotional, rather than material and tangible—as a zoologist's or a bricklayer's might be. In addition, however, evangelicals tend to love abstractions—reconciliation, justification, conversion, sanctification, and the like—instead of concrete, living things, like making enemies brothers again, a verdict of acquittal, a turn-round in your tracks, a clean and dedicated life. A sound motto for the evangelical preacher's desk would be: 'Shun every -tion.'

'How vile a thing is the abstract noun: it wraps a man's thought round like cotton wool' so Quiller-Couch, offering as example: 'One of the most important reforms mentioned in the rescript is the unification of the organisation of judicial institutions and the guarantee for all the tribunals of the independence necessary for securing to all classes of the community equality before the law.' Judicial institutions are courts; unification of organisation is a uniform system; the guarantee required is simply that all may be equally treated.

'The Chinese viewpoint, as indicated in this letter, may not be without interest to your readers, because it evidently is suggestive of more than an academic attempt to explain an unpleasant aspect of things which, if allowed to materialise, might suddenly culminate in disaster resembling the Chang Sha riots. It also ventures to illustrate incidents having their inception in recent premature endeavours to accelerate the development of Protestant missions in China; but we would hope for the sake of the interests involved that what my correspondent describes as "the irresponsible ruffian element" may be known by their various religious designations only within very restricted areas.' Cotton wool indeed! The only thing not 'allowed to materialise' is the meaning.

A little later, Quiller-Couch is warning against the vague and lazy habit of circumlocutions like 'as regards, with regard to, in respect of, in connection with, according as to whether'—

The special difficulty in Professor Minocelsi's *case* arose *in connexion with* the view he holds *relative to* the historical value of the opening pages of Genesis.

Quiller-Couch might well have added 'in terms of', for which the only appropriate treatment is to wring its neck. But in expressing his warning, he is not content to say 'Note carefully the grammatical imprecision of . . .', or 'Circumlocution and abstraction should ever be avoided, for the sake of clarity and force . . .' He says *'Train your suspicions to bristle up* whenever you come upon . . .' An invaluable asset in every public speaker: well-trained suspicions that bristle whenever things get lost in thoughts.

'The first virtue, the touchstone of a masculine style, is its use of the active verb and the concrete noun.'

Jesus never spoke of reconciliation—the abstract idea: He did say 'Go, and be reconciled to your brother'—an active step between persons. He never spoke of—'prayer' but of people praying; never of love for 'humanity' but of you loving your neighbour, your enemy; never of religious forces, 'the eternal', the power that makes for righteousness, the over-ruling providence that superintends history, but of God, the kingly Father.

The Master did say, 'It is always well that those who possess by nature the capacity for hearing and interpreting human speech should pay diligent attention to what is, from time to time, being uttered in public intercourse.' But He put it: 'He that hath ears to hear, let him hear.' It is in fact a characteristic of human experience, familiar to the wise observer of affairs, that the private possession of any valuable quality of personality, capacity of mind, or other advantage towards the enrichment of life, generally promotes the possessor's still further acquisition of similar qualities, capacities, and advantages, through wise and diligent exercise of the powers and opportunities so brought within his reach: that is, 'Unto him that hath shall be given, and he shall have abundance'.

A few paragraphs back, it was laid down as a general maxim of universal validity that intellectual understanding and response are stimulated not only by mental images evoked by audial sensations, but by images contributed by visual experience also. The reader may perhaps recall the statement. Or he may not. What we actually said was, 'the brain lies behind the eyes as well as between the ears'. If the concrete statement is so much more effective in reading, how very much more important it must be when the listener is merely catching sounds across an auditorium.

John Wood cites Brunner's 'Man's life is a defaced cheque, a yellowed photograph of what it ought to be'; D. L. Moody's 'The chains of habit are generally too small to be felt until they are too strong to be broken'; J. H. Jowett's remark that having creeds without faith is 'like hugging a timetable without making a journey'.

(iii) Imaginative power reveals itself equally in the briefest of all illustrations, the *metaphor and simile*. The simile states a likeness between two things: 'the kingdom of God is like leaven'. The metaphor implies a likeness: 'helmet of salvation', 'born again'. The speech of Jesus, like all Eastern speech, is practically composed of such figurative comparisons. 'Ye are the salt of the earth—the light of the world; a city set on a hill; what went ye to see, a reed shaken by the wind? whited sepulchres; blind leading the blind (of teachers); as Moses lifted up the serpent . . . so must the Son of Man be lifted up; knock and it shall be opened (of prayer); I beheld Satan as lightning fall . . .; if you have no sword, sell your coat and buy one; fear not little flock'. Metaphor is as natural an expression of emotion as tears or laughter, but more flexible, articulate, and communicative.

Descriptive metaphors bring two things together so that some quality in the one will illumine a similar quality in the other: 'faith as a grain of mustard-seed'—smallness combined with astonishing power of growth; 'Hope, an anchor of the soul'; 'Like as a father pitieth . . . so the Lord pitieth . . .' Or, we name a thing by some part of it, by something associated with it, by an image of it, to lend the thing we name a new colour, tone, or feeling: blind mouths; stoney-hearted streets; the power of the purse; his face fell; face like flint; the pen is mightier than the sword; bring down grey hairs to the grave (man in old age); the cup which we drink; they have Moses and the prophets (i.e., their writings); the Lord is my strength . . . my song . . . my salvation.

Or, we seek by picturing events to re-live the things we report, and to make the listeners re-live them. To say 'Warsaw has fallen' is to register a fact; to describe the seige, the bombing, the famine, the courage, the fear, the dwindling hope, the lacerated children, the burning buildings, the sleepless nights, the disease, the despair, is to create an image, a picture, an emotional involvement, in which speaker and hearers re-live in imagination what is being described, and are moved to pity, and anger, and resolve.

Transfiguring metaphors bring together ideas that already carry definite associations and overtones, so that something of the attraction or repulsiveness, the strength or the weakness, the joy or the sadness, of the one idea overflows on to the other, transforming it. Phrases like 'the lion of the tribe of Judah', 'the bride of Christ', 'the whole armour of God', 'the brood of vipers', carry as much of feeling as they do of strict meaning, and the feeling arises from word-associations. Statements like 'the judgements of the Lord are true . . . more to be desired than gold . . . sweeter also than honey . . .', and a description of a beloved woman as 'looking forth like the dawn, fair as the moon, bright as the sun, terrible as an army with banners', owe their force not simply to what they say but to the overtones of the words in which they say it.

By this use of colourful and emotional language the preacher's ideas take on warmth and weight, are made memorable, attain power to attract or repel, to make indignant, or stir pity. The metaphor is the instrument of innuendo. The speaker's approval or disapproval, admiration or disgust, personal attitude and intention, finds expression in the comparisons he chooses.

Consider, for example, the implied assessments in :
He clung steadfastly to faith, the star by which he steered, the rock on which he built his whole career;
He clung desperately to faith, the thin ice beneath all forlorn hopes, the last flimsy refuge of the timid and naive.

Or in descriptions of two groups of people :
You are a chosen race, a royal priesthood, a holy nation, God's own people, (used of a little group of *gentile* Christians);
These are blemishes on your love feasts, . . . waterless clouds, carried along by winds: fruitless trees in late autumn, twice dead, uprooted; wild waves of the sea, casting up the foam of their own shame; wandering stars for whom the nether gloom of darkness has been reserved for ever.

Why is it that 'her hair yellow as ripe corn' is poetic, and 'her hair yellow as ripe cheese' is merely comic ?—simply because of the imported associations of the metaphor. Consider, too, three versions of the same statement :

(i) (it is)   nigh upon that hour
When the lone heron forgets his melancholy,
Lets down his other leg, and stretching, dreams
Of goodly supper in the distant pool.

(ii) The curfew tolls the knell of parting day,
The lowing herd winds slowly o'er the lea,
The ploughman homeward plods his weary way,
And leaves the world to darkness, and to me.

(iii) It is evening.

And how the Song of Songs fixes a date :
lo, the winter is past,
the rain is over and gone.
The flowers appear on the earth,
the time of singing has come,
and the voice of the turtledove is heard in our land.

> The fig tree puts forth its figs
> and the vines are in blossom,
> they give forth fragrance.

Once more, for the point *cannot* be made too emphatically, note how much is added to careful analysis and moral assessment, by the way these are expressed in Edwin Markham's account of Abraham Lincoln:

> Here was a man to hold against the world,
> A man to match the mountains and the sea . . .
> The colour of the ground was in him, the red earth,
> The smack and tang of elemental things:
> The rectitude and patience of the cliff,
> The goodwill of the rain that loves all leaves,
> The friendly welcome of the wayside well,
> The courage of the bird that dares the sea,
> The gladness of the wind that shakes the corn,
> The pity of the snow that hides all scars, . . .
> The tolerance and equity of light.

Remove the metaphors, and you reduce the man.

Unhelped by the power of metaphor, the plain and prosaic spoken statement carries little conviction. Until an idea has passed through the speaker's imagination, it will not kindle the imagination of those with whom he strives to share it. Here once more, *awareness of the value* of figurative speech, evoking alertness to notice such writing and speaking in others, and stimulating the desire to grow proficient, is the chief source of growing skill. But as always, some dangers must be mentioned.

Extravagant metaphors defeat their purpose, provoking disbelief or ridicule; for example 'A blush suffused her cheek, as when the blood-red dawn floods with glowing crimson the snowy peaks of Kilimanjaro'.

Conventional metaphors lose their power through lack of the surprise which lends piquancy to all living figures of speech. Unfortunately, many early Christian metaphors, once vivid and compelling, are now dead through over-familiarity or misuse: the Christian Way, the Christian's cross, the seed of the word, the Lamb of God, and scores of others. Similarly dead, frigid and unmoving, through over-use are originally metaphorical phrases like: towering aspiration, sacrificial giving, passionate devotion, soldiers of Christ, the precious word, a passion for souls, red-hot evangelism, bitter persecution, suffering martyrdom, priestly intercession, deep (or, profound) faith, the Christian's Gethsemane. To compare *how such phrases are used* with *what once they really meant*, is to see how metaphors decay through thoughtless repetition.

Curiously, the careless use of a dead metaphor tends not only to add nothing to a statement, but actually to subtract from it. To say that a man 'practised exceptional generosity' (a plain, unfigurative statement) is somehow stronger than to say that he 'practised sacrificial giving'—which ought to mean more, but does not.

There is always, of course, the danger of *mixing* metaphors, causing unintentional, and costly, amusement. To speak of 'piercing the indifference of unbelievers with the blunt truth'; of 'the infant church, clothed in the armour of Christ, striding Caesar's world undaunted'; of 'hope, like a shining star, often indeed obscured by the racing clouds, but never hidden beneath a bushel'; of 'the Christian standing with one foot on the shore of this world and the other in that distant world beyond the Jordan'; of 'Christ the rose of Sharon, never a thorn in any man's side'; of the true believer 'burning his boats before he sets off upon the sea of life with Christ for Pilot'; of 'the onward march of the divine purpose, when the rain of God's blessing kindles the fires of revival' is not to add picturesque emotion to plain statement, but to provide fun where comedy is least appreciated.

But the admitted dangers of metaphor are no excuse for dullness. Until imagination fires language and illumines thought, the truest and best-intentioned sermon is likely to remain dark to the mind and cold upon the heart.

In all such ways imagination enriches preaching. A man should teach himself to watch, to listen, to read, with this purpose in mind. Numerous writers who will help have already been mentioned: many might be added—John Bunyan, H. E. Fosdick, J. S. Stewart, G. H. Morrison, A. J. Gossip, and scores of American writers and preachers with their marvellous facility for visual speech.

Special attention is due to the way in which great novelists create mental images, and poets make picture and symbol carry meaning, suggestion, mood, and even argument. An essayist like G. K. Chesterton used language as an artist uses brushes and paint. Who else would have so described the curvature of the earth, as one looks out to sea?—'The sea is a vast mountain of water miles high . . . rising in a solid dome like the glass mountain in a fairy-tale. To have discovered that mountain of moving crystal, in which the fishes build like birds, is like discovering Atlantis,' Again, 'We are all careering through space, clinging to a cannonball . . . An invisible force holds us in our own armchairs while the earth hurtles like a boomerang: and men still go back to dusty records to prove the mercy of god.' And again,

'I am sitting under tall trees, with a great wind boiling like surf about the tops of them, so that their living load of leaves rocks and roars in something that is at once exultation and agony. I feel, in fact, as if I were actually sitting at the bottom of the sea among mere anchors and ropes, while over my head and over the green twilight of water sounded the everlasting rush of waves and the toil and crash and shipwreck of tremendous ships. The wind tugs at the trees as if it might pluck them root and all out of the earth like tufts of grass. Or, to try yet another desperate figure of speech for this unspeakable energy, the trees are straining and tearing and lashing as if they were a tribe of dragons each tied by the tail.'

This is imagination: the power to see the grass grow, to feel the toothache of a child, to shudder at the fall of a bird, to thrill with fear at a blood-red sunset, to be so absorbed in music as to forget to breathe, to agonise with Jeremiah at truth frustrated by circumstance, to stand with David beneath the balsam trees and hear God pass by, to sing with John in exile and with ten thousand times ten thousand and thousands of thousands, Worthy is the Lamb that was slain.

Without it, the preacher merely bandies words with leaden minds; with it, he can move hearts more than with a trumpet.

15 BY WAY OF ILLUSTRATION

EVEN MORE important than vivid phrasing, concrete expression, or picturesque metaphor, is the carefully chosen and finely polished illustration. Imagination is at its most powerful in transfiguring truth into a tale, enlisting the fascination of a story on the side of serious reflection.

It is true that a certain kind of intellectual snobbery affects to disparage illustration, as needed only by untrained minds. A certain type of spiritual self-righteousness, too, sometimes pretends that a scriptural message, filled with sound doctrine, needs no titivating with engaging stories. Usually, those who so contend speak more than they listen: frequent listeners would never talk such nonsense. Persuasion, interest, and imagination apart, good illustrations have, to say the least, sound practical advantages.

(i) The *evidential* value of a good story, when it is historically true, is obvious. Illustrations gain enormously when they are also examples: not fictional parables of the power of faith but living testimonies; not imagined cases of good neighbourliness, or loyalty to truth, or self-sacrifice, but actual records of personal dedication. Such illustrations add powerfully to the truth they picture.

(ii) The *educational* value of illustrations may be as great. So much of the Bible, of Christian history, of the triumphs of faith, the exploits of Christian valour, the endurance of martyrs, the heroism of missionary enterprise, the secret saintliness of obscure souls who have been the salt of their generation, so much remains undiscovered for the average worshipper, until the preacher introduces him to the long and wide experience of the Church. Tempting his hearers to explore the past, to investigate the world-church around them. to reverence great souls in whom the gospel has borne abundant fruit, the preacher will incidentally, attractively and almost unconsciously, enlarge their knowledge, their vision, and their sympathy, by the many illustrations he gathers from many fields to press home the truth he presents.

(iii) The good illustration has also *psychological* value, relieving tension when the going is heavy and the thought intense. A sermon labouring uphill against the lethargy of the congregation, whipped by the dogged determination of the preacher that they shall get his point or slumber in the attempt, may catch new fire from a telling story deftly introduced. Sometimes the illustration will bring light where all has been obscure; sometimes it will kindle renewing emotion when the preaching has been flat; often it will give a poor sermon a fresh start, with hope of finishing better than it began.

But to press the utilitarian values of good sermon illustration is to plead the case on altogether too pedestrian a plane. The Master is our mentor. Whoever despises sermon illustration despises the master preacher. Though Jesus did not invent the religious parable, for prophets and rabbis were familiar with this method of teaching before Him, yet Jesus did bring it to perfection. But He also added to it other imaginative expressions of religious truth, in order to make His message plain and memorable. Christ's 'illustrations' demonstrate the wide variety of source, of use, and of form, that is available to the alert imagination and the retentive memory—or the pocket-book methodically filled.

Varied Types

(a) Jesus used, for example, *the literary parallel*, drawn in His case from the Old Testament, but in such manner as to strike chords of memory within the listener —echoes of days at home, or in synagogue school, when the matchless stories and thrilling passages were first heard and oft repeated. So Jesus linked His new truth to things already familiar, sacred, and beloved.

In this way, Naaman and Elijah creep into the sermon at Nazareth; Jonah illustrates the presence of the living voice of God within a generation; the queen of Sheba's visit to Solomon reads a lesson on grasping one's opportunity. 'Solomon in all his glory' recaptures a childish picture of the great and wealthy Sultan who once made Israel magnificent. Listeners are made to see John the Baptist through the pages of the Book of Kings and the soul-stirring defiance of Elijah against Jezebel and Ahab. The whole marvellous story from Abel to Zechariah is made to yield examples, reminders, explanations, evidence, encouragement and warning. All that Jesus had ever read or heard becomes preaching material in His sparkling mind.

Possibly, too, other sacred, or semi-sacred, books fed His thought. The parable of the Unjust Judge would follow very neatly the reading of Ecclesiasticus 35: 12–19 on some occasion of private or family meditation. And there are in Jesus' speech other echoes of extra-canonical Jewish literature.

Probably no aspect of the preacher's continuing development is more profitable, or more in need of attention, that an increasing facility in discovering in his general reading, incidents, stories, situations, characters, which illustrate truths he may wish at some future time to emphasize. He will learn to read at two levels, not enjoying less with the surface of his mind, but sometimes alerted to homiletic possibilities in a character, a fictional situation, a historical event, or a well-written passage. As suggested above (chapter 7) a note preserved on the fly-leaf or endpaper of the book is sufficient, until the notebook is at hand to cull the references for future consideration.

Dr F. W. Boreham exhibits this source of illustration at its perfection. English literature is combed, sifted, and indexed in an endless series of essay-sermonettes, each consisting of a single evangelical idea brought into relation with a series of literary extracts that explore or explain it, the whole woven into a charming meditation. One quite arbitrary example will suffice: an essay on Ready-made Clothes stresses the need for having a faith of one's own: it lays under tribute Carlyle's *Sartor Resartus*, Henry Drummond's biography, Professor James on Henri Bergson, David refusing Saul's armour, Carlyle's *Frederick the Great*, the epistle of Jude, Mark Rutherford's Clara *Hopgood*, James Chalmers of New Guinea, Robert Louis Stevenson, John Williams of Erromanga, Drummond on Bonar's *God's Way of Peace*, and on John Angell James' *Anxious Enquirer*, and Bunyan's *Pilgrim's Progress*. Boreham's pocket-book had become, as we know, a nest of drawers, and only a light and practised hand could have made such digestible pastry from so many ingredients.

A single book, Charles Dickens' *Tale of Two Cities*, yields in retrospect innumerable suggestions, of which selections may be given: the agony of inherited guilt, in Darnay; the sense of a whole universe pursuing the threatened soul, in the flight from Paris; the figure of a simple, ignorant woman sustaining domestic piety under the rough persecution of an erring husband, in Mrs Cruncher; the whole theme and title of the first 'book', 'Recalled to Life' and its account of the liberation of an old man long thought dead; the irony by which Dr Manette becomes the agent of his beloved daughter's suffering; the deeper irony by which the revolutionary mob which liberates is also the force which persecutes; the national movement for freedom is seen to produce the worst kind of tyranny, because it is freedom without moral restraint or responsibility, while the individual freedom given to the old doctor proves to be no freedom while he remains a prisoner in the habit of his mind; in the end the only free person is the one who goes by choice to the guillotine; Sydney Carton is the real Christ-figure who shows love by death in sacrifice; but he is also the symbol of redemption from worthlessness through the love of another.

Biography, of course, yields far more, and more direct, sermon–

illustration, both of the formation of character and the effects of character upon career. Accuracy is essential when real people are named or commented upon in the pulpit, and when the illustration is detrimental to them, it is more Christian not to publicise the name. Best of all are the biographical illustrations which afford examples of great truths as well as illustrations—adding evidence and argument to explanation.

Mention may be made here of a rather different source of illustration in great art. The painter, like the novelist, seeks to observe, to comment, and sometimes to preach: often his message is too deep, or too immediate, for words. The preacher who cares to become informed in this field will find immense resources of sermon-illustration which many of his hearers will appreciate, as he opens to them a new world of enjoyment, as well as instruction.

(b) Jesus used *the literary quotation*, again in His case from the only literature available to most of his hearers, the Old Testament. Usually the quotation cited scripture as authority for a principle or doctrine, but Jesus also used Old Testament phrases and sayings to illustrate His own thought, just as we quote beautiful, pithy, expressive or authoritative utterances of others, and lines of poetry, to reinforce our own.

Of such a kind, probably, are 'Go and learn what this meaneth, I will have mercy and not sacrifice' when used of friendship with sinners; 'Out of the mouths of babes and sucklings Thou hast perfected praise'; the Mountain Sermon is full of quotations from the Torah, and Christ's prophecies of the End explicitly refer to a passage in Daniel; 'How often would I have gathered thy children together even as a hen gathereth her chickens under her wings' echoes Psalm 91: 4, and the parable of the Rich Fool quotes Ecclus. 11: 17–19; Noah and Lot become illustrations of a state of things prevalent in Christ's day; the discourse after the feeding of the five thousand appeals to the Manna story; the parable of the Vineyard gains its power from its being a deliberate re-editing of Isaiah's on the same theme; the parable of the rich man and Lazarus has Egyptian and Jewish versions; 'Man shall not live by bread alone', and 'My God, my God, why hast Thou forsaken me?' are 'literary quotations'—the latter from well-loved poetry.

Such use of quotations is more than embellishment, and certainly more than conceited parade of knowledge: it lends grace to our own thought, and will sometimes win assent that might not readily be given to our own words. The notebook, and the sermon seed-bed, must accumulate such possible quotations, *and their sources*, accurately recorded for future use. A scrupulous honesty in quotation is essential, whatever the temptation to adjust, or reword, to make aptness more obvious.

By this means, again, the congregation can be introduced pain-
lessly to significant writers, great souls, scholars, commentators on
public affairs, Christian leaders and other preachers. Not least, the
whole treasury of Christian poetry, with all its deep insights and
moving beauty, is laid open to others to explore, as the preacher
shares from time to time the gems he has discovered.

(c) Jesus used also *the historical event* to illustrate His teaching.
The parable of the Pounds in Luke 19, where 'A certain nobleman
went into a far country to receive for himself a kingdom, and to
return . . .' was told in Jericho, and the hearers must have thought
of Archelaus, elder son of Herod the Great, to whom Judea was
bequeathed. He went to Rome to have the legacy confirmed, and
eighty subjects petitioned Caesar against him, accusing him of
misgovernment: 'His citizens hated him, and sent a message after
him, saying, We will not have this man to reign over us'. Similarly,
the parable of the Marriage of the King's Son probably had reference
to a recent royal event.

History is a fruitful source of illustrative material. One danger
lies in making facile judgements about past events or leaders without
sufficient knowledge or historical perspective. But most listeners are
glad to be reminded of the long story of the past, and the ongoing
purposes of God. And when the preacher has taken the trouble to
learn something of local history, and can illustrate his truth by
reference to place-names, traditions, characters, events of the
district, he can be sure of interest and appreciation.

Beside John Foster's excellent pamphlet, *Preacher's Use of Church
History*, such a book as Prothero's *Psalms in Human Life*, or
the books of Jane T. Stoddart (for example, *Great Lives Divinely
Planned*), show how history can be laid under tribute for the pulpit.
Mention may also be made of Edith Deen's *Great Women of Faith*,
and Kathleen Heasman's *Evangelicals in Action* for much directly
relevant, and pre-digested, material.

(d) Jesus used *the current local news* to sharpen the point of truth.
An accident in the Siloam district of Jerusalem, when a tower
collapsed, killing eighteen people, underlined the warning to be
ready at all times, in penitence, for the divine call. So did the news
of Pilate's ruthless attack upon certain Galileans at worship: 'the
funeral bell tolls for thee!' The death of the Baptist provoked a
public comment on the cunning of the Herods—'that fox!' The road
from Jerusalem to Jericho was called 'the bloody way' from the
many attacks there upon travellers, and a fort was at some time

built to protect passengers: a recent outrage could well have provided topical background for the Samaritan parable.

A prolonged court case, discussed in the bazaars, might have suggested the parable of the Unjust Judge, and the sudden death of a local landowner, the parable of the Rich Fool. The point here is not that such local incidents *did* evoke the teaching, but that they could have done so. Jesus was alert to the moral implications of things happening around Him, the weather signs, the passing seasons, the changing pattern of the countryside from seedtime through harvest, the hiring fair, the current public discussions, whether over the rules of cleanness, the fewness of the saved, or the laws of divorce.

The preacher's temptation may be to drag in references to topical events and local gossip, indiscriminately, sometimes without discretion, and possibly without realising the extra weight which pulpit mention will give to conjecture, rumour, or criticism. A mind awake to life around him, open to things that are interesting his hearers, will be disciplined and restrained by a great care not to hurt, and a gracious attitude at all times—even towards evildoers. With this safeguard, the preacher who finds in local affairs occasional illustration or application for his message will win respect from old and young as a man with his feet on the ground.

(e) Closely related to this is Jesus' use of *the village tale*. It is indeed impossible to be sure when Jesus is alluding to current local events, and when He is inventing stories to make a point, as Aesop did. Our uncertainty itself shows how very close to everyday life His illustrations are. It does not matter whether Jesus actually knew a farmer whose younger son squandered half the capital in a wild sowing of oats; whether He remembered a domestic crisis provoked by the unexpected arrival of midnight guests; whether the house that was burgled stood near His own home in Nazareth, or the ill-planned wedding when half the bridesmaids got themselves shut out was a boyhood village scandal.

Nor whether He ever saw the ill-fated house that fell down in a storm, or only heard of it—or imagined it. Or whether He had visited the family whose two sons were so different, the one pliable but disobedient and unreliable, the other stubborn but right at heart. The significant thing is that all such illustrations might well have been reminiscences, just as the baking of bread, the patching of garments, the brewing of wine, the fishing, sowing, shepherding, were all drawn from the daily world He knew. For Jesus, all human life was eloquent of eternal truth: all life and nature spoke to Him rememberable things, and He made them speak to others.

Beneath this habit of thinking lies more than 'the years that bring the homiletic mind'. It springs from a deep interest in people, in their ways and their work, in their hopes and their problems, in the things they handle, in their crises and tragedies, their varying experience and sudden changes of character. When a man's illustrations keep thus close to life, and make his people aware of his sympathy and knowledge, they are the readier to believe what he says of another and higher life to which they can rise. But if concerning the world they know the preacher shows himself uncomprehending and out-of-touch, they will wonder what he can usefully say about a world that neither he nor they have yet experienced.

Admitted Dangers

Amid all the advantages of vivid and imaginative illustration, certain dangers must be noted. It is possible to *overdo* illustration, so that truth becomes obscured rather than illumined, and the sermon a trivial retailing of anecdotes. Serious Christians intent upon worship do not really want to be entertained, except as an aid to concentration or understanding.

Surprisingly, too, it is possible to be *too clear,* too easy to listen to, so that the laboured effort to make things simple becomes offensive, a talking-down to people well able to follow a speaker without nursery aids! C. E. Montague, in his striking chapter 'Only too Clear', protests against the 'indiscriminate cult of clearness', the overdose of lucidity.

'You must, at some time or other, have groaned dumbly under a flood of clearness from a pulpit. First the giving out of a text, clear as noon, perhaps the words, "A city set on a hill". Then the illumination of this heavenly lamp by setting out, all round it, pound after pound of tallow candles. From word to word of the text the hapless divine struggles onward match-box in hand. "A city", mark you. Not two cities! Not twin cities like Assisi and Perugia, each set on its Umbrian hill. Not one of those potent leagues of cities which shine in the storied page of history like constellations in the natural firmament! And yet a *city*! No mere village! No hamlet perched on a knoll, as the traveller today may see them in the Apennines . . . and so on and on till the martyred Christian below has to ask, in his heart, "Shall I never hit back?" . . .' 'Even in his most explicit moments,' comments Montague, 'a courteous writer will stop short of rubbing into our minds the last item of all that he means.'

There is no need to illustrate the obvious, making what was already plain into something puerile.

A third danger in illustration is *distraction*. This is mainly a matter of timing, of placing a good illustration where it will be most effective. A dramatic, telling story at the end of a sermon can entice the thought away from all else that has been said, just as easily as it can clinch the whole with unanswerable argument. A good story told too soon can make all that follows anticlimax. And there is always the danger that the good story will seduce the mind from further listening. There is considerable skill in knowing how to use an illustration, and when to refrain.

For a fourth warning: illustrations can sometimes *irritate* because the preacher conceitedly assumes—and even says he assumes—that everybody knows what he himself is only hazy about, or has just looked up. To 'drop names' in a sermon, in order to exhibit one's erudition, is unpardonable. But sometimes it will seem to others that the preacher is doing this when he has merely forgotten to add the phrase which would clothe the name with meaning. A congregation may be pardoned for interposing, as judges are supposed to do, 'Pray, who *is* Mr Calvin—Bonhoeffer—Kagawa—Tillich? What *are* the catacombs, the Qumran community, the Moravians?'

A simple phrase giving background, period, place, may be enough: Calvin, the great theologian of the Protestant Reformation; Savonarolla, the courageous Christian reformer of Florence—and that's a city, not his wife! To take too much for granted is to forfeit the educational value of illustrations. It is also to forfeit the goodwill of the congregation, who resent being rudely reminded of their ignorance. The need of identifying background can be as great, in these days, if the illustration be drawn from scripture: Micah,—the socialist prophet of ancient Judah; 'from Dan to Beersheba'—the extreme north and extreme south of Palestine at that period.

Illustrations may be *too long*, usurping more important matter. They can be *too complicated*, requiring so much explanation as to defeat their own purpose. They can be *too controversial*, making references to gambling, Communism, Trade Union activities and the like, which will give offence and distract from the real theme. Illustrations can be *too trivial* in themselves—too many angelic little girls make cute remarks loaded with profound theological import! And they can be *too personal*, until the congregation gets weary of the preacher's children, pets, in-laws, holidays, former homes and churches, college chums, and all the rest of the intimate family details fascinating to himself but boring as holiday snapshots to everyone else.

Finally, illustrations can be *too elaborate*. 'Reading a short passage of scripture every day will help to keep the soul healthy and strong, just as it used to be said by our grandmothers, "Eat it up sonny; an apple a day keeps the doctor away".' Why munch through the trivial idea so laboriously? 'A passage a day keeps the devil at bay' sufficiently recalls the familiar adage without mentioning it, makes the point without blunting it, and awakens in the listener a mild pleasure at having recognised your allusion without your help.

Such *instant-illustration*, the allusion to something too familiar to need explanation, is always useful. 'No man puts new wine into old wineskins . . .' says Jesus, without going on laboriously to explain in detail just why the kingdom of God, like fermenting wine, needs new and elastic containers of religious patterns and customs to give free and flexible expression to its newness. The leaven, the mustard-seed, the pearl, the hid treasure, are all instant-parables: so is 'Physician, heal thyself!' 'Where the carcase, there the eagles', and much beside. The illustration dragged out to the last conceivable element of its spiritual significance is worse than no illustration at all.

Indeed, the illustration which is elaborately introduced by 'There is a splendid illustration of this point in Charles Dickens' account of how . . .', or by 'To make my meaning crystal clear, may I turn for a wonderfully apt illustration to . . .' begins already to defeat its own purpose. It should not be heralded, prepared for, announced, and then slowly led in by the hand. It should arrive promptly, and with impact. The illustration which has to be commented upon, explained and explicitly applied to reveal its 'moral' is a deadly failure. Unless unaided it makes its own point, brings its own illumination, *any* illustration, however dramatic, sentimental, or amusing, wastes time and squanders attention.

Nevertheless, the dangers of misuse do not outweigh the immense value of imaginative illustration.

> Were not God's laws,
> His gospel laws, in olden times held forth
> By types, shadows, and metaphors? Yet loath
> Will any sober man be to find fault
> With them, lest he be found for to assault
> The highest wisdom. No, he rather stoops,
> And seeks to find out what by pins and loops.
> By calves and sheep, by heifers and by rams,
> By birds and herbs, and by the blood of lambs,
> God speaketh to him; and happy is he
> That finds the light and grace that in them be.

So Bunyan defends his 'similitude of a dream':

> Sound words, I know, Timothy is to use,
> And old wives' fables he is to refuse;
> But yet grave Paul him nowhere did forbid
> The use of parables; in which lay hid
> That gold, those pearls, and precious stones that were
> Worth digging for, and that with greatest care.

16 A HIGH RATE OF INTEREST

'WE MIGHT as well be dumb as dull.' So we said while discussing what a sermon should contain. Some would insist that a sermon's most important ingredient is truth, for without that the message would be misleading, even dangerous. Others would say the most important element is purpose, for without it the sermon is futile. But it might be contended that the most important ingredient is interest—since without that, the sermon will not be listened to, and can do neither good nor harm.

It is possible to go further: what is often admired as great spiritual power is usually, in sober fact, the capacity to hold attention, to interest the listener to the point of persuasion. True spiritual power demands more, but it certainly begins there.

The ability to be interesting, like imagination, is not a gift which a man either has or will never have. Most men who begin to preach at all have some power to awaken interest, or they would never be invited to address a congregation. But the initial capacity develops astonishingly with cultivation, and no preacher, however experienced, can ever let up on the effort to discover new sources of interest, or on the discipline of criticising his own preparation in this respect.

When all the stages of preparation have been carefully followed, and the travail of composition is almost over, it can be disheartening to look over the result with this irritating question in mind: Will this message really interest anyone other than myself? But the man who can bring himself to ask it, and honestly to answer it, will be on the way to becoming a compelling speaker.

Most of what has been said about imaginative preaching is pertinent here. Only an alert mind will keep others awake. But beside imagination, the sources of interest are at least three, which we notice in turn.

An Interesting Purpose

No sermon can possibly be interesting if it is irrelevant. However fascinating as an academic study, however charming as a religious essay, the sermon that never touches the listener's faith, problems,

life-situation, or human need, will always be a waste of his worship
time; a futile, frustrating, sometimes infuriating, exercise in trivial-
ity. Relevance is indispensable if people are to go on listening:
lack of it makes 'being preached at' an intolerable trial of patience.

One cannot conceive a dull sermon from Harry Emerson Fosdick.
In a review of Fosdick's preaching through three decades, Robert
A. Phillips highlights the changing subjects to which the 'pastor to
millions across America and the world' addressed himself. Phillips'
assessment, 'The primary focus of his preaching was the burning
concerns of human beings' is amply confirmed by the constant
sensitiveness of Fosdick to the questions people were asking, the
challenges being offered to faith, the social and economic changes
people were facing, the discouragements and disillusionments,
temptations and moral distress, of economic depression followed by
devastating war.

Fosdick 'preached to the down-to-earth problems in his congregation' and became, so it is asserted, for many 'the master com-
municator and interpreter of the Christian faith of this century'.
Few would agree with all of Fosdick's opinions: but no one who
reads the opening paragraph of any of his printed sermons would
willingly put it down unfinished. Other factors contribute to the
absorbing interest of his style, but the chief, compelling attraction
is the feeling that all the time he is *saying things that matter*.

Freelance journalists. and other hopeful contributors to popular
journals, are usually advised to study the advertising in order to
discover the readership aimed at, and the needs, interests, background and motivation which the advertising experts believe those
readers will respond to. In Vance Packard's *The Hidden Persuaders*
a similar investigation uncovered the techniques of advertising which
appeal most powerfully to the buying public.

One crucial realisation—it can hardly be claimed a discovery—
was that advertisers must offer emotional satisfaction with their
goods: the sense of power in possessing a big car, the sense of comfort
with a well-heated home, the sense of security conferred by sound
insurance investment, the sense of personal pride in a pretty dress
or well-groomed hair. Eight specific emotional wants have been
identified as points of contact for the salesman: emotional security,
reassurance of worth, ego-gratification, creative outlets, love symbols, the sense of power, the need for roots, the desire for immortality.

John Wood relates this study to preaching—'their point of
need is our point of contact'. But, strangely, he remarks that some
of these emotional wants 'are entirely irrelevant to our purpose.'

Are they? The Christian approach, of course, is not that of commercial advertising, but every basic human need provides a point of relevance to which the gospel of Jesus may appropriately be addressed.

The list is certainly not to be confined to these eight. Many people feel a deep need for:

1. forgiveness, peace with themselves, acceptance, reconciliation;
2. courage and hope, when life confronts them with tragedy, or menaces them with death;
3. illumination of the perplexities of moral life;
4. satisfying explanation of the religious facts of history;
5. succour when they reach the limits of endeavour, of emotional expression, of intellectual enquiry, or of endurance;
6. escape from profound self-distrust;
7. a way of adjusting to life as it is—to reality;
8. the antidote to uncontrollable fears;
9. the underpinning of their creaturely sense of dependence;
10. the answers to social problems, and some cohesion and direction in social attitudes;
11. meaning in life to make sense of experience;
12. discipline in the self-destructive conflicts that rage within the soul;
13. something to dedicate themselves to;
14. re-assertion of remembered pieties and loyalties that bind them inescapably to early training;
15. acceptance in some group that will support and complement their individuality;
16. satisfying expression of their innate, mystical awareness of the divine.

Each of these 'religious interests' is a legitimate target for the preacher. As he addresses himself to any need to which the human heart is vulnerable, he is assured of a hearing from someone, provided he preaches not the need, but the provision for the need which God has made in Christ. And provided he does so with a positive and personal sympathy towards individual inadequacy.

The best instructors for the preacher who would speak to needy hearts are a watchful eye, a listening ear, a sensitive spirit, a wide circle of friends, and pastoral experience. General literature, and reflection upon the newspaper, can also widen his understanding. If he trains himself constantly to notice the things that men and women will pay for, give their time to, discuss, protest against, or defend, he will know the needs that people are aware of. And if he will teach himself to see beneath their weaknesses, failure, vices, and anti-social attitudes, the deeper needs that they themselves do not yet understand, he will rarely fail to capture interest and hold attention.

Interesting Content

Not the sermon's purpose, only, but its material and content must be interesting, lest the disappointed listener comment 'He was on to a good theme, if only he could have handled it properly!' Yet the sources of human interest are so numerous that any classification of them is a mere convenience of arrangement.

(1) *Personal interest* is universal: only the dreariest people are not interested in other people. This makes news fascinating, gossip irresistible, gives power to the novel, and fascination to biography. A strong interest in persons arises in part from the natural impulse of sympathy, as the hearers identify themselves with the hopes and fears, the romance, remorse, or problems, of the person studied. Sometimes the interest lies in wish-fulfilment, as the hearer receives vicarious courage or strength from watching another wrestle with situations similar to his own.

It is always absorbing, too, to watch the process of development in another's life, from the limitless aspiration of early days through the testing which brings deeper understanding, to a modified achievement all the more admirable for the obstacles it has overcome. This is the basis of the personal 'documentary' and can be powerfully used in preaching, provided the approach is not academic. When, with sympathy and insight, a life-story is analysed to show what influences and accidents, what motives and principles, governed its course, the process takes on all the fascination of a detective story.

Of all this, the preacher will take advantage. But the *method* needs attention. If the character, or the story, be not too well known, and the narration be lively and imaginative, the straightforward Bible biography, tracing a life from the earliest to the latest reference, may be interesting. More often, to start with some crisis in the life, and work backwards, and then forwards, lends added attractiveness. Another treatment, and often more valuable, is to see the person under consideration as a symbol, an outstanding example of a truth: Barnabas as Mr Greatheart, to whom people were more important than abstract principles; Timothy as an earnest servant of Christ whose chief struggle was with himself.

The interplay of circumstance with character is another approach —specially appropriate for Joseph, or Gideon. To imagine (in the study, only) how Elijah, or Hezekiah would have appeared if set in another age, will bring out the strength, or the tasks, which were fashioned for them by their individual circumstances. The interplay of relationships, too, can cast new light on a story: would Esau have been a better man had Jacob not brought out the worst in him? How much did David owe to Jonathan's selflessness? or Peter to Andrew? As a study in relationships, Abigail offers a tantalising problem in detection!

To challenge the commonly accepted explanation of a triumph or a tragedy, is sure to win attention, provided the explanation offered is at least as convincing as the one rejected. Was greed the whole explanation of Judas' conduct? (it may have been—for greed is deadly). Was fear of being thought a fool the real explanation of Jonah's disobedience (as one famous commentator said)—or was it his Jewish nationalism? Is it enough to trace Peter's final triumph to his 'Thou knowest that I love Thee'?—were not Christ's sternness and refusal to let him go, equally potent factors? If the denouement be both surprising and credible, and the analysis kept close to the hearers' own experience, such studies can be very influential.

The more strict character-study explores the person more than the story, and shows the key to development, the reason for breakdown, the interplay of motives. Jeremiah, Hosea, Thomas, offer challenging examples. To show Esau sympathetically, as a 'hairy man', masculine and untutored, profane, impatient, and inevitably self-impoverishing; to study Demas the worldly-hearted, ambitious for gain, counting his losses in the end; to picture Andrew the self-effacing evangelist, or Dorcas who clothed the naked—all such themes will hold a congregation by the sheer interest of persons. And inconsistencies of character are always intriguing: David's great sin demands fairly deep investigation—mere lust hardly explains it: was political power, or religious pride, part of it too?

Sometimes twin sermons offer themselves: one delineating a character, and the effect of what he was on what he did; the other, tracing the sources of that character in what the man believed, the things that happened to him, the choices he made. Jeremiah, Paul, offer almost too much scope here: Jehu, Joshua, Mary of Nazareth, represent similar possibilities. When the person is well known, but not the story, it may be well to use three sermons. On Luke, for example, one sermon would trace the story; the second would describe the character within the story; the third, the experiences that made the character. If the inevitable overlapping be carefully controlled, such a series could hold attention firmly, and throw much light on the formation of Christian character.

Such studies need not be confined within scripture, marvellous gallery of portraits though the Bible is. To consider St Francis of Assisi as a Christian psalmist, John Wesley as 'doing the work of an evangelist'; to represent Augustine, or Bunyan, as later seers on other islands of Patmos; to see Erasmus as a Christian humanist, and place Kagawa within the parable of the sheep and goats; to describe Nansen as the friend of the Friend of little children—all such attempts will win attention. In this way, without forsaking the fundamental principle that preaching, to justify its place in worship, must be scriptural, we may draw upon the long, long story of Christian enterprise and adventure for material certain to arrest and hold attention. The human heart is much the same in all generations: and man's curiosity about man —not to mention woman's—is a useful hook upon which to hang many a spiritual message.

(2) A distinctively *moral interest* will strengthen the personal one for certain types of listener. These are deeply concerned with the problems and the explanations of human behaviour. They may be involved with such questions professionally, or sensitive to the problems and dilemmas of society, and well aware that moral uncertainties and inadequacies underlie most social perils. A more academic interest in moral questions may arise from discussion of plays, films, reports, or proposed legislation, or from conflicting political philosophies. Differences of moral attitudes among denominations, or between different religions, will also attract attention to sermons which seriously examine moral issues.

Earnest people of this kind do attend worship. But beneath this moral perplexity of the thoughtful lies the widespread crisis faced by our generation in the collapse of moral authority. The permissive society of the publicists, and the more sensational examples of 'ultimate liberty' as asserted by small sections of the community, are not as significant as journalists pretend, but a genuine concern for the shaken basis of moral discipline, a sense of being at sea without chart or compass in a society increasingly willing to allow exploitation of the weak and the vicious for private gain, do give to serious moral discussion a new importance for many people.

What the church has to say, and why it so speaks, are subjects to which some will pay attention who firmly reject merely traditional standards and prohibitions, but who have no desire to be either immoral or amoral. Earnest and up-to-date expositions of the great commandments, the deadly sins, the moral problems of democracy, the implications of war, race, family planning, the new medical dilemmas and similar themes, are never despised in the ethical climate of our time.

But it is to be feared that in this field the Christian pulpit has a reputation for dogmatism and condemnation, far outweighing its reputation for discussion, exposition, and reasonable explanation. Inadequate ethical preaching is largely to blame for the confusion of the young about what Christianity demands. Thorough study of homiletic treatment of moral questions—such as that of R. W. Dale —would do most congregations and preachers 'a power of good' in every sense of those words.

(3) A *narrative interest* is universal too. The story-teller can be sure of an audience in all generations and at all ages. But the ability to tell a story well is not to be assumed. It is a complicated talent—attention to order, to detail, to the management of suspense, to the best point at which any necessary background information may be given without forfeiting interest, to the delaying of surprise, and the introduction that provokes curiosity, are all part of the gift. One might learn much from careful analysis of the technique of Hans Andersen or W. W. Jacobs. The preacher whose clumsiness throws away a good story never fails to exasperate his audience.

With the Bible in his hands, no man can lack material for story-sermons. He will play sometimes upon the intricacies of plot and counterplot (as with David and Joab, Elijah and Ahab, Nehemiah and Sanballat); sometimes upon the element of adventure (as with Abraham's probing journeys); sometimes upon action and excitement (the Old Testament has enough battles, journeys, escapes, and personal conflicts for imaginative reconstruction); sometimes upon characters themselves (as with Samson). What cannot be made of Moses and the Egyptians, Gideon and the Midianites, Jehu's military reformation, the return from Exile, Peter's escape from prison, Paul's conversion, the Philippian epic, Paul's shipwreck, the conflict of Jesus with Caiaphas, and with Pilate, the whole confrontation of church and state in Revelation ?

Sometimes the story will concentrate upon suspense. The record of Moses' argument with Pharaoh presents a classic situation where great events hang too long upon an individual decision. So the narratives of Jephthah, of David's struggle with Saul, of Nehemiah's plea to be allowed to go home, of the Maccabean heroism, are all gifts to the lively imagination. Most of the other sources of interest add something to the story's power to hold attention: but well-told narrative is interesting in its own right and the wise preacher often exploits the congregation's love of a good tale, new or old.

(4) Scripture has several *tragedies* on the epic scale that fascinated men like Shakespeare, Milton, Dumas, and that never fails to hold the rapt attention of theatre-goers, opera-lovers, musicians and novelists. Something dramatic, fearful, awe-inspiring, marks the towering ambition, or avarice or jealousy that overreaches itself and destroys a life. The nemesis that falls upon great wrong can always stir the deepest feelings.

Here again, the identification of the listener with the characters concerned, by sympathy with their struggles, their failures, their remorse, brings deeper spiritual understanding. Such a tragedy as that of Samson, illuminated by Milton's great study; the story of Saul, of Solomon, of Judas, and the tragedy of Isaac's home-life; perhaps Moses' failure to reach Canaan; the fate of the churches at Ephesus and Laodicea; and numerous other scriptural dramas may be so treated as to stir pity, regret, and a kind of vicarious remorse. In such ways, conscience is educated, and the ways of God are better understood.

(5) The infection of *deep feeling* will lend another interest to sermon material. *Compassion* can be compelling, when stirred by such a story as that of Mary Magdalene, or Bartimaeus, or Peter in disgrace, or David's sorrow for Absalom. *Indignation* is a powerful moral force, when evoked by such stories as Naboth's, or that of Jacob's treatment of his father and brother, or David's treatment of Uriah. *Romance* lies to hand in Isaac's wooing, even more in Jacob's, in Ruth's immortal idyll, and even in the Cana story—though the most imaginative preacher will be hard put to it to describe what the bride wore!

Emotions of *combat* are pleasurable, especially from the sidelines. Sport's hold over spectators is the sublimation of the old battle-joy, and the eternal attraction of David versus Saul, Gideon versus the Midianites, Hezekiah versus the Rabshakeh of Assyria, Peter versus the Sanhedrin, Paul versus Felix, draws something from this interest in a good fight. Where the tyrant and the little man are involved, as in David versus Goliath, Jezebel and Naboth, Assyria and Israel, the exhilaration of combat is reinforced by the interest all feel in the triumph of justice.

Hannah, and Sarah, provide opportunities for studies in *jealousy*, always a human preoccupation. Samuel is the superb illustration of loyalty, but so is Moses, in his alternate exasperation with Israel and his self-denying devotion to her. Dead must he be of soul who cannot make such emotional themes—and many like them—kindle again for his congregation.

(6) Of an opposite, and rarer, kind is the *intellectual interest* which some listeners look for in good preaching. New information, a new approach, an enlightening, balanced discussion, will win respect from the listener whose professional training makes him appreciate intellectual competence and integrity.

Such men and women value a sound and persuasive exposition of a doctrine, or an ethical principle, based on truly relevant scripture passages, gathering up the insights of the historic church, setting the truth in contemporary context and relating teaching to experience and to life. Such an expert teaching-sermon will hold the attention of worshippers who want to understand what the great festivals stand for in Christian faith and obedience, or what the Christian position is on some tremendous question—immortality, monogamy, the future of the world, atonement, Christian citizenship.

On a less exalted, but still intellectual, level are the occasional sermons that deal with difficult passages of scripture, perplexing Bible stories, or other traditional matters which modern judgement evaluates in new ways. Problem sermons, also, interest such listeners, those which (like the detective novel) set a question to be answered, a puzzle to be solved, and then approach it step by step, following clues or hints that reveal character or expose failure. Why did Pilate, sworn to uphold the still unsurpassed standards of Roman justice, consent to Jesus' death? How does one explain the conversion of Saul of Tarsus? What really went wrong with the Pharisee movement, the original fundamentalists, Puritans, and evangelicals of Judaism?

Modern problems will be even more interesting. Whether the Protestant Reformation must be complemented (or undone) by Reunion; what is the alternative to the export of denominationalism to non-Christian areas of the world by the separate Missionary societies; what new insights must guide the Christian reaction to transplant operations, and to space exploration? The trouble will lie, not in kindling interest in such sermons, but in providing convincing and representative answers, with biblical foundation.

An intellectual interest attaches sometimes to imaginary situations, posed to illustrate the truth of actual situations, or to bring out comparisons. One can imagine conversations between say, Paul and Gamaliel, or Paul and Peter (see Galatians 1); between

Jacob and the prodigal son: between the writer of Psalm 91 and Job; even between Peter after the denial and Judas after the betrayal. There is obvious danger in losing sight of any real message or religious purpose, in the intellectual exercise: but carefully handled, the appeal to the widespread love of puzzles can throw new light on old stories.

(7) A purely *religious interest* may safely be assumed in anyone present at Christian worship, though to presume upon it, as though any ill-digested and ill-presented message must therefore be acceptable, is costly and wrong. But the religious motive for being present does offer further sources of interest of a welcome kind. The earnest restatement of old and beloved truths is never resented by such listeners—provided it is something more than the repetition of hackneyed words by a lazy mind.

New light on the scriptures, if it truly illumines and does not merely bewilder, is especially welcome, while the explanation of perplexities, the reassurance of the discouraged, fresh reminders of the resources available for Christian living, anything at all that makes Jesus more real, more understood, more wonderfully relevant to Christians today, can count upon the alert attention of Christian people.

To provide such fare, the preacher must often go to great scholars, historians, and thinkers, becoming in himself a mediator between the princes of Christian research and 'ordinary' worshippers. They will *not* want to hear about his studies, or the great names he can just pronounce, or the struggles he has had to understand: but for every new gleam of insight that he brings to their faith they will be deeply grateful. And he will often become aware of the congregation's increasing concentration whenever he touches upon some old theme which they have loved and which he is making wonderfully new.

Nothing in this rough classification of the many available sources of interest suggests that the preacher's first priority is to entertain. But he must first get a hearing: and a relevant theme, elaborated with interesting material, is the least a congregation may expect when they invite a man to speak to them about the things of God. A third source of interest remains, without which even these two gifts may lose value: an interesting presentation. Even interesting matter can be stultified by a dull mind intoning prosy paragraphs in a monotonous harangue. But that raises questions of style which demand wider treatment.

17 WORDS—OUR TOOLS

THE SURE sign of a good craftsman, 'a workman that needeth not to be ashamed', is his care of his tools. Ill-kept tools indicate a man with no pride in his creativeness, no love for his own handiwork. The preacher's tools are—words.

With words he expresses eternal thought, moves deep emotion, kindles high faith, rebukes the wayward, uplifts the downcast, restores the fallen, reclaims the wandering, re-awakens the dead. With words he worships, prays, preaches the everlasting gospel. 'Words finely used are in truth the very light of thought' said 'Longinus'.

The two meanings of the word 'spell' are not a coincidence: to 'spell' the right words in the right way is to 'cast a spell' over mind and heart and will. Of course, facility with words can betray, if it be glibness, words without thought, without sincerity. But truthfully employed, carefully chosen, arranged and polished, they become arrows in the quiver of the Lord's marksman, feathered to find their target in the human heart.

> 'Words are, in fine, the only currency in which we can exchange thought even with ourselves. Does it not follow, then, that the more accurately we use words the closer definition we shall give to our thoughts?' So Quiller-Couch.

Even more are words the currency of communication. How can thought pass from mind to mind, except by the vehicle of words chosen, not only to *express* what the speaker has in mind, but to *convey* that identical idea to the listener's mind? If our words are few, poor, or imprecise, then thought itself is hindered, and the impression called up in the listener's mind is obscure, uncertain, unconvincing. Continually to improve our stock of words, in number and in quality, is thus both an excellent intellectual investment, and equally good for trade, the commerce of minds.

Command of language does not come to any man by nature. Acquired in the first place by imitation, it can be improved only by endeavour, discrimination, and practice. Attention has to be paid both to *diction*, increasing the number of words a man has available and improving his grasp of each word's proper use; and also to style, the skilful combination of words in phrase and sentence. For the moment we concentrate upon the former.

'By diction,' said Aristotle, 'I mean . . . the expressive use of words . . . The greatest virtue of diction is to be clear without being commonplace.' For this, a copious vocabulary, and an appreciation of the width and depth and ring of words, are the main requirements.

One source of *new* words will be a man's constantly widening reading in literature of all kinds. Every workman in words needs to cultivate the mental habit of noticing a word new to him, whenever one crosses the page, nodding to it with pleasure, even shaking hands with it, and asking a dictionary to introduce him.

Another fertile source will be the new technical terms constantly produced by increasing specialisation in many fields, but passing rapidly into common speech—*nuclear, complex, fissionable, fiscal,* (musical) *texture, molecular, conservationist, sidereal,* and hundreds more. A preacher may need such expressions rarely, but he does need to understand them before he ventures to use them. For one or another of his congregation, the newest coinage will be 'a household word'.

Yet another source of enlarging vocabulary is the daily invention of new words in the vigorous impatience of common speech. 'Good slang,' says G. K. Chesterton, is 'the one stream of poetry which is constantly flowing . . . Every day some nameless poet weaves some fairy tracery of popular language . . . blue moons, white elephants, men losing their heads, men whose tongues run away with them . . .' Stephen Potter suggests three motives behind the creation of slang: novelty, vivacity, and intimacy—qualities of speech which any preacher might covet. Many expressions begin as slang and attain complete respectability. The Roman soldier's sneering description of his pay as 'salt-money' became our 'salary'; 'hoax' is the modern version of a conjurer's slang, 'hocus pocus' for the showman's diversionary chatter.

C. E. Montague notes *to run for it, make it up. hard put to it, we did him down, up to you to do it, up against it,* as similar native inventions that came to stay. 'A list of American slang words and phrases should gladden anyone who delights in the way Elizabethan English was made.' To be *all in,* to *beat it home,* to *get away with it,* and *put it across,* to *fall for him, boob, grouch,* are examples, while the publisher's advertisement, *blurb,* is a peach of the first order'.

More learned examples are *recalcitrant* from Latin, 'to kick back with the heel'; *wag* from 'wag-halter', one who will 'wag-a-noose' one day, if he persists; to swing *a cat* for 'cat o' nine tails', and *chap* for 'chap-man', merchant or pedlar.

Grammarians and purists will protest at the use of 'low language' in the pulpit, and the protest must be weighed. *Purity of diction*, the avoidance of vulgarisms, technical, obsolete or foreign words, and harsh or ugly-sounding words that offend the educated ear, is a great contribution to persuasive speech. Nothing is gained, if you provoke resistance to what you say by the way you choose to say it. On the other hand, a merely correct and respectable style can be very dull. The vividness and force of new words and expressions, especially some of the picture-language and compressions that make American speech so memorable, may add considerable interest and vigour to any sermon.

One must weigh the dangers of seeming vulgar, and giving offence to people of taste, against the advantages of a forceful, modern-sounding style. Great caution is needed, in these days, lest a phrase or a word be borrowed from popular usage without knowing its origin or associations. Some expressions, apparently adopted as respectable, arose in unpleasant, cruel, even coarse connections. They may convey, to some younger listeners, meanings or innuendoes of which the preacher, if he realised them, would be ashamed. As a general rule, a remark of Stephen Potter may suggest a safe maxim: 'Good conversation lies behind much of the best literature in the world.'

Precision in the use of words is a rewarding habit, adding sharpness and strength to what is said. Professor Raleigh pleads 'Let the truth be said outright: there are no synonyms, and the same statement can never be repeated in a changed form of words.' That is why legal documents and scientific statements can never be 'translated into ordinary speech' without sacrificing all the exactness and accuracy which give them authority.

In preaching, the aim of precise speech is 'to take care, not that the listener may understand if he will, but that he must understand, whether he will or not' (Quintillian). Such an aim will awaken a great care for words, and a sensitive conscience concerning their misuse.

Thus, we shall never say 'the average population of Africa is tall' when we mean 'the average African'—the average *population* is a mere number, neither tall nor short nor fat.

'He had no other object but to get his money' mixes together 'he had no other object than . . .' and 'He had no object *but* . . .' 'I don't hardly know . . .' intends to say 'I hardly know . . .' 'Quite' does not mean 'very'. 'Quite expensive', means 'expensive'; 'quite a place' means (presumably) 'an important place'; 'quite a sermon' probably means 'a good, or striking sermon' (accurately used the phrase would refer to an address, a political speech, or after dinner speech which strayed from its proper function into a religious message, becoming 'altogether, quite, a sermon.')

'Very unique,' 'almost unique,' is nonsense; 'unique' means 'there is only one, and this *is* it'. There cannot be degrees of oneness.

'Open entry equalises advantages, making the advantage of each the advantage of all' is nonsense: *all* cannot be ' a step in advance' of others. So 'privilege' means a 'private law', an opportunity or protection private to some person or class. 'The privilege of everyone' is self contradictory.

To 'aggravate' is to increase the gravity of, not to annoy; 'alternative' means either of *two* (only); 'beneficent' means *achieving* good, a good *intention* is 'benevolent'; 'complex', in psychology, means an *unconscious* morbid reaction, not a conscious obsession; 'converse' means opposite, not contradictory; 'to doubt' is to disbelieve, not to fear; 'decimated' means 'reduced *by one tenth*'; 'innate' (depravity) means inborn, not due to wrong decision or habit; 'mutual' means *between* two or more persons named, not *jointly* by them all together (e.g. 'mutual enmity'; cf. 'common enmity'); 'nice' means fastidious, dainty, precise, requiring discrimination: the colloquial extension to cover all forms of 'agreeable' makes the word meaningless; a question is 'asked', only a proposition, suggestion, is 'proposed'; 'verbal' means 'in words', spoken or written: a spoken agreement is 'oral'; 'import' means significance, meaning, not properly importance; 'literally' means 'to the letter, in the plain, exact meaning of the words': it never means 'utterly, completely'. To say that a preacher is 'literally at sea' means he is journeying over the waters. 'One' (as in 'one does like comfort') means 'anyone'—it is *not* a shy substitute for 'I'.

The list of words often carelessly used could be indefinitely extended. Says T. S. Eliot, in Burnt Norton—

> Words strain,
> Crack and sometimes break, under the burden
> Under the tension, slip, slide, perish,
> Decay with imprecision, will not stay in place,
> Will not stay still.

And every word used imprecisely blunts the edge of speech, blurs thought, and misses its target in the listener's mind.

The value of knowing the *origin* of words is already obvious. Etymology is a rewarding hobby: there is no more effective way of enlarging one's vocabulary, or of learning to use words with discrimination. One must remember that words and usages change: original meanings may be only clues to a word's history, and may not determine present definitions. Even so, to know how a word was first used very often illumines its own breadth of meaning, and its relation to cognate words.

All kinds of odd information is buried in the development of words. *Glamour*, for example, is a corruption of *grammar*. The root-word, *gramma*, a thing written, a letter of the alphabet, gave rise to *grammar*, the art or science of words, and so of learning; a later form, *gramarye* signified the power which such learning bestowed, especially in magic words and spells; and *glamour* is a modern descendant, meaning strictly the magic 'enchantment' exercised by beauty over the beholder.

Some trace *giddy* to the same root as *godly*: *giddy* = possessed by (a) god in a distracting way; *godly* = possessed by God so as to be godlike; enthusiasm, likewise, means divine indwelling or possession.

Disaster originally signified ill-*starred*; *pedigree* recalls the foot of the crane (or stork), symbol of natural descent in old French genealogical tables. *To astonish* is related to the verb *to stun*, and both appear derived from a root meaning to strike with a thunderbolt.

To prevent used to mean to go before (so 1 Thessalonians 4: 15 KJV 'precede' RSV); only later 'going before to hinder others, to get in others' way'. *Iniquity* originally meant unequal, unfair, and so, unjust: the claim of undue favour or liberties for oneself (compare, *inequity*). *Chance* and *cadence* both come from a root meaning to fall. *Aptitude* is first-cousin to *attitude* ('a settled/natural posture'). *Antic* and *antique* both indicate something grotesque, fantastic. *Etiquette*, another form of *ticket*, deriving from 'a label stuck on', links 'that is good etiquette' with 'that's the ticket!'

Stephen Potter says that *to bear* has forty related words, ranging from *birth* to *overburdensome*. *Splutter* combines *splash* and *sputter*; *twirl* combines *twist* and *whirl*.

If such information seems idle, it does at least foster a critical appreciation of language, without which neither force nor clarity of speech is attainable. And when the same etymological analysis is applied to a word like *Comforter*, uncovering its root in *fortify* and its relation to *fort*, *fortification*, *fortitude*, and *fortissimo*, the familiar title for the Holy Spirit takes on a new significance. So does the Christian ministry of mutual comfort.

Provision means looking ahead, foresight, 'pre-vision'; in the plural things laid aside for future use, the results of foresight; *improvidence* is failure thus to look ahead. God's providence is His looking and planning ahead for us.

A *companion* is one who eats bread with you; *fellow, fellowship,* imply joint enterprise involving money or partnership; *comrade* means chamber-fellow; a *friend* is one who loves; a *neighbour* simply means one who is nigh.

Other words whose history and relationships are of special interest:

alms, from eleemosune, compassion: eleemosunary gifts

amen, from Hebrew for certainty, originally strength; no connection with amenity

anthem, from antiphona, responsive singing (of psalms)

atone, to set at-one, unite

Bedlam, (madhouse) from Bethlehem (16th century asylum of St Mary, at Bethlehem); bedlamite = lunatic

benediction, to say well, opposite of malediction; (compare edict, verdict, interdict, contradict, jurisdiction, dictator, etc.)

Bible, from biblion, a scroll, biblos a book; compare bibliography, bibliophile; (the only book to be called just 'The Book')

blaspheme, from damage + speech; originally speech which damages others; later, abbreviated also to *blame*

church, from kuriakos, 'house—*of the Lord*'

deacon = server, used of Mary at Bethany and of Jesus—'The Son of man came to *minister*' is literally, 'to deacon'

disciple = scholar, student, from *to learn*

dominion, from dominus = Lord, (compare dominate, predominate, also dame, damsel, domineer etc.)

duty, from *debere*, to owe, hence debt, debenture, debit, due, endeavour

faith from *fides*, so linked to confide, defy, defiance, fidelity, fealty, infidel, perfidious, diffident, affiance

gossip = God + sib (relation): godparent, etc., a sponsor before God (in baptism); so familiar acquaintance, and hence one who talks much, etc.

forgive = for (apart, away) + give (act generously, bestow freely, without payment); to give away generously one's claim, or revenge, or accusation

magnanimus, from *animus*, soul + great; compare animated, animosity, equanimity, unanimity, pusillanimous

martyr, a witness

maudlin = mawkish, tearful, sentiment; from (Mary) Magdalene (sometimes pronounced maudlin)

Peter, rock, compare petrify, and lamprey (licker of rocks)

prayer, a derivative of *precem*, prayer, and so linked to *precarius*, that which is obtained by entreaty, and so precarious, that which is held during the pleasure of someone else; and imprecation, deprecate

preach, derived from *praedicare*, proclaim or speak before; compare predicate

prodigal, derived from *to squander*, apparently 'instead of work, drive'; compare prodigality

prophet, one who speaks on behalf of someone

psalm, originally from the twang of the bowstring, and so to sing to strings, to a harp; a song so sung

righteous = rightwise

sacrifice, make sacred, holy; compare desecrate, consecrate, sacerdotal, sacrament, sacrilege, and also (with intrusive *n*) sanctify, sanctimonious, sanction, sanctuary, saint.

This highly selective list is offered merely as temptation to pursue the treasures of meaning and association discoverable in the history of words.

Neither a full stock of words, nor accuracy in their use, is however quite sufficient, without a developing sense of the colour and the weight of words, their tone and breadth, their psychological context and their texture. 'In youth you fall in love with words, written and spoken,' says C. E. Montague; 'each word's evocative value or virtue, its individual power of touching springs in the mind and of initiating visions, becomes a treasure to revel in.'

The *associations* of words can betray a speaker, too. A famous left-wing politician received a chilly reception when he sought to rally the British Trade Union Congress with the cry 'You are our rock . . .' forgetting that the chairman for the year was the *Seamen's* leader. 'Pipe', as Stephen Potter points out, evokes different images in the minds of the smoker, the plumber, the civil engineer, the geologist, the organist and the boatswain. 'The *line* means a clothes-line to a laundrywoman, a fishing line to the fisherman, the equator to the seaman, a communication wire to the telephonist, a succession of descent to the genealogist and a particular kind of article to the man of business.' We might add it means a note, or certificate, to a Scotsman, and in the plural, the script of a play.

Like the birds, Grierson says, words are 'winged messengers' of thought, possessing body, colour, and music. A thought, simple enough in itself, may by the excellence of its expression become 'a Pan's pipe to enchant us'. The 'colour' of words includes qualities like vulgarity, homeliness, poetry, smoothness: it may include the pedantry which airs scholarship, or the atmosphere of words like *argent, incarnadine, dervish, imbroglio, peccadillo, parasol, carousel, argosy, ottoman*. Colour, also, may arise from association: *Gethsemane, Nazareth, Immanuel, Calvary, immortal, pastures, mystic,* (the) *Name, spiritual,* (the) *Word, profound, sublime. Comforter, blood,* the *breaking of bread, priestly, sanctuary* are only few of many terms which possess in addition to religiously significant meanings, rich associations which lend them emotional colour.

As G. G. N. Wright says, such words as grace, or charity, have a long history in several languages during which their meaning has been enriched in the growth of religion, art and philosophy. But 'charity' has declined from admiration to reproach.

'Insomnia' dignifies an uncomfortable experience, whereas 'sleep-lessness' has in it something of the endless round of idle thoughts and fears, a suggestion of sleeplessnesslessnesslessnesslessness . . . on till morning.

'Corpse' is a callous word; 'cadaver' has for British ears the re-minder of haggardness, hollowness; 'body' is the kinder word. 'Humane' means more than 'human'; 'sympathy' is wide, reasonable; 'compassion' is moved with emotion; 'pity' is personal and tender; 'commiseration' is condescending; 'ruth' survives only in its opposite, 'ruthless'.

Some words possess melody, rhythm, sweetness; *the murmur of innumerable bees; lustre, beatitude, dawn,* 'the tide of pomp that beats upon the high shore of this world',

> 'She walks in beauty, like the night
>   Of cloudless climes and starry skies;'

cadence, chalice, remembrance. Other words are 'jaw breaking, pebble words'—awkward sounding and rough on the tongue. Milton's account of the progress of Satan across hell is famous:

> Through many a dark and dreary vale
> They passed and many a region dolorous,
> O'er many a frozen, many a fiery Alp.
> Rocks, caves, lakes, fens, bogs, dens, and shades of death.

Montague speaks of words that 'hiss with sibilant letters, or scrunch and jolt with grinding lumps of harsh consonants': *neces-sarily, sussuration, suspicion; jangling, grudge, breakneck, gradgrind, crossgrained, dungeon, obdurate, concatenation.* Others again are insignificant, pauper-words, that weaken anything they seek to express—'dribbling off into weak trickles of unaccounted syllables': *incomprehensibility, ordinariness, unspirituality, ineffectiveness, volu-bility, insipidity.* Thus the precise word is not always the most effective, for in persuasive speech tone and overtone must reinforce meaning, to captivate the listener's mind.

Unnecessary words only weaken impact: as in *entire* monopoly, *voluntarily* offered, *decline* to accept (ie refuse), restored *again*, return *back*, *new* discovery, *novel* innovation, *mutually* encouraged each other, tidings of good *news*, having leisure *on his hands*, dis-simulation *and deceit*, rail *aloud*, danger and *hazard*, the *first* ag-gressors. One of the surest signs of an efficient command of language is awareness of the nice distinction between additional words that add emphasis, and additional words that subtract force. To say

'the men readily offered' is to emphasize their freedom and willing-
ness; to say they 'voluntarily offered' is tautologous: saying the
same thing twice halves the impact.

Occasionally repetition can be useful, and numerous common
phrases employ it: *forms and ceremonies, free and easy, heart and
soul, house and home, high and mighty, all intents and purposes,
jot or tittle, over head and ears, safe and sound, stuff and nonsense,
well and good, through and through, first and foremost.* The Old Testament used repetition in an especially memorable way, in the em-
ployment of parallelism:

> What is man, that thou art mindful of him,
> Or the son of man, that thou visitest him?

> He will not always chide,
>   Nor will he keep his anger for ever.
> He does not deal with us according to our sins,
>   Nor requite us according to our iniquities.

Less formally, 'Christ, being raised from the dead, dieth no more:
death hath no more dominion over him'; 'A man of sorrows and
acquainted with grief'; 'Surely He hath borne our griefs and carried
our sorrows' illustrate the emphasis of repetition.

On the other hand, the *careless repetition* of words is jejune,
flat, disappointing. 'The bushmen's story is just the sort of story
we expect from bushmen, whereas the Greek story is not at all
the kind of story we expect from Greeks,' is tedious. 'It is necessary
to hear soon to make the necessary arrangements'; 'he means to
plan what means to use'; 'in his letter, the latter had written hastily';
'the wrangling of tongues and the jingling of bells jarred upon the
jollity', are verbal discords that needlessly offend the sensitive ear.

H. W. Fowler offers numerous examples, including 'Dr L. seriously
maintains opium-smoking will be as serious as . . .'; 'meetings at
which they passed their time passing resolutions . . .'; 'the founders
of the study of the origin of human nature'; 'the secretary of State
would have to form an informal one if not a formal one'; 'I agreed
that the evidence disagreed'; 'amassed a mass of figures'; 'I awaited a
belated train'; 'invalidity caused by a technicality'. Fowler rightly
warns that sentences can be spoilt by ill-advised avoidance of repetition, too. The article on 'Elegant Variation' in Fowler, and the
list of 'elegancies' used to avoid repetition, given in Partridge, are
important reminders that conscious repetition has its uses, and deliberate avoidance of it can lead to absurd circumlocutions.

Brevity and *simplicity* are hallmarks not only of earnestness and
economy but of clear thought and mastery of language. Says Horace,

of the orator, 'He lays aside bombast and many syllabled words if he wishes to touch the heart of his hearer.' Strangely, there is a widespread assumption that 'talking like a book' is appropriate to the pulpit: it is in fact always the sign of the half-educated. A *too* colloquial style may detract from worship, but a too pedantic style may destroy it.

G. G. N. Wright points out that in George Herbert's poem, *Love*, there is no word or phrase which would need to be explained to a child, and yet 'there can be no more tremendous meaning than is conveyed in its last two lines':
   'You must sit down,' says Love, 'and taste my meat.'
                    So I did sit and eat.
—the last line, with no word of more than three letters, being the superb culmination of a debate between God and the soul. Nesfield likens the ill-formed mind that indulges in big words and phrases to the 'drum in the fable, that gave a booming sound but was found on inspection to be hollow within'. He offers as examples, *lunar effulgence,* the *amorous affection, caudal appendage, nasal organ, partake of refreshment, tonsorial artist, maternal relative, the sacred edifice, the sacred day of hebdomadal rest, eventuate, he breathed his last in indigent circumstances;* the *noose was adjusted and he was launched into eternity; votes were taken by members exhibiting their hands above the heads of dissentients.* Quiller-Couch adds: *adverse climatic conditions, envisage,* the *psychological moment, true inwardness, adumbrate.* To all such pomposities, a weary listener might well reply 'the intellectual content and intention of your verbal expressions do not come within my comprehension'.

The worst form of this pedantry is *jargon,* high-sounding, pseudo-technical, but meaningless 'in-speech', understood only by the initiated. Quiller-Couch has a devastating chapter on the use of jargon: in politics, 'The answer to the question is in the negative'; in petty officialdom, 'In the case of John Jenkins deceased, the coffin provided was of the usual character'; and in journalism, 'there can be no doubt that the accident was caused through the dangerous nature of the spot, the hidden character of the by-road, and the utter absence of any warning or danger signal'; 'he was conveyed to his place of residence in an intoxicated condition'. But nowhere is jargon more zealously cultivated, more meaningless, or more deceitful, than in religion.

An anonymous discussion of Gobbledygook, Maverick's wonderful term for 'pompous or pretentious unintelligible jargon', says that its essence is to dazzle without illuminating, and impress without leaving any impression. *Encounter,* or *'meeting up with', dialogue, participation, structuring, implementation, tension, involvement, con-*

frontation, dimension, are slightly old-fashioned now, and so are *meaningful, transcendental, open-ended commitment, existential, eschaton, integrated, viable, ambivalent*, and *orientation*. But *agapeistic, insightful* and *religionless* are still on the way 'in', as are *polarity, mutuality, dichotomy, heuristic, noosphere, zymotic*.

The writer suggests that the future lies with those who can invent new terms (*agorization*, for bringing truth down to the level of the shopping precinct; or *theothanatoism* to describe the theme of the 'God is dead' school); or who can form what we might call innovative and import-bearing recombinations—*disclosure situations*, the *polarity of dichotomous orientation*, the *totality of the fragmentation of motivation disclosed in fluid and openended contextual dialogue, producing a creative and meaningful tension in the mutuality of intellectual confrontation.*'

A single religious magazine-article in 1970 yields:

'a remarkable convergence of thinking . . . it spite of the fact that research has stemmed from different theoretical orientations and different empirical referents.' 'Because of the polarity of the universal and the unique, there is structure-maintenance. Then being proclaims being!' 'Without the polarity of potentiality and actuality, there can be no change. Then becoming ceases to become!' 'A cosmology provides us with our most overarching organisation of meaningful reality. This image of the universe arises from the undifferentiated ground that, by virtue of its very groundedness awakens in us a sense of awe in the presence of the mysterious power of life itself.' *Awakens* is optimistic!

In all such prostitution of the divine gift of speech, language returns to barbarism, thought to unreason and religion to the unintelligible incantations of jungle rites. As Quiller-Couch remarks, 'If your language be jargon, your intellect, if not your whole character, will almost certainly correspond. Where your mind should go straight it will dodge: the difficulties it should approach with a fair front and grip with a firm hand it will be seeking to evade or circumvent. For the style is the man . . .'

And when the preacher's style is that of pedant, coxcomb, showman and fool, dressed in lexicographical conceits—who can wonder if the congregation's reaction passes from amusement to exasperation? Stephen Potter well says of Tyndale: 'he wrote simply *because he was in earnest.*'

The force of a *brief, terse style* depends mainly on the selection of precise and significant words, each one of which is made to earn its place in the sentence. There are dangers: most preachers can echo Horace's complaint 'I try my hardest to be succinct, and merely succeed in being obscure.' On the other hand, 'prolixity is lifeless'. The sharpness of proverbs lies in their shortness: 'penny-wise, pound-foolish' becomes, when expanded to a complete sentence, a, somewhat trite remark. 'If a thought can be expressed in five words, there is a waste of strength in employing ten' (Bain). As Nesfield adds, the best known quotations from distinguished authors are usually those that say the most in fewest words. The same is true of remembered sermons, and pre-eminently of the words of Jesus.

'The progress of civilisation has been from status to contract' would require many words to elucidate: yet it completely expresses its thought.

So do 'Man is the only animal that blushes, or that needs to blush', 'there are several safeguards against temptation, but the surest is cowardice'; 'a grief too deep for tears'; 'It is more blessed to give than to receive'; 'they that take the sword shall perish by the sword'; 'you cannot serve God and mammon'.

This is not the place to dwell upon the right use of words in grammatical and euphonious ways, but a few *common mistakes* may be illustrated:

Which prepositions follow incomplete words is largely determined by idiom, or by etymology: the only safe guide is a good dictionary. For examples: at his disposal (not *in*); resistance to (not *of*); presented *to* (not *before*); sympathy *with* (not *for*); treats *of* (not *with*); concur *with* a person *in* an opinion (not concur *with* an opinion). The same *as* (not *with*); prevailed *upon* (not *with*); interfere *in* affairs, *with* people (not with affairs); different *from* (not *to*, nor *than*); characterised *by* (not *with*).

Not only . . . but also must conjoin similar ideas, similar parts of speech:
  'He *not only bought* the book *but also read it*'
  'He bought *not only the book but also a pen*'
are correct. But
  'He *not only bought the book but also a pen*'
has muddled the construction. The effect can be confusion. as in
  'He not only was saddened but disgusted by his reaction'
which probably means he was not only saddened but he was disgusted by someone else's reaction, though it actually says that he was saddened, and disgusted others by his reaction.

That does not mean *when, though, if, whether, unless,* or *because*, In 'If I did not mention Jane, it is not that I dislike her' *that* should be *because*. In the lines
      'The fault, dear Brutus, is not in our stars,
        But in ourselves, *that* we are underlings'
does Shakespeare mean *if, because,* or *namely that*?

Only is a troublesome word. Strictly, it should precede the word it qualifies, or (when it means *but*) the clause it introduces:
  Only he promised to read the scriptures (no one else did)
  He only promised to read the scriptures (he failed to do so)
  He promised only to read the scriptures (not to preach)

He promised to read only the scriptures (to read nothing else)
He would not have come, only (= *but*) *he promised to read the scriptures.*

Nevertheless, usage, habit, and the clarity which voice inflexion can impart, lead to many exceptions, which Stephen Potter defends as natural and 'psychological' even if not strictly logical. 'He only died last week' sounds natural; 'He died only last week' seems pedantic; 'I have only been to China twice' is preferable to 'I have been to China only twice'. The need is, to be aware of the difference, so as to avoid ambiguity.

A *double negative* makes an emphatic affirmative, and not an emphatic negative. 'No one doesn't care' means 'Everyone cares'. 'There is no one who does not in his heart believe' means 'Every single one believes'. 'Not infrequently' = 'often' (but with an implied hesitation?). 'I don't know nothing about it' is a colloquial, and clear, but strictly illogical, form of emphasis. On the other hand, 'I shall never consent, not in any circumstances' is clear and logical. Any proposed rule here must be very complex. Again the prime need is to be clear.

It assists clarity, sometimes, to complete a sentence mentally even when the whole is not spoken. 'The Presbyterians disliked the Independents more heartily than the Royalists' may mean either 'The Presbyterians disliked the Independents more heartily than (they disliked) the Royalists', or 'The Presbyterians disliked the Independents more heartily than the Royalists (did)'.

'He does not love Mary as much as me' (means, as much as *he loves me*). 'He does not love Mary as much as I' (means, as much as *I love her*).

How far it is wrong, or inelegant, to end a sentence with a preposition, is much debated. Fowler said it was a cherished superstition that prepositions must be kept true to their name and placed before the word they govern; and he cited exceptions from classic writers, together with examples of the great clumsiness that sometimes results from obeying the supposed rule. Partridge cites Fowler's attitude with approval. 'What are you hitting me for?'; 'A state of dejection such as they are strangers to'; and 'that depends on what they are cut with', are not improved by the inversions and relative pronouns necessary to tuck the preposition inside. (Fowler offers for the last given example the 'correction', 'that depends on with what they are cut'!) Potter likewise rejects any universal rule, claiming scripture ('I will not leave thee, until I have done that which I have spoken to thee of'), Shakespeare ('the table round'), and others, in support—including Sir Winston Churchill's reputed comment 'This is the sort of English up with which I will not put'; and the nurse who demanded of a child 'What did you choose that book to be read to out of for?' The important thing, always, it to be clear and forceful.

From all that has been said one thing is clear: no preacher can afford to be slovenly, ill-provided, or unskilful, in the use of his verbal tools. He will read and listen attentively; he will not be too hurried, or ashamed, often to consult authorities on the use of English. Books like those of Fowler, Partridge, Potter, and others by Onions, Curme, Empson, Richards, as well as the invaluable Roget's *Thesaurus of English Words and Phrases,* will be on his desk and frequently in his hands. Not in any hope that facility with language will of itself confer spiritual power: but because he wishes to offer no hindrance to the clear expression of the truth, and no offence to the educated taste of his hearers, in his preaching of the everlasting *Word.*

18 THE STYLE IS THE MAN

WE ARE brought by two paths to the consideration of preaching style. One path is the realisation that mastery of words demands more than a rich vocabulary; dexterity in the handling of our tools extends not only to right choice but to deft use—the assembling of the right words in efficient ways. If the total impression left by speech is to be sharp and memorable, some attention has to be paid, however reluctantly, to sentence construction, arrangement of paragraphs, clarity and pleasantness of style.

The other pathway is the endeavour to be interesting. 'Even interesting matter,' we said, 'may be stultified by a dull mind intoning prosy paragraphs in a monotonous harangue.' Says Pope, sarcastically, 'Dullness is sacred in a sound divine.' On the other hand, Cowper declares

> He that negotiates between God and man
> As God's ambassador, the grand concerns . . . .
> Of judgement and of mercy, should beware
> Of lightness in his speech.

And not only of lightness: Cowper loathes, most of all in ministers, affectation; 'I seek divine simplicity in him who handles things divine'; 'in language plain, and plain in mind, decent, solemn, chaste, and natural in gesture'. 'A man's style is his mind's voice,' wrote Emerson, thinking of the matter from the speaker's viewpoint; Amiel, thinking of the listener, declares 'Style is what gives value and currency to thought'.

It is far easier to caricature bad preaching style than to prescribe for its cure. Novelists are often merciless. Dickens has Mr Chadband:

'My friends,' says he, 'what is this which we now behold as being spread before us? Refreshment. Do we need refreshment then, my friends? We do. And why do we need refreshment, my friends? Because we are but mortal, because we are but sinful, because we are but of the earth, because we are not of the air. Can we fly, my friends? We cannot. Why can we not fly, my friends? . . . Is it because we are calculated to walk? It is. Could we walk, my friends, without strength? We could not. What should we do without strength, my friends? Our legs would refuse to bear us, our knees would double up, our ankles would turn over, and we should come to the ground. Then from whence, my friends, in a human point of view, do we derive the strength that is necessary to our limbs? Is it . . . from bread in various

forms, from butter which is churned from the milk which is yielded
unto us from the cow, from the eggs which are laid by the fowl, from
ham, from tongue, from sausage, and from such like ? It is. Then let us
partake of the good things which are set before us . . .'

Ridiculous as it sounds, Dickens is determined we shall take him
seriously: he adds the comment, 'The persecutors denied that there
was any particular gift in Mr Chadband's piling verbose flights of
stairs, one upon another, in this fashion. But this can only be received
as a proof of their determination to persecute, since it must be
within everybody's experience that the Chadband style of oratory
is widely received and much admired.'

Anthony Trollope is scarcely kinder: 'No one but a preaching clergy-
man has, in these realms, the power of compelling an audience to sit
silent and be tormented . . . can revel in platitudes, truisms and
untruisms, and yet receive, as his undisputed privilege, the same
respectful demeanour as though words of impassioned eloquence or
persuasive logic fell from his lips . . . jejune words, useless, empty
phrases . . . He is the bore of the age, the old man whom we Sinbads
cannot shake off, the nightmare that disturbs our Sunday's rest, the
incubus that overloads our religion and makes God's service distaste-
ful . . . an amount of tedium which ordinary human nature cannot
endure with patience . . . I yawn over your imperfect sentences, your
repeated phrases, your false pathos, your drawlings and denouncings,
your humming and hawing, your ohing and ahing . . . To me it all
means nothing.'

It would of course be easy to cite recent criticisms from writers
inimical to religion itself. But if even friendly caricatures like these
appear extreme, the spectacle of natural, sociable, easy conversa-
tionalists becoming wholly unnatural, didactic, overbearing,
portentous and parsonic, in voice, style and manner, immediately
they mount the pulpit, is too familiar to doubt. Speech, look,
diction, tone, speed, even the hortatory cough, become homiletic,
funereal, false—all the more offensive for being paraded as religious
reverence!

Anyone tempted to dismiss a discussion of style as irrelevant to
the spiritual work of preaching, may ponder the words of the Public
Orator of Cambridge (England) University, Dr T. R. Glover,
describing the writing and speaking style of the apostle Paul
'Here, if anywhere, the style is the man . . . We have to realise that
he is one of the great writers of Greece, and of the world. "Paul",
said Erasmus, "thunders and lightens and speaks sheer flame."
Luther noted that "his peculiar phrase or kind of speech is not after

the manner of men . . . a very strange and monstrous way of speaking, which phrase is sweet and comfortable".'

Norden says that in Paul the language of the heart is born again. Since the hymn of Cleanthes nothing so intimate, nothing so splendid, had been written as Paul's hymn to love. Those two hymns of love to God and love to men (Romans 8: 31f.; 1 Corinthians 13) have given again to the Greek language what had been lost for centuries, the intimacy and enthusiasm of the mystic.

'Other men', Dr Glover continues, 'have caught in Paul's style the ring of other languages, the popular, the legal, the tones of the mysteries, and of magic . . . He owes more, certainly, to the scriptures in Greek—the habit of making clauses balance and ring back, the parallelisms, the easy interchange of prose form and metre form, the massing of words without copula . . . He has a great range of living allusion and metaphor. The flaming individuality of his mind is all through his style, in the tangent, in the hyperbole . . . he piles up his superlatives . . . Paul *talked* his letters . . . If his similes and allegories miss fire now and then in print, he made them effectual *viva voce*. In Galatians his argument is a series of explosions . . . the amazing vocabulary, the striking metaphors, the compressed word-pictures, popular phrase, Septuagint echo, terms of his own . . . You have . . . wondered why he was not a poet, and why he was so much more than any poet. . . .'

When a Christian of high authority can so discuss the style of an apostle, we need not apologise for drawing attention to the need for care in this too. Paul might turn away from the tricks of oratory, disown excellency of speech and renounce the hidden devices of dishonesty and craftiness; but when the passion for Christ and for men burned high in him, all the gifts and talent, all the training and intellectual discipline of those earlier years, *were there*, to be wielded in the service of the gospel. Paul would never deceive men with rhetoric: but he had no scruples about persuading men to accept the truth by every honest means at his disposal.

No preacher can seriously question the necessity of self-watchfulness in this direction. With all else in the complex art of.preaching, style is only a handmaid to the saving truth, a subordinate and useful gift of pleasant persuasiveness. But it is that, and not to be despised. Our concern is first with the clarity and ease of a good, easy-to-listen-to speaking style, and secondly, with the qualities of presentation that enhance the interest of earnest purpose and sensible, informative matter.

An Easy Speaking Style

The simplest of all styles of speech or narration is that of the breathless child pouring out an excited story in gasping assertions, each a simple sentence, the whole linked together by 'and-and-and-and'. Some of the Old Testament stories illustrate this method, and so does the Gospel of Mark, substituting *straightway, immediately,* for 'and'. This paratactical style, as it is called, is easy to follow, clear, and sometimes dramatic: but the ear tires of it quickly, and the mind becomes bored.

The period, on the other hand, reserves its main statement until an atmosphere has been created, and the mind prepared, by a number of preparatory clauses. Grierson quotes a sentence of John Donne's

> The soul that is accustomed to direct herself to God upon every occasion, that as a flower at sunrising conceives a sense of God in every beam of His, and spreads and dilates itself towards Him in a thankfulness for every small blessing that He sends upon her; that soul that as a flower at the sun's declining contracts, and gathers in, and shuts up herself, as though she had received a blow, whensoever she hears her Saviour wounded by an oath, or blasphemy, or execration; that soul who whatsoever string be strucken in her, base or treble, her high or low estate, is ever tuned towards God, that soul prays sometimes when it does not know that it prays.

Here, in 120 words, only one thing is affirmed—in the last twelve. When full allowance is made for sixteenth century prolixity and pace, the sentence drags, yet the cumulative effect of the introduction is to set the statement, when it comes, in a well defined, emotional context. Modern taste would reject this length entirely; and in any case the listener, unlike the reader, cannot glance back to refresh his memory, or pause to regain his breath.

Yet the periodic sentence is useful. Stephen Potter well cites Gibbon:

> It was at Rome, on the 15th of October 1764, as I sat musing amidst the ruins of the Capitol, while the bare-footed friars were singing vespers in the temple of Jupiter, that the idea of writing the decline and fall of the city first started to my mind

and comments: 'The word-picture is brief, but it is artistically perfect. The reader is held in suspense to the end.'

This is the value of this type of composition: its danger is that the listener may lose the thread, even if the preacher does not.

Two preparatory clauses are probably all that speaking style permits. Preparatory statements are better expressed in short sentences explicitly leading up to the main affirmation. Even 1 Corinthians 13: 2 with six preparatory clauses and a brief, three-word assertion, would today be broken into four separate sentences: 'I may have prophetic powers. I may understand all mysteries, and all knowledge. I may have all faith so as to remove mountains. Yet if I have not love, I am nothing'.

The basic sentence may also be varied by adding qualifying or explanatory statements which modify the assertion even while it is being made. The simple statement 'I may have all faith' was just now extended to include a foreseeable *result*—'So as to remove mountains'. The simple statement 'I am nothing' was modified by the naming of a *condition* 'if I have not love . . .' Sometimes the added clause defines the *timing* of the main statement '*When I was a child* I spake as a child'; or a *concession* that was involved '*Though I give my body to be burned* . . . I am nothing'; or a *cause* may be indicated: 'We love him, *because he first loved us*'. Often the additional clauses indicate *attendant circumstances*: '(1) And supper being ended, (2) the devil having now put into the heart of Judas Iscariot, Simon's son, to betray him; (3) Jesus knowing that the Father had given all things into his hands and (4) (knowing) that he was come from God and went to God, He riseth from supper . . .' Here the simple sentence 'Jesus riseth from supper' is enlarged by four separate clauses of attendant circumstances, making a *complex* sentence. But while accurate statement sometimes demands these careful qualifications, too complex sentences only confuse the listener; they are better broken down into shorter ones.

It is true that speech can call to its aid inflexions of voice, gestures, variety of tone, and of speed, to help out its meaning, where print has only ink-marks on the page. But most men need to check over-elaborate sentence construction, of which they are usually quite unconscious, and which may arise simply from the habit of writing out sermons. For a small effort of self-discipline in this respect, their listeners will be quite disproportionately grateful.

The rules of style, so far as they affect preaching, are three: (i) *The rule of Unity* simply requires that each sentence shall say one thing, and attempt no more. 'The *tall fair-haired, blue-eyed* boy *who lived along the road*, loved Jane' says only one thing—'The . . . boy . . . loved Jane.' 'The boy *secretly* but *with great sincerity,* and *in a kind of despairing idol-worship, passionately* loved Jane' still says only one thing: 'The boy . . . loved Jane.'

Compare this with loose, disunited sentences like:

On hearing this news he got off his chair, went out of the room, took down his hat, brushed it, put on his greatcoat, went round to the stable, saddled his horse, mounted, and after giving a few directions to the cook, rode off into the nearby town which was decorated with banners and badly overcrowded because of some local religious festival. (Thirteen separate statements).

Or this:

But now we must admit the shortcomings, the fallacies, the defects, as no less essential elements in forming a sound judgement as to whether the seer and artist were so united in him as to justify the claim, first put in by himself and afterwards maintained by his sect, to a place beside the few great poets, who exalt men's minds and give a right direction and safe outlet to the passions through the imagination while insensibly helping them towards balance of character and serenity of judgement by stimulating their sense of proportion, form, and the wise adjustment of means to ends. (Seven separate thoughts).

And this:

And it is pleasant also to have heard Lord Lyndhurst, when ninety years of age, the son of Copley Fielding, who was born in Boston in the United States of America, an English subject before the independence of America, speaking on a Canadian question, and his voice ringing as clearly as a bell.

These are not complex sentences, in which single statements are made with necessary, or useful, enlargements. They are swollen sentences, bulging at their seams with all the thoughts which the writers can lay hand upon, packed into a strained net of words.

Two other causes of over-strained sentences are parentheses, and afterthoughts. Consider:

After his last illness (when you remember he had a tumour and the doctors said he could never get over it, though he did, and went to Bermuda for a long holiday, and came back and started work again, in a quiet way) but he never was the same.

The parenthesis here is itself a tumour, and (as the *but* clearly shows) it is fatal to the sentence. For a more reasonable example consider:

The history of Natal during the past year has been (except for agricultural depression caused by rinderpest and locusts) the happy history of a colony which has none.
The *none* comes confusingly after rinderpest and locusts. The parenthesis interrupts disastrously. The sentence could begin with these words: but it would be better to place the important *exception* in a separate statement.

Parentheses are bad in principle, and especially troublesome in speech, despite the help of voice inflexion. They should be confined to short phrases of explanation, or exception, and never used simply to interrupt oneself.

> The senior scholars (of sixteen years and over) are a fine crowd.
> I gave all I had (just ten cents) to the child.
> All the players (except those disqualified) will travel to the ground.

Afterthoughts are final parentheses which will not let the sentence end.

> In America, before the trade recession, in districts that had enjoyed a war-time boom, cars were plentiful and hire purchase the habit among less far-seeing workers—not that I have anything against hire purchase for I do not know what we would have done without it, or how we ever should have got married, with Jim's low wages, and his father dying so suddenly and all.

Clearly, here are four sentences telescoped into one. The result is a sign of mental indiscipline, as well as a sin against the rule of unity.

The rule applies also to the paragraph, which should be a series of sentences all relating to one main idea. The first sentence of a paragraph may indicate the paragraph's theme, the remainder exploring it. Or, the first sentence may summarise the previous paragraph (in more technical works), and the second sentence will carry the new theme. Skilful use of conjunctions and conjunctive particles (*so, however, yet, nevertheless*), will bring out the connection of each sentence with the preceding. Modern style tends to briefer and briefer paragraphs; but this application of the rule of unity affects writing much more than speaking.

(ii) *The rule of proximity* is usually stated in Spencer's dictum: 'Things which are to be thought of together must be mentioned together.' Humorous breaches of this rule abound:

> The chair cost ten dollars on which he sat.
> I perceived it had been hammered with half an eye.
> Erected to the memory of John Phillips, accidentally shot as a mark of affection by his brother.
> A wise doctor does not endeavour to cure diseases but to prevent them. (Does he not?)
> 'He hath made him to be sin for us who knew no sin ...' (KJV)

All such confusion arises from scattering through the sentence words and phrases that belong closely together, and that should be kept together.

(iii) *The rule of variety* applies equally to sentences, and to general tone and pattern. Most speakers have a favourite sentence-structure, simple, complex, periodic, antithetical, long and sonorous, or short and epigrammatic. Most of the soporific 'parsonic' style which comedians ridicule is essentially the repetition of one sentence-construction, with balanced clauses and 'rounded' polished periods that lull the mind. The cure is to vary deliberately the pattern, the length, the rhythm and balance, of one's individual sentences, in order to break monotony. The best self-discipline in this respect is to take a favourite book and to watch, through a complete chapter, just how the author works to achieve his variety: count carefully the words in his sentences, and the changes in sentence-pattern and order of words.

Deliberate variety of tone and general pattern is especially important when any congregation must attend to the same preacher on innumerable occasions. Here once more, habit is the snare: and habit is only economy of effort corrupted into laziness. A man should consider what, in any given sermon, he is seeking to do, and then adopt a manner and tone appropriate to that purpose.

Sir Winston Churchill, writing of his close friend the English barrister F. E. Smith (Lord Birkenhead), said: 'For all purposes of discussion, argument, exposition, appeal, or altercation, F.E. had a complete armoury. The bludgeon for the platform; the rapier for a personal dispute; the entangling net and unexpected trident for the Courts of Law; a jug of clear spring water for an anxious perplexed conclave.' And 'he was always great fun' (V. Bonham-Carter).

So the preacher occupying the same pulpit week after week will earn the attention, and the gratitude, of his people, beyond his expectation, when they perceive how his approach and style vary with his matter and aim. He will be quiet, pensive, slow, for meditation, offering rich but restful reflections on a great theme or passage. He will be strong, assertive, clear, on some central truth or issue needing positive witness. He will be winsome, tender, appealing, sometimes, as he preaches to the conscious need of salvation.

But he will be bold, challenging, uncompromising, when the sharp decisiveness of Christian commitment is his theme. Yet again, he will be argumentative on some topics, quietly reasonable and judicious on others; patient, thorough, practical, in exposition; persuasive in exhortation. This is not play-acting: it is sincerity—the absorption in one's theme that controls even diction, voice, emotion and style. But it can never happen if a man is so habit-bound, or so complacently self-satisfied, that he will not change his usual approach, or admit the need for variety. Nor will it happen if a man never consents to listen to himself.

'I shall aim', said Horace, 'at a style that employs no unfamiliar diction; one that any writer might hope to achieve, but would sweat tears of blood in his effort and still not manage it—such is the power of words that are used in the right places and in the right relationship; and such the grace that they can add to the commonplace when so used.'

An Interesting Presentation

'Unquestionably a good man, earnest, well-read, and evangelical: but I fear the pulpit does not show him to advantage!'

'Good matter, but difficult to follow. If you listen attentively, you will get something—but he does not make it easier for you.'

'I really believe that man would make a proposal of marriage sound boring!'

'When he began I thought he was on a good theme—I felt I would get something worth while. But I just could not concentrate.'

So the precious truth is lost, dribbling away through the profusion of words—

In a style, to be sure, of remarkable fullness
But which nobody hears, on account of its dullness.

And all the effort, earnestness, and prayer, are wasted. Not clarity, careful construction, or variety, alone or together, will suffice to hold attention: there are refinements of style by which these can be reinforced so as to rivet attention—or to recapture it when lost. The determination to be interesting has to extend to presentation—to liveliness of expression, to unexpected turns of phrase, memorable epithets, arresting epigrams and paradoxes, and every other device for turning thoughts into barbs that cling in the mind, and ideas into goblins that haunt the memory.

All that has been urged about vividness and concreteness of language, about illustration, metaphor, quotation, poetry, and apt allusion, is relevant also here, for these are aids to sustain interest as well as expressions of imagination and helps to exposition. With them should be cultivated certain other excellences of presentation which may lay hold of the listener, and leave the truth lingering even in unwilling minds. No device can be neglected which might arm the truth to effect an entrance and possess the soul.

Yet because the skills of rhetoric, and the studied methods of presenting arguments and winning assent, are always suspect among cautious men—who know only too well how vulnerable is the mind to the unscrupulous orator—we shall notice only those features of a lively, interesting speaking style which are to be found within the scriptures themselves.

C. E. Montague points out that there are three ways of saying things: 'You may state them about twice as big as they are, or about half as big as they are, or—if you have the skill, and complete confidence in your skill—you may state them only just as big as they are.'

Understatement, stating things half as big as they are, would describe the Sahara as 'very light soil'; someone deserving highest admiration as 'pretty decent'; and a luxury cruise around the world as 'not cheap'. It can be effective, especially when the opposite is expected. As a typically western idiom, it is rare in scripture, though we do find Tarsus, which in Paul's eyes was proud and important, described as 'no mean city'.

Exact statement is much more rare in public speech. C. E. Montague recalls the effect of a sermon by Benjamin Jowett of Oxford, urging a wise stewardship of time. Other preachers would have drawn highly coloured pictures of the daily uncertainties of life, of the tragedy of lives cut off in unfulfilled, wasted, fruitlessness. Jowett cited the insurance actuaries' figures for expectation of life in men of twenty-one. 'Our young minds were electrified by this quaint piece of precision.' Such 'Quakerish finesse of accuracy' can be amusing, but also, in the heat of controversy, extremely convincing. This again is rare in Hebrew writing, with its gift for poetic, imaginative description: so we are startled to attention by the precise age of Jairus' daughter, and of the lame man at the Temple gate, and the number of fish caught from Galilee.

Exaggeration, or hyperbole as it should be called, is much more frequent in political speeches, advertisements and all kinds of propaganda. A party's policy is 'the most monstrous hash of crude and undigested proposals remembered in a long political career'. The newest brand of soap is positively the most efficient, cheapest, most up-to-date, most scientific, nicest-smelling, easiest to handle, most harmless to hands, most romantic and attractive to men, ever placed upon the market!

As a typically eastern form of emphasis, hyperbole finds ample illustration in scripture. David's lament for Saul and Jonathan includes the claim, 'they were swifter than eagles, they were stronger than lions'. The psalmist declares, 'a thousand shall fall at thy side, and ten thousand at thy right hand, but it shall not come nigh thee.' Jesus says, 'the hairs of your head are all numbered.' He speaks too of the difficulty of the rich man entering the kingdom as equal to that of a camel squeezing and wriggling through the eye of a needle. He warns that 'every idle word that men shall speak they shall give account thereof in the day of judgement'. He pronounces faith, even like a grain of mustard-seed, to be powerful enough to remove mountains. And He declares: 'Think not that I am come to send peace on earth: I am not come to send peace, but a sword.' Paul says he *robbed* churches.

> John's gospel ends with the supposition that if everything Jesus did were written down, the world itself could not contain the books that should be written. Jeremiah's 'Oh that my head were waters, and my eyes a fountain of tears, that I might weep day and night for the slain of the daughter of my people' is paralleled by Charles Wesley's 'Oh for a thousand tongues to sing . . .' Grierson well remarks, about the rhetorical use of exaggeration. 'The question of the truthfulness of such writing must always be taken as relating to truth of feeling. Do the words reflect what the speaker feels ? and is what he feels extravagant, or does it represent what human nature would, or should, feel if men clearly realised the circumstances ?'

Exaggeration is dangerous, as we shall presently see, when used in argument: but as a means of emphasis and of vividness it is extremely useful and widely effective. Nevertheless, as 'Longinus' says, 'one must know where to draw the line. If one overshoots the mark one spoils the effect of the hyperbole, and if such expressions are strained too far they fall flat and sometimes produce the opposite effect to that which was intended.'

Personification ascribes personal qualities, actions, and even speech, to inanimate things. In Romans 7 Paul says that sin took occasion, worked in him, revived, slew him, deceived him, dwelt in him, and consented to evil—as though sin were a living and personal entity. In 1 Corinthians, he says that love suffers, envies not, does not behave unseemly, thinks no evil, rejoices, believes, hopes, endures . . . Elsewhere he says that Jerusalem is the mother of us all. Isaiah says the wilderness shall be glad and the desert rejoice; that the mountains and hills shall break forth into singing and all the trees of the field clap their hands. Another writer can speak of the blood of Christ speaking better things than the blood of Abel, as James talks of the wages of the labourers crying out to God. Sometimes things so personalised are then addressed with question,

counsel, or warning, in a figure called *apostrophe*. Psalm 114 offers
a vivid and sustained esample:

> When Israel went forth from Egypt . . .
> The sea looked and fled.
>   Jordan turned back.
> The mountains skipped like rams,
>   The hills like lambs.
>
> What ails you, O sea, that you flee ?
>   O Jordan, that you turn back ?
> O mountains, that you skip like rams ?
>   O hills, like lambs ?
>
> Tremble, O earth, at the preserfce of the Lord . . .

Feeling here obviously runs high, as it does in Paul's superb—

> O death, where is thy sting ? O grave, where is thy victory ?

Not many preachers would attempt flights of fancy quite so
dramatic as these, but when feeling and occasion prompt the
vivid picturing of one's theme, personification can be very effective.

In both of these latter examples, the *rhetorical question* adds a
still greater degree of emotional emphasis. Scripture is full of this
figure of speech:

> Who hath believed our report, and to whom is the arm of the Lord
> revealed ?
> How shall we escape, if we neglect so great salvation ?
> What shall we then say to these things ? If God be for us, who can be
> against us ? . . .
> What shall we say then ? Are we to continue in sin that grace may
> abound ?
> Why judge ye not even of your own selves what is right ?
> Do men gather grapes of thorns, or figs of thistles ?
> What think ye of Christ ?
> How think ye ? . . . . How readest thou ? . . .
> What shall it profit . . . ? What shall a man give in exchange for his
> soul ?

The examples are numerous, and it should be noted that while
we have them in written records, they are drawn from the preaching
style of prophet, apostle and the Master. This vivid, imaginative
questioning of the audience makes preaching very personal, and
searching. Rudeness, and too frequent use, can make the method
fail, and even provoke resentment: but given a gracious and earnest
manner, with no assumption of superiority in the questioner,
'those who are being questioned by others are stimulated into
answering spontaneously, with energy and complete candour'
('Longinus'). Many a crucial decision for Christ has been registered

in a heart moved by such searching questioning—though the preacher never knew.

Antithesis consists simply of setting a statement side by side with its opposite, as though imagining the listener's comment. The effect s to say a thing twice, in disguised form. 'The Lord knoweth the way of the righteous, but the way of the ungodly shall perish.' 'That which is born of the flesh is flesh, and that which is born of the spirit is spirit.' 'The letter killeth, but the spirit giveth life.' 'To be carnally minded is death, to be spiritually minded is life, and peace.' A similar effect is often obtained in even briefer form: 'The foolishness of God is wiser than men, and the weakness of God is stronger than men . . .' 'When I am weak, then am I strong.' The contrast here is not between statements but between ideas: the nail is hit twice quickly, and the thought is safely home.

Irony states the opposite of what is meant, the tone of voice, the gesture, the drift of the argument, or the obviousness of the truth, being relied upon to make the intended meaning clear. It is often confusing to slow minds; and often mistaken for sarcasm, or a sneer. In the context of worship it is frequently condemned for that reason. Yet irony is often used in scripture, very effectively. Perhaps the greatest sustained example is Isaiah's description of the idol-maker at work, an account full of mock-sympathy and understanding, but in effect pouring ridicule upon the whole process.

> Job says to his friends, 'No doubt you are the people, and wisdom will die with you.' Micaiah says to Ahab, who pretends to seek counsel of the Lord before a battle, 'Go up, and triumph; the Lord will give it into the hand of the king.' But the king, discerning the ironical tone, bursts out 'How many times shall I adjure you to speak to me nothing but the truth . . . ?' Paul says to the Corinthians, 'Already you are filled! Already you have become rich! Without us you have become kings! And would that you did reign, so that we might share the rule with you!' When Peter asks 'Lo, we have left everything and followed you. What then shall we have?' Jesus answers, 'Truly I say to you, in the new world, when the Son of man shall sit on his glorious throne, you who have followed me will also sit on twelve thrones judging the twelve tribes of Israel.' Was Peter's face red! (Those who would cling to these words as literal prophecy have difficulty in explaining the 'twelve'). See, also, 2 Corinthians 12: 13.

Listeners necessarily take time to react, and the speaker who would make a deep impression must learn how to give them time, by mounting his thoughts in order of breadth and intensity, step by step—a figure of style usually called *climax*. Many of the most

H

memorable passages of scripture have this form—and are memorable because of it.

'Blessed is the man that *walketh not* in the counsel of the ungodly, nor *standeth* in the way of sinners, nor *sitteth* in the seat of the scornful . . .' 'Ask, and it shall be given you; seek, and ye shall find; knock, and it shall be opened unto you; for every one that asketh receiveth; and he that seeketh findeth; and to him that knocketh it shall be opened.' 'Whosoever is angry with his brother without cause shall be in danger of the judgement: and whosoever shall say to his brother, Raca, shall be in danger of the council: but whosoever shall say, Thou fool, shall be in danger of hell fire.' 1 Corinthians 13: 1–3 is a similar, though more complicated, progression of thought through stages to an unanswerable climax.

To the attentive mind, eager to learn how to preach, such refinements of presentation slowly become the easy and habitual accompaniments of lively and earnest speech. To realise their value, to notice them in others' writing and speaking, to explore the whole field of effective oratory (with Bain, Grierson, Quintillian, Aristotle among others) is to grow in versatility and eloquence at cost of very little effort, and so to increase one's basic competence as a preacher of the word.

'The perfect orator is he who speaks to the souls of his hearers, and delights them, and moves them' said one of the greatest the world has ever listened to, the Roman statesman Cicero. 'And delights them' is no mere flourish, unnecessary, meretricious, a waste of time in serious worship. For through that delight of the hearer in listening, all other impressions are reinforced, the mind convinced, the emotions stirred, the will persuaded. Interest is the beginning of that delight, and glad assent is its fruition.

19 CLEAR THINKING CARRIES CONVICTION

MIRACLES APART, a muddled sermon cannot well be sound in theology, interesting to listen to, effective in persuasion, memorable as an experience, or make any useful contribution to worship. Unclear speaking dissipates attention, destroys persuasiveness, defeats the intention of the speaker from the outset. To any man in earnest about communicating truth, the necessity of clarity is clear enough.

But there are several kinds of clarity. *Clearness of description* depends upon precise observation, on the power of imagination to recall and reproduce impressions, and on selection of relevant details while ignoring those which would blur the image described. *Clear narration* requires, in addition, the ability to control emotion (as of shock, or excitement, after some great experience now being retold), and a firm sense of order and proportion.

Clearness of argument requires exact use of terms and carefulness about the logical rules of inference. *Clearness of persuasion* demands a well-defined intention, leaving no possible doubt what the speaker wants us to do; a lucid explanation why we should do it; and a plain indication where we can start. Clarity, it is evident, is more a quality of mind than a trick of style.

There are several kinds of obscurity, too. We often persuade ourselves that we know what we want to say but just cannot express it; we know what we mean, but 'the words stay on the tip of the tongue'. Occasionally this is true, and we shall need to say something further about words. But usually we speak or write just as clearly as we think. When words dry up, and our writing runs into a tangle or becomes turgid and diffuse, the cure is to sit back and think out clearly what it is we are trying to say. When we have sorted out our muddled thinking, have corrected our preconceptions, hasty generalisations, hidden assumptions, false analogies, exaggerations and contradictions, then words come readily enough. Sometimes, however, our difficulties lie deeper, in faulty logic, sophistries, and fallacies: these need more radical correction.

It is exasperating to see the earnestness and zeal of a godly man with a good message defeated by his inability to marshal his

219

thoughts and make his meaning clear. It is distressing when the young student, rejoicing in the developing powers of his own mind, newly aware of the pitfalls that beset all discussion, can justly criticise his pastor's misuse of words, invalid arguments, unwarranted conclusions, and so find easy excuse for evading the truth presented. It is even more serious failure when carelessness, or want of honesty in thought, betrays a preacher into exaggerated claims, unjust condemnation, or misrepresentation, into special pleading, or fallacy, or foolishness.

Very few men can afford to be complacent, or contemptuous, about their own thought-processes. A constant self-discipline in clarity will pay attention to all causes of confusion, obscure language, slipshod thinking, and unsound logic. To examine either thoroughly would carry us far beyond the scope of a primer of preaching: we must be content with erecting danger notices.

Obscurity of Language

We are concerned here not with the preacher's vocabulary and style, but with certain types of words that tend to muddle thought itself, and to obscure the speaker's meaning.

(i) *Beware of ambiguous words*. Most arguments turn at some point upon the phrase, 'It depends what you mean by . . .' Many theological controversies arise simply from unwillingness to define terms. The same words mean different things to different people, and to the same person at different times. The man who would communicate must always consider what his words will convey to other minds; the man who would persuade must also consider how his chosen words will *feel* in other minds.

'Spiritual' can mean ghostly, visionary, religious, refined, an attitude ('spirit of chivalry'), anything not material ('the spiritual world'), anything relating to the spirit of man (valour, honour, the spiritual values), anything relating to the Spirit of God (spiritual gifts), anything ethereal (spiritual music), a religious song, a quality or mood (spirit of fear, or contention), independence of mind and action (a woman of spirit), unusually intense religious attitude ('he that is spiritual'), or anything mystical. The word can mean almost anything a speaker chooses; all clarity evaporates in 'a spiritual mist'.

The ambiguity of the word 'love' is a serious disadvantage to Christianity. Love of country, of money, of poetry, of ice-cream soda, of art, of the sea, of God, of an old friend, of a sweetheart, of lifelong husband and wife, of a mistress, of sex experience, of parents, of adolescent singers, of humanity, of games, of speed, of charitable actions, of self, of attention, calf-love, 'for the love of Mike'—no conceivable definition of the word could possibly cover all its usages. The strictly Christian meaning, unconditioned and absolute goodwill, is *rich* rather than vague; the common name for it, 'love' is almost useless.

The similarity of words can be especially misleading. For example,
  curable means *able to be* cured,
  but vulnerable means *liable to be* wounded
  admirable means *worthy to be* admired
  returnable means *under obligation to be* returned
  negotiable means *permitted to be* negotiated
  laughable means *deserving to be* laughed at
  debatable means *needing to be* debated (not assumed).

The whole argument of Utilitarianism was once built upon such an ambiguity:
  (a) All men desire happiness
  (b) What all men desire must be desirable
  (c) Therefore the happiness of all is what all men ought to pursue—the chief end of man.

But in (a) 'happiness' means *the happiness of each man*, not as in (c) *the happiness of all*. In (b) 'desirable' means *able to be desired*, not as assumed in (c), *ought to be desired*.

Beside muddling discourse, ambiguous words are sometimes deliberately exploited to bolster an argument: this is dishonest.

'Everyone familiar with the riot-stories of the late '60's realises the cruelty, the irresponsibility, the lack of intelligence, manifested by any crowd stirred to united action. It is elementary mob-psychology that mass-activity invariably brings out the worst in people. Democracy, therefore, which by definition is rule by the biggest crowd of all, must inevitably degenerate to the most cruel, irresponsible, unintelligent and debased form of human government.'

This seems cogent because of the ambiguity of the word 'crowd', which one moment means 'rioters', the next means any mob stirred to united action, and the next means 'a majority of voters expressing informed opinions by ballot' (democracy). The speaker hopes this will not be noticed, and slips in the splendid appeal to 'definition', and the word 'therefore', to make the argument more specious.

(ii) *Beware of abstractions.* These provide a convenient shorthand for large, comprehensive ideas such as civilisation, equality, liberty, justice, culture, nature, law, humanity, mankind, progress, higher things, happiness, the church invisible, revelation, sin, science, the average man. *But not one of these actually exists.* Each is a notion in the mind: the trick of giving some of them a capital initial (Nature, Sin) does nothing to confer existence upon them.

To make entities of our abstractions, and attribute speech, action, attitudes, praise, or blame to them, is nonsense. They mean something only when reduced to known instances. 'Science says . . .' means 'some scientists say . . .'; 'liberty demands . . .' means 'men who prize liberty demand . . .' What sociological, historical, and logical puzzles are revealed in a phrase like 'the fall of man' if we ask 'What man?'

> 'Sin is the root cause of all the evil in the world' is plausible only in that abstract form. If we mean 'Evil choices are the root cause of evil living' it may possibly be true, but it is scarcely illuminating. If we mean 'Evil living is the root cause of all unhappy lives' it is quite untrue.

Sometimes, the whole thought is too abstract and incomplete to mean anything at all:

> 'Pacificism is a destructive creed'—destructive of what? Of national honour, of manliness, or just of war and armaments? 'Oratory is a more expressive art than music'—expressive of what? Boxing is more 'expressive' of pugnacity than either. 'Communism is more productive than capitalism' means nothing, until you specify what it produces.
>
> G. K. Chesterton remarks: 'All our controversies are confused by certain kinds of phrases which are not merely untrue but were always unmeaning; which are not merely inapplicable, but were always intrinsically useless. We recognise them wherever a man talks of *the survival of the fittest,* meaning only the survival of the survivors; or where a man talks of *going on towards progress,* which only means going on towards going on; or when a man talks about *government by the wise few,* as if they could be picked out by their pantaloons. *The wise few* must mean either the few whom the foolish think wise, or the very foolish who think themselves wise.'

(iii) *Beware of emotive words.* The language of religion necessarily carries strong overtones of feeling: a wholly unemotional expression of religious truth would be a distortion, or at least an understatement. In any case, to exercise persuasion without touching the emotional springs of action is impossible.

The emotional weight of words is thus inescapable. But because their feeling-tone differs for speaker and hearer, communication may become complicated by emotion. Indeed, the unscrupulous can employ 'emotionals' deliberately to obscure truth and to load his argument unfairly. It is possible by this means for a speaker to evoke a desired reaction without the hearer clearly understanding why he should so react, or why he does react at all.

According to emotional prejudices, without any reference to the facts involved, the *same* circumstance may be

a shrewd thrust	or a sarcastic sneer
a responsive audience	or a mob of hecklers
deep patriotism	or narrow nationalism
profound Christian conviction	or fanatical dogmatism
popular appeal	or vulgar sensationalism
trenchant criticism on all sides	or a vicious campaign of personal abuse
a long-winded harangue	or a painstaking and thorough examination
a subtle insinuation	or a delicate hint
a dedicated pressure-group	or a clique of wire-pulling agitators
an eloquent leader	or a ranting demagogue
a profound and steadfast faith	or a stubborn incredulity.

The economist, warning of troubles ahead, will stress that starving women and children will pay the price of economic folly. So will starving stockholders and bookmakers—but he does not mention them! Consider this description of a young preacher: 'A young man of a religious turn of mind and consumptive habit of body, not quite sick enough to die nor healthy enough to be wicked.' Add that it is by the notorious critic of all things religious, Robert Ingersoll; and note how our sympathy with the preacher, our antipathy towards the author, and our personal interest in the defence of preaching, make it extremely difficult to admit that Ingersoll's cynical description could possibly be correct. Yet it is perceptive, and quite possibly true.

Only a fair mind, exercising candid self-criticism, and disciplined to check each strongly expressed sentence for possible dishonesty, will avoid using emotional language in place of valid argument. If you have first proved your case, of course, you may justly use what emotional persuasion you wish.

(iv) *Beware of negatives.* Negative forms of statement can be useful for emphasis: 'No man is immortal'; 'There is no one who does not in his heart hate tyranny.' But unless deftly handled, the negatives can bewilder:

There are not meanwhile critics wanting here who assign this victory to Russia.
I doubt whether the reverse be not the case.
All orders not issued by the manager must not be attended to.
There can be no doubt that nothing will be done.

Say things positively if you would be instantly understood. When a sermon begins, 'There is probably no one of our generation, who bestows any thought on the problems of the time, who will not acknowledge their acute difficulty . . .'; or begins with 'There is

no one—and I mean no one—who does not in his heart believe that
to live without faith is not a self-impoverishment . . .' is it surprising
that the ordinary listener is bemused, wondering whether the preacher has not lost his way, or never found it, or not ?

These are but some of the ways in which unthinking use of language obscures meaning and hinders communication. They suffice
to warn that if we wish to be understood we must take care to say
exactly what we mean.

Slipshod Thinking

Careless habits of thought, often quite unconscious, can cost
us the respect of listeners with better disciplined minds. Prolonged
watchfulness of our own mental processes is not easy, but true
thinking demands it. One helpful exercise is deliberately to read
authoritative books with which we do not agree, that we may
practise debate with sharper minds. For the rest, to be aware of
the more common examples of slipshod thought can alert our
intellectual conscience.

(i) *Selective observation* means seeing only what we want to see.
A hasty conclusion having been reached, only those arguments
which support it are noticed and carefully assessed. In preaching,
a theme being chosen and 'hot in the mind', only those texts which
serve it, only those biblical characters which illustrate it, come to
mind. The balancing texts, the later scripture comment which
qualifies the point which we wish to emphasize, are ignored. The
student of scripture, convinced that his general theological opinions
are right, has constantly to guide against highly selective and
prejudiced exegesis. A settled conviction almost inevitably pre-
disposes the mind to biassed reasoning and the suppression of
inconvenient information: few ardent people have patience with the
impartiality of scholarship.

> Two drug addicts, a wild party, and a few illegitimate births, 'prove
> the universal decadence of modern youth'—ignoring the vast number
> of healthy-minded, socially sensitive, and often Christian young
> people; a student riot 'proves' the wastefulness of all expenditure on
> education —ignoring the many serious, and often brilliant, students
> who pour from modern universities; some well-publicised heretic
> 'proves the sad decline of a great denomination'—ignoring the piety
> and faithfulness of thousands of ordinary members who are equally
> bewildered by their leaders' utterances; the Spanish Inquisition shows
> that no Roman Catholic could ever be a Christian—ignoring the
> Protestant persecution of Roman Catholics; the enormous crowds

who gathered to hear Dr Billy Graham demonstrate that he is a man of God—ignoring the still greater crowds who gather before the Vatican to do homage to the Pope: all such arguments illustrate the danger of selecting evidence to support a prejudged conclusion.

The slum areas in any great city will provide evidence of poverty, of misery, and of drunkenness. The Temperance preacher will declare emphatically: 'Any one can see that the misery is due to poverty arising from drunkenness!' The preacher with a taste for economics will declare equally emphatically: 'Any one can see that the drunkenness arises from the misery due to poverty!' The preacher whose compassion controls his thinking will plead still more emphatically: 'Any one can see, if he has a heart at all, that the poverty arises from the drunkenness to which these poor victims are driven by the misery of their lives!' Even more disturbing: the same congregation may well hear the same preacher use these three 'explanations' on successive Sundays, as his theme or his mood may require.

The perceptive listener soon distrusts the preacher who, whether deliberately or unconsciously, descends to such 'special pleading'.

(ii) *Exaggeration* is a form of emphasis beloved by forceful speakers; but used unguardedly, it seriously undermines confidence. It has many forms:

The sweeping statement—'Women are emotional thinkers, and therefore illogical'; 'no woman has ever been a great architect'; 'the Germans were Nazis . . .' Always distinguish *all* from *some, ever* and *never* from *often*, and say which you mean. That *all* women are emotional thinkers, and *all* Germans were Nazis, is plainly false.

The illegitimate generalisation from limited information—An irate hospital matron declared: 'This generation of student-nurses is hopeless. I do not know what the training schools nowadays teach them. They have no care, no responsibility. The whole pampering system is wrong; they should be trained the hard way, as I was. This week alone I have had three valuable instruments broken on one ward; and one girl has just not turned up at all on ward seven.' The facts were: from an output of eighty graduating nurses, the matron received twenty, placing two in each of ten wards. One in ward seven was homesick, and had been removed to sickbay; one in ward four had quarrelled with her boy-friend, and dropped three things in a week. So far as matron knew, only two out of eighty girls were unsatisfactory, each for reasons unconnected with training. Always consider the unobserved instances, the facts not covered by the information offered in evidence.

The concealed exaggeration—'Science says that . . .' usually means that a leading scientist and his assistants are investigating the possibility that . . . 'Modern philosophy has abandoned metaphysics' is true only if it means that one modern school of philosophy questioned the logical status of metaphysical statements. 'Modern parents simply do not care how their children behave' is slanderous (especially if the preacher means 'except, of course, my wife and me'). 'That France has had twenty-eight governments in thirteen years proves that democracy is unworkable' says too much. The fact cited *suggests* the conclusion; it also "tends to prove" that the French were singularly determined to make it work; that some forms of democracy (like the French proportional representation) may incur especial difficulties; and that the speaker hopes that it will not work.

The extreme example—'Puritanical censorship of plays and books destroys individual liberty: wherever liberty is destroyed, slavery reigns—look at Russia!' Analysed, the truth here would seem to be: the censorship of (obscene) plays and books destroys *one* individual liberty, that of exploiting the lust of others for one's own material gain. Liberty as a whole is not thereby destroyed, but safeguarded from corruption. Nor does slavery reign—no one is bought and sold in the market-place. The reference to Russia is tendentious but irrelevant: Russia does not buy and sell captives for purposes of unpaid labour and sexual promiscuity, nor is her censorship of literature which criticises Communist leadership at all 'puritanical'. The argument is dishonest. And so is the following: 'The higher critics set out to destroy the Bible and undermine the Christian faith, and so produced atheism, and a neo-pagan society which despised Christian values: that is what happened to Germany, with dire consequences for the whole western world.' Even the speaker must see that this makes the 'higher critics' somewhat important! But all the economic, political, and psychological consequences of the 1914–1919 war are here deliberately ignored in the explanation of Nazism; so is Nietzsche, who was not a biblical scholar of any school. 'Set out to destroy the Bible' is a concealed exaggeration for 'tended by their writings to have this unforeseen and unwelcome effect'—it is as fair to presume that men who devoted their lives to biblical study found their conclusions uncongenial, as to assume the opposite. The emergence of Nazism, and the tragedy of the second European war, are—to say the least—extreme examples of the dangers inherent in certain theories about the origin of the Old Testament!

By such gross misrepresentation and overstatement, exaggeration defeats its own purpose of emphasis, and provokes disbelief. A mere habit of exaggeration is soon evident to a congregation, and rapidly undermines their confidence in a speaker's judgement.

(iii) *False analogy.* We sometimes imagine we have established a truth by an illustration, which in fact only restates it more clearly, or which arouses sympathy, indignation, or anger, towards it without in the least confirming its truth. Sometimes the illustration itself is not valid: the analogy 'breaks down'.

'If the housewife finds the family budget getting overstrained, she sensibly concludes (a) that she will have to wait for some things that she wanted; (b) that some things she must just go without; (c) that the weekly income must somehow be increased. That is just what your government is seeking to do—follow the sensible housewife's example! We must wait for new roads and hospitals; we must cut down on overseas commitments; we must raise taxes a little—just as the housewife does.' A hungry and deprived family reluctantly yielding up their own pocket-money in order to increase their own income!

'The mind of the child is a blank slate, upon which society writes its conventional codes; everything in the child's later life will depend upon the writer and the code.' Is the wriggling, resilient, flashing, unpredictable, wayward, absorbent, transfiguring, tempestuous, and lovable chaos we call the mind of a child really as passively receptive as inert slate?

The central Christian analogy of the family, when taken as a complete description of the divine-human relationship, becomes sentimental and false. Biblical teaching never makes the Father-son relationship *natural*: it is moral; never *inevitable*: it is covenantal; never *universal*, but always conditioned by voluntary response to the divine initiative. In the Bible, the family-analogy expresses divine providence, God's response to prayer, and the unbroken fatherly love of God towards the wilful prodigal, enduring a broken sonship far from the Father. The necessity of new birth, the reality of divine judgement, and even Christ's most frequent term for God (the King), fall outside this *partial* analogy of 'the divine family'.

Here, too, the only cure is self-watchfulness. The honest thinker will ask himself what his illustration is intended to do. If to enforce to emphasize, to clarify, or to make memorable, a truth already established, he will use it. But if it is to take the place of argument, because the speaker is unable to justify what he contends for, or too lazy to do so, or too arrogant—then the illustration is deceitful.

(iv) *Unwarranted assumptions.* Every man has his own list of things which he takes for granted and presumes that everyone else accepts. He is surprised, and even angry, if one of them is challenged, and he will probably abandon argument in impatience. When, as in preaching, such unspoken assumptions cannot be challenged, they need to be examined all the more carefully. A few examples out of many must suffice:

'A man must live' (is self-sacrifice, or martyrdom, *never* right?)
'The majority must be right!' (provided I am in it!)
'Every man has a right to his own opinion' (that $2 + 2 = 5$ for example?)
'It must be one thing or the other: of two contrary statements one *must* be true!' (For example, Either all cats have six legs or all cats have seven—you cannot have it both ways!)
'There is no argument against taste' (Are all men and women, then, equally competent judges of music, or poetry, or morals?)
'The exception proves the rule' (A real exception always disproves a supposed rule. An apparent exception to a stated rule, when ex-

amined, often reveals that the rule is too loosely framed, or that the seeming exception is not really covered by the rule, when properly understood. In such ways, an apparent exception serves to clarify the rule. This was the original meaning of the phrase—the exception *tests* the rule).

'Truth lies ever in the middle way' (A persuasive appeal to the sweet reasonableness of compromise: $2+2 = 3$ is obviously inadequate; $2+2 = 7$ is plainly exaggerated; $2+2 = 5$ is the happy mean, on which both sides can agree!)

(v) *Tabloid thinking*—the lazy reiteration of slogans as the substitute for thought—is encouraged by the severe limitations of space and time imposed upon modern advertising and propaganda. Exact statements require measured assertion, with exceptions, qualifications, and uncertainties, all allowed for: but we are impatient, and precision is rarely persuasive. Summary statements are memorable, and avoid discussion; slogans are summaries of summaries, useful to clinch an argument, but deceitful when they take the place of argument.

There is nothing wrong in reiterating 'Higher taxes mean dearer food', if that assertion has been established by facts, figures, and argument; if it is offered instead of argument, it is a confidence trick. 'Evolution, the stupid theory that man is descended from monkeys . . .'; 'Freudianism, the dirty idea that everything is governed by sex . . .'; 'Communism, which believes no man will do anything he is not paid for . . .' are all falsehoods wrapped in slogans.

'The prosperity of a nation is based on the sanctity of its home-life' might be true, if sufficient mineral resources, skilled and energetic workers, inherited capital to invest, fertile soil, a good climate, and opportunities to trade, are all taken for granted.

'Evangelise or perish!' is valid as a defence mechanism, meaning 'let the evangelist evangelise if he wants to stay in business'; as a motive for evangelism, it is of course selfish, desperate, and unchristian.

For the earnest preacher, slipshod thinking of any kind is a serious occupational hazard, a fault in the technique of persuasion that may cost him many hearers. But it is also an indication of character. It may betray carelessness concerning truth, which is fatal to spiritual influence. We shall not, by intellectual dishonesty, commend ourselves to any man's conscience, either in the sight of God or in the light of truth.

Faulty Logic

The third enemy of clear thinking is want of a technical training in logic, a deficiency from which the great majority of people suffer, except perhaps for the introduction to the subject provided by school mathematics. A preacher conscious of the insufficiency of his education in this respect would do well to make his way through one or two textbooks and learn something of the principles of sound argument. The pulpit is not the place for contention, but whenever appeal is made to reason, it ought to be made in a reasonable way. All that can be done here is to indicate some of the grosser fallacies of which we who preach are occasionally guilty.

In the fallacy called *begging the question*, the reason alleged in support of a statement already assumes the statement to be true. 'The Bible is infallible, for every honest scholar knows it to be the word of God.' Here the reason offered merely reiterates the original statement. More subtly: 'All Christians accept the Bible as infallible.— But Dr A. and Rev. B. do not.—Ah! but I mean all *true* Christians.' (That is, all who accept the Bible as infallible).

The *circular argument* resembles this. 'I believe in all the miracles, because I believe that Jesus was the Son of God. He must have been— look at all the wonderful things He did!' Or, 'I believe the Bible is God's word, because of what it has done in my life. Some people say it has no effect upon them, but that is because they do not read it in faith, as the word of God; so of course it does not work for them!'

The fallacy of the *complex question* insinuates some very doubtful statement in order to raise a spurious question. King Charles II of England is said to have asked the Royal Society for the Advancement of Learning, Why does a vessel of water receive no weight from a live fish being put into it, though it does if the fish be dead? Other examples: Science having proved that there is no God, how can Christianity survive? How can the inherent divisiveness of Christianity be reconciled with its own gospel of reconciliation? So much is assumed in such questions that a straight answer is impossible.

The fallacy called *the false dilemma* appears to show that, since all possible alternatives to a given statement are plainly untrue, the statement offered must be true. For example: 'Christianity may be a perfect way of life, but it is useless. For unless you have perfect people, it is impracticable; and if you do have perfect people, it is unnecessary. Thus Christianity is valueless.' This dilemma is false, because there is a third possibility, namely that some imperfect people may find the Christian way their only hope of becoming perfect—which in fact is what redemptive Christianity is all about!

Two statements may be joined together so that if the first ('the antecedent') is true, then the second ('the consequent') must also be true. 'If John is a Christian, then he will be honest; John *is* a Christian —therefore John is honest.' This is clear, and valid. But often we try to prove the antecedent by *affirming the consequent*: we say 'If John is a Christian then he will be honest; John is honest—therefore John is a Christian.' This is a fallacy: John may well be honest and not a Christian. Sometimes, too, we try to disprove the consequent by *denying the antecedent*: we say, 'If John is a Christian he will be

230 A GUIDE TO PREACHING

honest; John is not a Christian—therefore he is not honest.' This
again is a fallacy: we are told nothing in the premise about what
follows if John is *not* a Christian, only what follows if he is. The only
valid inference from any conditional statement is, that if the antecedent condition be fulfilled, then the consequent statement will be
true.

Everyone can see something is wrong with the following argument:

    All cowards pray in time of danger
    All Christians pray in time of danger
    Therefore, All Christians are cowards.

To explain the mistake, we must notice that 'middle term' which
links the first two statements: '(those who) pray in time of danger'.
This can be taken to mean '*All* those who pray in time of danger—
the whole class of them.' The argument then runs:

    All cowards = the whole class of those who pray in danger
    All Christians = the whole class of those who pray in danger

Therefore All Christians are cowards;

    and also: All cowards are Christians!—the two classes of people
coincide. But this is clearly not what the first two statements really
mean. They mean:

    All cowards are *some* of those who pray in time of danger
    All Christians are *some* of those who pray in time of danger

and these two classes do not coincide. Among those who pray in
time of danger *some* are cowards and *some* (others) are Christians
—and some of course may be both cowards and Christians. To be
valid, this type of argument must have its 'middle term' *distributed
over its whole class*, applying to all its class, in at least one of its statements, when, as here, it refers in both statements to only part of its
class ('some'), then the argument goes wrong: we have the fallacy
technically called the *undistributed middle term*.

The chief value of this somewhat daunting chapter is to illustrate
how much there is to learn if preaching is to be clear, cogent, and
convincing. We have already suggested that the earnest preacher of
the gospel, anxious to commend his message to every man and to
give no offence in anything, will try to overtake any deficiency in
his general education in this respect. If that seems too much to ask,
he might at least re-read occasionally this catalogue of pitfalls:
and he might practise his logical skill in criticising the obscure and
the illogical in all he hears and reads. He can be sure of plenty of
exercise-material, and of a source of constant amusement. But he
should try not to forget that clarity begins at home.

20 HOW SHALL THEY CONTINUE PREACHING?

THE PASSING years demand not only increasing facility, skill, and resources, but a continuing zeal, a constantly renewed sense of commission to this work of preaching. When Paul asks 'How shall they preach?' he is not thinking of the theme, the content, the technique of preaching, but—as the implied answer shows—of the much deeper question of call and motivation.

The great F. W. Robertson of Brighton is reported to have once complained of 'the degradation of being a popular preacher'. It is hard to guess what mood prompted such a protest: a half-conscious sense of being superior to such work; a momentary loss of faith in the whole process of transforming people and society by the proclamation of truth; or just depression, bred of criticism by others, or by oneself. Probably no minister is entirely free from periods when his inspiration fails, his regular work descends to drudgery, his conviction that he was called of God to preach is shaken, and his soul is undermined with misgivings. At such times, a man's safety and resources lie in a planned routine. in his solemn engagement to his people, and in a character sufficiently mature to persevere from principle rather than from impulse.

If such fluctuations of faith and infirmity of purpose are not to become an emotional habit—or indulgence—to the point where a man's will to preach is broken, and his power in preaching destroyed, he must take himself in hand. Only he will know the real causes of his despondency and frustration. But they may become easier to handle if he realises more clearly the tensions necessarily inherent in such a calling; if he achieves a sound level of self-understanding and self-evaluation; and if he can learn to see his task of preaching in the light of objective truths that have little to do with his own emotional susceptibilities.

Inescapable Tensions

If a man ever did come to feel himself too good for this kind of work—if, that is, he ever lost the sense of privilege and of call— then he should give up preaching. Before that happens, however, he should reflect on the numerous possible sources of his disillusion. How far, for example, is he merely accepting the judgement of society upon his work? The role of the preacher is undoubtedly undervalued, if not wholly rejected, in wide circles of culture, not only in Britain and Europe but even increasingly in America. The loss of social and intellectual status is especially painful to some men. But has the faithful preacher of the Gospel any real ground for expecting otherwise? 'If they have rejected me, they will reject you' Jesus said. And to let the denigration of the world at large destroy one's zeal for preaching is to confess to a scarcely worthy motive for preaching at all.

An opposite pressure upon the preacher's spirit is the exalted ideal, the well-nigh impossible ideal, by which the Christian preacher feels himself to be judged. Bishop Ken sketches the requirements of the perfect priest:

> Of an Ambassador the just address,
> A Father's Tenderness, a Shepherd's Care,
> A Leader's Courage, which the Cross can bear,
> A Ruler's Awe, a Watchman's wakeful Eye,
> A Pilot's skill, the Helm in Storms to ply,
> A Fisher's patience, and a Lab'rer's Toil,
> A Guide's Dexterity to disembroil,
> A Prophet's Inspiration from Above,
> A Teacher's Knowledge, and a Saviour's Love.

Any man may feel it unfair that so much may be demanded of one soul: yet the expectation is in truth a high compliment to his calling. Besides, is it so surprising if the posture adopted by the preacher,—the assumption of divine authority to exhort, instruct, rebuke, and warn on issues affecting intimately the life and conscience of others—should leave him subject to searching criticism? Luther includes among the qualities needed by a preacher 'the readiness to suffer himself to be vexed and criticised by everyone'. The pulpit is inevitably an exposed position; and its occupant will ever be sensitive and vulnerable—if he were not that kind of man he would probably not be preaching. Paul, at any rate, was aware of, and hurt by, others' criticism of his preaching.

It would be pathetic weakness to preach only for others' praise: but it is arrogant conceit to despise, or affect indifference to, your hearers' reactions and response. If it be good to accept your peoples' gratitude as encouragement given by God, it must be equally just to accept criticism as a lesson from God. To be despondent simply for want of compliments is as naïve as to be elated by flattery. One must learn to weigh one's critics, as well as their criticism, and to assess their motive in criticising. As for one's family, it is well to remember ruefully that no prophet is wholly without honour except among his own kindred.

Self-criticism is likely to sharpen with experience. It is the price of improvement, and often the unconscious cause of much dissatisfaction. Painfully, we realise the enormous potentialities of pulpit ministry just as we become more convinced of our own inadequacies. In truth, both are signs of progress—though they do not feel like that.

One deeper disappointment lies in store for those who fancied that a life of preaching must bring endless new supplies of grace to one's own heart, relief from the pressures of 'ordinary' temptation, shelter from the rough and tumble of Christian life in an unsympathetic world. Much of this is true: the disappointment lies in finding that there is nothing inevitable about it, and in discovering that preaching brings its own temptations.

> The great Bishop Butler long ago warned in his sonorous way, that 'going over the theory of virtue in one's thoughts, talking well, and drawing fine pictures of it, this is so far from necessarily and certainly conducing to form a habit of it, that it may harden the mind in a contrary course, or render it gradually more insensible—that is, form a habit of insensibility to all moral considerations.'

A still more serious warning was sounded by Paul: 'I do not run aimlessly, I do not box as one beating the air; but I pommel my body and subdue it, lest after preaching to others I myself should be disqualified.' It is a fear many have felt. For the public profession of Christian truth, in order to persuade others to live by it, obviously increases responsibility.

But more is involved: the constant exposure of his inmost thoughts and feelings to others can create unusual spiritual tensions in any man. That others wait week by week for his counsel and instruction can foster exaggerated self-importance—which he himself will mistake for spiritual influence. Responsiveness in some group of 'faithful' sympathetic listeners can rapidly become the adulation of a fan club, to whose approval and delight the unwary preacher will increasingly address himself. Even Paul's reference to subduing the body must not be lightly ignored. The nervous tensions, emotional involvement, spiritual reactions, and social opportunities of a life spent in church leadership have been the moral undoing of good men, who foolishly thought themselves immune to grosser temptations.

Modern conditions have created two new sources of tension, which some find especially painful. Few contemporary preachers have ever known widespread spiritual revival, or can remember anything of the atmosphere in which the great preachers worked at the turn of the century and afterwards. The thrilling inspiration of vast congregations, the radiance of preaching 'success', the stimulus, challenge and encouragement which made men of ordinary talent into eloquent pulpiteers, are not even sustaining memories. Instead, young preachers of today are far more likely to suffer the back-lash of scornful dismissal.

Dr Henry Cook of London once remarked that evangelicals tend to react to the changed conditions with despair; the Roman Church reacts with detachment and patience; Jesus would have reacted, as always, by continuing to seek and to save those who are lost. More accurate assessments of 'past glories' might dispel some spiritual romanticism and nostalgia. But the only relevant reply to the gloom and despondency evoked by historical comparisons is simple. A man must preach to his own contemporaries, serve God's kingdom in his own generation, acquit himself faithfully in the circumstances in which God has set *him*—and not make weak, futile excuses.

More subtle is the undermining uncertainty that afflicts some preachers. Desperately anxious to be clear and authoritative yet inwardly aware of unresolved problems and unanswered questions on many theological subjects, they wrestle daily with the doubts of maintaining at once both their evangelical loyalty and their intellectual integrity. Escapist bolt-holes are available: a species of evangelical double-talk which does not really mean what it seems to say; a forthright proclamation of denials, as the best apologetic in an age of unbelief—'relieving Christianity of its unnecessary intellectual lumber'; or—at the opposite extreme—a retreat into ultra-conservativism, and obsessive Calvinism, which (like the Roman dogma) imposes still heavier burdens upon belief as faith becomes progressively more difficult.

Absolute honesty of mind, persistent prayer, and determination to live out to the full those things that *are* clear, is probably still the wisest course. Plainly no man should preach what he does not believe. But neither should he proclaim his doubts and difficulties—which will help no one. To make a publicity-gimmick out of your own scepticism is cheap showmanship. Be positive, be practical, and be persistent in following through what God has shown you: and

> God stooping shows sufficient of His light
> For us i' the dark to rise by.

Those who have never faced the intellectual challenge of our age will be impatient with a faith so hesitant and cautious: but honest and earnest listeners will respect their preacher's integrity and accept what he does affirm with greater confidence. Until the next intellectual revival shall illumine the modern mind, in a new age of spiritual enlightenment, there is no escaping this tension between the Christian's central certainty and the many questions to which he cannot honestly pretend to know the final answers.

Many preachers claim to find in manual hobbies a relief from trying to handle that more intractable, cross-grained, unpredictable raw material, human nature. To be engaged always, creatively, remedially and redemptively, in the realm of ideas, traditions, emotions, motivation, ideals and human perverseness, *must* impose strains beyond even those met by the educator and the psychotherapist. It is worthy of remark that great souls, like that of Paul, rarely achieved the serenity, the 'balanced norm' that is the modern ideal of integrated personality. Instead, they held their varying tensions in control and drew from them phenomenal psychological and spiritual strength. But that requires considerable self-knowledge, and some clear objective dedication, to discipline the soul.

Self-understanding

Something is gained when a man realises that the pressures he feels are part of the task, and not some personal inadequacy peculiar to himself. But he needs also to distinguish moods of despondency and frustration, which are merely subjective reactions, from more reliable, because impartial, assessments of his work.

It is altogether natural, and right, for example, that a man should find considerable enjoyment and self-fulfilment in the conscious use of his gifts and training; that he should enjoy, too, the public recognition of success; even more that he should feel elated at the evidence of God's blessing. The lack of either, or all, of these personal satisfactions is great personal disappointment. *But it is not failure.* In all probability, it bears no relation of any kind to the real value and effectiveness of his preaching. It is well for a man to know precisely what has disappointed him.

It is well, too, for a man to defend, as Job did, his own integrity and truth. There is no spiritual health in accepting undeserved self-blame. 'We commend ourselves to every man's conscience in the sight of God,' Paul manfully protests—'having renounced the hidden ways of dishonesty, not walking in craftiness, nor handling the word of

God deceitfully.' What more can any man do? 'We are not, like so many, pedlars of God's word;' Paul says again: 'but as men of sincerity, as commissioned by God, in the sight of God speak we in Christ.'

There is in such words the dignity of a clear conscience—a precious resource when things are not going well. Paul has in mind those familiar figures in the ancient world against whom Socrates also warns: those who hawk their wares—intellectual or material—with all the tricks and persuasiveness of the travelling salesman, intellectual hirelings, mercenary minds making merchandise of ideas, trimming their message for the tastes of the prevailing market. Paul protests the 'transparency' of his own motives, appealing to Him who alone knows the sincerity of hearts—'in the sight of God'; to Him to whom alone he is answerable—'as commissioned by God'.

But God never claps. The inner voice of divine approval is often drowned by self-criticism. A man ought to be his own best critic, listening to himself as impartially as he can, and often applying all he has learned about preaching to his own performances. Only, let him do it intelligently, objectively, by accepted standards, and not in moody self-denigration. The 'Decalogue' which sound preaching must obey can be simply stated and precisely applied to decide the merits of a sermon:

1. The sermon shall possess definite scriptural warrant and definable religious value for the cause of God and the heart of the hearer.
2. The sermon shall be directly relevant to the congregation to which it was preached.
3. The sermon shall possess, and shall be seen to possess, a clear, practical purpose.
4. The sermon shall be interesting, to the hearer as well as the preacher, and this shall be measured only by the degree of attention aroused and sustained during its preaching.
5. The sermon shall be intellectually cogent—making its point, demonstrating its chosen truth, by methods of proof that satisfy reflective analysis afterwards.
6. The sermon shall aim at a style of presentation appropriate to theme and purpose but in every case retaining the personal and persuasive note demanded in public speech.
7. The sermon shall be orderly.
8. The sermon shall be effectively introduced.
9. The sermon shall be effectively and firmly concluded.
10. The sermon shall be illumined, enriched, applied and made memorable by imaginative speech and telling illustration aimed at delighting, educating and wooing the inattentive listener.

By such canons of self-criticism a man may be delivered from the morbid emotional and introspective self-examination which has more to do with his mood and temperament than with his work. The result will be profitable self-improvement, rather than insincere self-punishment, especially if he can balance candour with laughter at himself.

Nor should the preacher forget that dissatisfaction is often a sign of growth. Preached sermons, like clothes, can become too small for us—indeed they ought to do so, even though the symptoms involve personal discomfort. If a man's spiritual life halts, his preaching stagnates, and he will find himself repeating many times not only the main ideas of his faith but the same sermons he was happy with twenty years ago.

Unless a man finds that his themes, his emphases, his favourite passages of scripture, his exegetical and moral interests, his areas of urgent concern, change from time to time, he ought seriously to ask himself if he is still *alive*—mentally, or spiritually. His dissatisfaction may be growing pains, his alternating moods of aspiration and despondency simply the pulse that testifies to an eager, questing, not-easily-satisfied spirit.

The preacher's self-knowledge will however probe into recesses of experience which have little to do with preaching technique or pulpit manuals. Yet the point cannot be entirely evaded. Times of severe spiritual drought, and even of intellectual barrenness, may, or may not, have moral and spiritual causes. They can arise from tiredness, ill-health, adverse circumstances, prayerlessness—or sin. Only the man himself will know, though a trusted counsellor may wondrously help to clear his mind. Certainly the preacher should never conclude he is 'unworthy' unless he can quite clearly specify to himself the disobedience which is making him so. Then the cure lies plainly to hand.

The knowledge that one has to preach to others, in a service of Christian worship, on the approaching Lord's Day, and will need the help of the Holy Spirit to do it, furnishes a searching discipline for any soul. The spiritual responsibility involved extends backwards through the week an extra carefulness of conduct and prayerfulness of spirit, lest the effectiveness of his public service be prejudiced by private unpreparedness of heart. Such is the inner, secret price that must be paid by anyone who aspires, however humbly to be a man of God.

But this is already to anticipate the second personal requirement for a steadfast and prolonged preaching career: a clear subjective self-understanding must be balanced by an equally clear objective dedication. The sources of persistence and patience are by no means wholly within oneself.

Objective Truths

At the very least a man should have sufficient objectivity of mind to see his personal task, and his performance within it, against the wide background of the church's life. The pattern of the original, essential church in Acts 2:42 already includes a teaching and preaching function—'they continued steadfastly in the Apostles' doctrine'—as well as in fellowship, worship and prayer.

It is of the nature of the church to preach. She is, and always will be, a proclaiming institution, her corporate life the 'ground of the truth' and her articulate witness 'the pillar (or bill-board) of the truth' within society. If it remains timelessly true, that 'this Gospel must be preached', it follows that the commission to preach abides in all generations. Thus far more is involved than a man's private sense of call, or of privilege: he continues in the work, as he took it up, as a necessary part of his service of Christ. He cannot lay it down without disloyalty, and disobedience. He knows exactly how Paul felt: 'necessity is laid upon me; yea, woe is unto me, if I preach not the Gospel!'

This general truth is *felt*, by the man who yields to its implied obligation, as a personal destiny. He discovers himself to be a vehicle for forces and purposes beyond his own. Sometimes he will know that this is so—feel it within himself and have evidence of its effect in other lives. Often he will be unaware of it, for God is under no obligation to tell us how He uses us. *The exercise of power and the sense of power are quite separate experiences.*

This is the meaning of Paul's astonishing reaction to his own illness. Though he had thrice prayed for deliverance, and restoration, he came to see that he was in fact more effective for God in his infirmity: 'when I am weak, then am I strong'. For 'the transcendent power belongs to God and not to us'. So, too, Paul faces the affliction, perplexity, persecution and despondency that he feels as sharply as any man: but all the time, and at the same time, the life of Jesus is being manifested through his ministry. 'Death is at work in us, but life in you.' And so, yet again, Paul faces advancing age and dwindling natural powers: 'though our outer nature is wasting away, our inner nature is being renewed every day'.

The simple truth is, 'we have this treasure in earthen vessels' —in the cheap, rough brittle pottery that perishes with use. With Paul, the treasure and the pot are never confused. Philips Brooks may speak grandly of preaching as truth through personality,

Paul's characteristic metaphor is that of buried treasure surprisingly discovered—gems in old jars!

'The exercise of power and the sense of power are quite separate experiences.' Luke tells of Paul's arrival and departure at Thessalonica in nine verses. Only one speaks of any success. 'Some of them were persuaded, and joined Paul and Silas; as did a great many of the devout Greeks, and not a few of the leading women.' The rest of the passage tells of 'wicked fellows of the rabble', stirred by Jewish jealousy, of uproar, attacks, accusations, civic disturbance, official action by the authorities, and the few converts hastily sending Paul away.

But Paul's own memory of these days is very different. 'Our gospel came to you not only in word, but also in power and in the Holy Spirit and with full conviction . . . you received the word in much affliction, with joy . . . they report what a welcome we had among you, and how you turned to God from idols . . . You yourselves know that our visit to you was not in vain . . . when you received the word of God . . . you accepted it not as the word of men, but as what it really is, the word of God which is at work . . .' Paul's remembrance of persecution and affliction at Thessalonica is clear, but it is suffused with happier memories of a sense of power and great joy.

On the other hand, Paul's references to his visit to Ephesus are full of pain. 'We fought with beasts at Ephesus . . . there are many adversaries. We were so utterly, unbearably crushed that we despaired of life itself . . . We felt that we had received the sentence of death . . .' The one word he writes over the Ephesian mission is 'affliction'.

Yet the rest of the New Testament makes abundantly clear that the Ephesian mission was the greatest of all Paul's undertakings. Luke records successful debates in the synagogue, and then two years public teaching 'in the hall of Tyrannus . . . so that all the residents of Asia heard the word of the Lord, both Jews and Greeks'. Moreover, God did 'extraordinary miracles' by the hands of Paul—many were healed, and one demonstration of the power of Christ's name brought fear upon all the residents of the city, and a public burning of charms and books of magic.

'So the word of the Lord grew, and prevailed mightily' is Luke's excited comment, answering Paul's word 'affliction'. The existence of the Ephesian church for two centuries, the scene of great ministries at the cultural centre of Asia, and the family of daughter churches—Colossae, Hierapolis, Sardis and the rest, spread through the surrounding province, show Luke's estimate was justified.

At Thessalonica, the sense of power amid much effective opposition; at Ephesus, tremendous accomplishment, with a sense only of affliction, perplexity and being 'unbearably crushed'. 'When I am weak, then am I strong': when I feel I fail—then by God's grace, I may be doing more than I can ever know. In this field, what is success, what failure? Success is to be doing what God wills, letting Him take care of results. Failure lies only in giving up.

'If you utter what is precious, and not what is worthless, you shall be as my mouth.' So said God to Jeremiah. And so Jesus sent his men, 'ahead of him . . . into every town and place where he himself was about to come', giving them His own message to preach and His own authority to preach it. 'Whenever you enter a town and they do not receive you . . . it shall be more tolerable on that day for Sodom than for that town . . . He who hears you hears me, and he who rejects you rejects me.' The commission, the intention of Jesus, the authority conferred, and the promise, 'Lo I am with you always' are objective facts beside which a man's fluctuating moods of elation or despondency have little significance.

Our sufficiency is of God: the sole condition is the unwavering, unconcealed attitude of dependence. Without Him we can do nothing, whatever our talent or technique, our personal drive or eloquence. But as the bearer of truth and the vehicle of the Spirit, preaching the gospel in the context of worship, the humblest man becomes transfigured, and weak things of the world confound—and convert— the mighty.

To be servant of the church in her most sacred hours; servant of the Word, mediating timeless truth to a new generation; servant of the Spirit, who so takes of the things of Christ and reveals them to men; and servant of the living God in a crucial time; that is the sufficient reward of those who, in unpropitious days continue, with true heart, tenacious faith, and stubborn dedication, to preach the everlasting Gospel.

SOURCES, BIBLIOGRAPHY AND ACKNOWLEDGEMENTS

Books and Lectures used and recommended:

BEASLEY-MURRAY, G. R., *Evangelising the Post-Christian Man* (Diamond Jubilee Lecture, London Baptist Preachers' Association 1969); quoted by permission

BLACK, JAMES, *The Mystery of Preaching* (Fleming H. Revell Company, New Jersey 1924)

BUTTRICK, G. A., *Jesus Came Preaching* (Charles Scribner's Sons, New York 1931)

CANN, RICHARD DU, *The Art of the Advocate* (Penguin Books, Harmondsworth 1964). Copyright, quoted by permission

CHAMPION, L. G., *Biblical Preaching in the Contemporary Situation* (Diamond Jubilee Lecture, London Baptist Preachers' Association 1966); quoted by permission

DOBSON, J. O., *Worship* (SCM Press, London 1941) Copyright, quoted by permission

DORSCH, T. S. (Translator) *Classical Literary Criticism* (Penguin Books, Harmondsworth 1965)

FARMER, H. H., *The Servant of the Word* (James Nisbet & Co., London 1941)

FORD, H., *The Art of Extempore Speaking* (James Clarke and Company Ltd., Cambridge n.d.). Copyright, quoted by permission

FORSYTH, P. T., *Positive Preaching and the Modern Mind* (Independent Press Ltd., London 1949)

GRIERSON, H., *Rhetoric and English Composition* (Oliver and Boyd, Edinburgh n.d.)

JONES, ILION T., *Principles and Practice of Preaching* (Independent Press, London 1958)

MENZIES, ROBERT, *Preaching and Pastoral Evangelism* (Warrack Lectures, St. Andrew Press, Edinburgh n.d.)

MICKELSEN, A. BERKELEY, *Interpreting the Bible* (Wm. B. Eerdmans Publishing Co., Grand Rapids 1963)

MONTAGUE, C. E., *A Writer's Notes On His Trade* (Penguin Books, Harmondsworth 1949) Copyright, quoted by permission of Mrs. Rose Elton and Chatto & Windus, London

OMAN, JOHN, *Concerning the Ministry* (SCM Press, London 1936)

POTTER, STEPHEN, *Our Language* (Penguin Books, Harmondsworth 1950, 1966). Copyright, quoted by permission

RATTENBURY, J. E., *Vital Elements in Public Worship* (Epworth Press, London 3rd edition 1954)

SANGSTER, P. E., *Speech in the Pulpit* (Epworth Press, London 1958)

SANGSTER, W. E., *The Craft of Sermon Construction* (Epworth Press, London 1949)

SPURGEON, C. H., *Speeches at Home and Abroad* (1878)
  Lectures to My Students (1875, etc.)
STEWART, J. S., *Heralds of God* (Warrack Lectures, Hodder and
  Stoughton, London 1946)
STIBBS, A. M., *Expounding God's Word* (Inter-Varsity Press, London
  1960). Copyright, quoted by permission
WARD, R. A., *Royal Sacrament* (Marshall, Morgan and Scott Ltd.,
  London 1958)
WOOD, JOHN, *The Preacher's Workshop* (Tyndale Press, London 1965)
WOOD, A. SKEVINGTON, *Luther's Principles of Biblical Interpretation*
  (Tyndale Press, London 1960). Copyright, quoted by permission

Sources:

PREFACE Horace, from the Art of Poetry, in Dorsch p. 89

CHAPTER 1 Rattenbury op. cit. p. 115; Ernest Barker *National
  Character* (1927) p. 191; F. W. Gotch in S. Pearce Carey *William
  Carey* (1923) p. 78; Spurgeon in *Speeches etc.*, and compare *Lectures,*
  1st series, introduction to lecture iv; Dobson op. cit. p. 165 and
  compare p. 90; Temple, cited often, without source (as in Stewart
  op. cit. p. 73); F. S. Leahy article in *Christianity Today* September
  12 1960, Copyright, quoted by permission; Stewart: from a reported
  lecture

CHAPTER 3 Stibbs op. cit. pp. 15, 11; Herman Sasse in E. G. Selwyn
  (editor) *Short History of Christian Thought* p. 87 (Geoffrey Bles,
  London 1949); Mickelsen op. cit. p. 366; C. E. B. Cranfield *1 Peter,*
  p. 98 SCM Press, London 1950. Copyright, quoted by permission;
  Calvin, cited by Leahy op. cit.; Stibbs op. cit. pp. 17, 7; L. Nelson
  Bell in *Christianity Today* September 12 1960 Copyright, quoted by
  permission; John Robinson's words are discussed in E. A. Payne
  Free Church Tradition in the Life of England pp. 37f., (SCM Press,
  London 1944); L. G. Champion op. cit. pp. 6f. and 8; Mickelsen
  op. cit. pp. 365f.; for excellent discussion of modern attitudes, see
  Klassen and Snyder (editors) *Current Issues in New Testament
  Interpretation* pp. 38f. (SCM Press, London 1962); L. G. Champion
  op. cit. pp. 9, 10f.

CHAPTER 4 Stibbs op. cit. pp. 47, 62; Skevington Wood op. cit. pp. 24f.
  21, 23, 11, and passim; Spurgeon *Lectures* 1st series vii; Luther cited
  in Skevington Wood op. cit. p. 13

CHAPTER 5 Grierson op. cit.; A. Quiller-Couch *On the Art of Writing*
  p. 30 (Guild Books edition 1946), this and other extracts used by
  permission of Cambridge University Press; E. Dickie article,
  Chaplaincy in War Time (Expository Times); Fosdick in *Harper's
  Magazine,* July 1928, quoted in Blackwood *The Preparation of
  Sermons* p. 127 (Church Bookroom Press, London 1951); Grierson
  op. cit. p. 15; Gilbert Laws in *Christian World Pulpit,* May 23 1946;
  Dickens *Bleak House* ch. xxv; John Pitts, transcript of article in
  Christianity Today on Dr Campbell Morgan; Du Cann op. cit.
  p. 160; Chesterfield *Letters,* 1746; W. J. Bryan in Hibbern *The
  Peerless Leader*; Spurgeon *Speeches etc.*; Cicero from Plutarch
  Roman Apothegms; Byron *Lara* (canto i stanza 19)

CHAPTER 6 Wesley the quotation is untraceable, possibly apocryphal; Trollope *Phineas Finn* ch. 18; V. Bonham Carter *Winston Churchill as I Knew Him* p. 118 (Reprint Society edition 1965) Copyright, quoted by permission of Collins, London

CHAPTER 7 John Wood op. cit. p. 8; Ingli James, lectures to ministers, never published

CHAPTER 8 Gilbert Laws op. cit.; John Wood op. cit. p. 33

CHAPTER 9 Maclaren *Sermons Preached in Manchester* 1st series, vi; R. Menzies *Magnet of the Heart* p. 89 (James Clarke)

CHAPTER 11 J. J. McNeil in magazine article; Bradley *Shakespearean Tragedy* lecture 2

CHAPTER 12 G. R. Beasley-Murray op. cit. pp. 8f., 10; R. Menzies *Preaching and Pastoral Evangelism* pp. 14f. (The other characteristics of evangelistic preaching which Menzies considers are: preoccupation with the sin dilemma, the summons to repentance (i.e. a burden to be removed, a change of heart, a new direction), the importance of conversion, a Christo-centric message, and the place given to personal experience)

CHAPTER 13 P. E. Sangster op. cit.; Thomas Fuller *The Holy State* p. 169; T. R. Glover *The Jesus of History* p. 49 (SCM Press, London 1917); H. Ford op. cit. pp. 11, 13 compare pp. 65–68

CHAPTER 14 Einstein essay *On Science*; Bonaparte in Bourienne's *Life*, ii 2; Quiller-Couch op. cit. p. 28; Grierson op. cit. p. 54; J. S. Stewart op. cit. p. 142; H. H. Farmer's dictum is elaborated in *The Servant of the Word* pp. 114f. (Nisbet, London 1941); Quiller-Couch op. cit. pp. 157; 66f., 69; John Wood op. cit. p. 26; G. K. Chesterton *The Defendant* pp. 77f., 49, (Dent 1940) Copyright, quoted by permission J. M. Dent and Sons Ltd. London; *Tremendous Trifles* p. 69 (Methuen, London 1920) Copyright, quoted be permission of Miss D. E. Collins and Darwen Finlayson Ltd

CHAPTER 15 F. W. Boreham *Mushrooms on the Moor* (Epworth Press, London 1925); C. E. Montague op. cit. p. 58; Bunyan, introduction to *Pilgrim's Progress*

CHAPTER 16 Robert A. Phillips in *Foundations* xiii no. 3 (American Baptist Historical Society); Vance Packard *The Hidden Persuaders* (Longmans Green, London 1957); John Wood op. cit. p. 25

CHAPTER 17 'Longinus'—see Dorsch op. cit. p. 139; Quiller-Couch op. cit. p. 29; Aristotle in Dorsch op. cit. pp. 41, 62; G. K. Chesterton *The Defendant* (see above) p. 142; Stephen Potter op. cit. p. 133; C. E. Montague op. cit. pp. 21–24; Stephen Potter op. cit. p. 131; Quintillian, quoted in Nesfield *English Grammar and Composition* p. 178 (Macmillan, London 1925); T. S. Eliot *Collected Poems* 1909–1962 (Faber and Faber) Copyright, used by permission; Stephen Potter op. cit. p. 83; C. E. Montague op. cit. p. 9; Stephen Potter op. cit. p. 109; G. G. N. Wright *Teach Yourself to Study* p. 167 (English Universities Press, London); C. E. Montague op. cit. p. 11; H. W. Fowler *Modern English Usage* (Oxford); G. G. N. Wright op. cit. pp. 176f.; Nesfield op. cit. pp. 190f.; Quiller-Couch op. cit. p. 63; J. B. Ashbrook in *Foundations* (above) on *The Search for a Usable Image*, quoted by permission; Quiller-Couch op. cit. p. 75; Stephen Potter op. cit. p. 54; Horace, in Dorsch op. cit. p. 79; Nesfield op. cit. p. 195; Stephen Potter op. cit. pp. 100f.

CHAPTER 18 Pope *Dunciad* ii 352; Cowper *The Task* ii; Emerson *Journals* x p. 457; Amiel *Journal* (introduction); Dickens *Bleak House* ch. xix; Trollope *Barchester Towers* ch. vi; T. R. Glover *Paul of Tarsus* ch. 8 (SCM Press, London 1938) Copyright, quoted by permission; Donne *Sermons* selected passages edited by Pearsall Smith p. 125 (Oxford 1919); Stephen Potter op. cit. p. 97; V. Bonham Carter op. cit. p. 147; Horace, in Dorsch op. cit. p. 87; C. E. Montague op. cit. pp. 44, 48; Grierson op. cit. p. 73; 'Longinus' in Dorsch op. cit. pp. 148, 128

CHAPTER 19 G. K. Chesterton, extract from a Digest; this chapter owes much to R. H. Thouless *Straight and Crooked Thinking* (English Universities Press, London 1936). This book, with L. Susan Stebbing *Thinking to Some Purpose* (Pelican Books) may be recommended for practical studies in logic

CHAPTER 20 Butler *Analogy of Religion* i ch. 5